THE FICTIONS OF DREAMS

To Ollie,
Have the dreams of
your life

THE FICTIONS OF DREAMS
Dreams, Literature, and Writing

Otto M. Rheinschmiedt

KARNAC

First published in 2017 by
Karnac Books Ltd
118 Finchley Road
London NW3 5HT

British Library Cataloguing in Publication Data

A C.I.P. for this book is available from the British Library

ISBN-13: 978-1-78220-420-6

Typeset by V Publishing Solutions Pvt Ltd., Chennai, India

Printed in Great Britain by TJ International Ltd, Padstow, Cornwall

www.karnacbooks.com

deo concedente
dominus illuminatio mea

To Liz and Daniel

CONTENTS

ACKNOWLEDGEMENTS

In gratitude to the ancestors and pioneers of dream consciousness:

Freud who courageously employed the gift of dreams for the task of self improvement and, by doing so, dreamt into existence psychoanalysis; Artemidorus, the foremost psychosocial chronicler of dream life of the Graeco-Roman world; and Aristotle whose dream philosophy was nothing less than the dawn of the science of dreams.

Thanks to my first dream guide, Margi Robinson, who took great care of my soul life. Thanks to my first teacher of object relations, John Gravelle, who believed in me from the beginning. Thanks to my analyst Lionel Kreeger, who, with his wealth of Jewish jokes, made me crack up with laughter and thus made me see the beauty of the world.

In gratitude to Liz Greene, who introduced me to Jungian psychology, and to Howard Sasportas, by far my most inspirational teacher. I am also indebted to my friend Herbert Hahn, who opened the doors to social dreaming. And I owe it to my friend Antje Netzer Stein that I had found a theoretical home in Kleinian theory so many years ago. A home that gave way to the wider world of dreams and literature.

And, by ways of reading, Australian writer Patrick White taught me about the love of words and the freedom of imagination. My writer friends Sarah Hall, Samantha Harvey, and Sam Burnside gifted me ways of finding my own range in fiction writing.

And as to non-fiction writing, I'm grateful to my wife Liz, who encouraged me to write a book on dreams. And thanks to my friends Andrew Pullin, Farhad Dalal, Mark Stein, and Nigel Williams, and their critical reading of my ideas, that the book became a solid reality.

And, at the core of my life, always, my family. A huge thank you to my wife Liz and my son Daniel, my ardent and patient teachers of love, beauty, and soul life, who are living life according to their dreams.

ABOUT THE AUTHOR

Otto M. Rheinschmiedt is a training group analyst, psychotherapist, and psychologist in private practice in Bath. He also works as a consultant with staff teams and organisations, and is an associate lecturer at the UWE in Bristol. He has analysed dreams for over thirty years, taught dream analysis at Bath University, presented his ideas on dreams on BBC Radio programmes, and given talks on dreams and literature in the UK and abroad. His twin passions are dream research and critically reading world literature.

INTRODUCTION

"We are such stuff
As dreams are made on. And our little life
Is rounded with a sleep"

—Shakespeare, *The Tempest*

Dreams and literature are closely related. The dream's essence lies in its storytelling capacity. Dreams are autobiographical fictions that tell the story of the dreamer's life history, her insertion in transgenerational family themes, and her ethnic and cultural identity. In that sense dreams are psychosocial depositories and makers, not unlike world literature, which recreates interiority and historicity of a given time period. Literature is a dream gone solid. And the process of fiction writing duplicates the dream's inherent narrative facility.

The basis for my book lies in over thirty years' experience of dream analysis and being a critical reader of world literature. Theories employed are, in the main, psychoanalysis, literary criticism, and dream theories of fiction writing. But I will also move outside of the psychoanalytic and literary paradigms by referring to the dream's inherent creative nature, the base condition for its narrative mastery, as reflected in the universal design of creation (strategies of genius, quantum physics, and chaos theory), sleep research, the study of dreaming and historical consciousness, and theories held by the ancient dreamers (Aristotle, Artemidorus). Case studies, actual dream fictions, will be frequently used to illuminate the dream theories presented. Themes of loss, bereavement, traumatisation, and depersonalisation predominate.

The origin of my thinking goes back to Freud's foundation myth, which is linked with his father's death and a subsequent flurry of dreams in the face of loss that led him into self-analysis, prolific writing, and a lifelong love of words, winning the prestigious Goethe prize for literature on the way. By dreaming himself and the discipline of psychoanalysis into existence, he set the tone for our understanding of the psyche as a poetry-making organ and the affinity between dreams and literature.

The poetry of dreams and the poetry of world literature employ the same writerly devices. Patrick Modiano, in his memorial mode of writing, takes us into broken memory at the time of the French occupation, in a reflection of a dreamer slowly but not entirely recovering from traumatisation. Gabriel Garcia Márquez uses the method of multi-temporality, which is the simultaneous occurrence of past, present, and future, a feature which gives credence to the non-chronological, cyclical nature of dreams. Kafka, the "poet of his own disorder", writing directly from dreams, gave expression to human alienation. His writing style of obscure lucidity comes close to the *poetic* nature of dreams, bringing forth the unknown and the unthinkable from the recesses of the mind. Irene Némirovsky, writing in the midst of France's Nazi occupation during the exodus from Paris, became a writer steeped in historical consciousness, which is also a dream conception. Australian author Patrick White's notion of writing, "infinite connectivity", is duplicated in the dream's capacity to dismantle ego identity, and by doing so reaches into the domain of interrelatedness of all beings and we-consciousness, the spiritual dimension of dreaming.

The poetry of dreams and the poetry of world literature also share the exposition of human motivation, as can be seen in the complex interiority of dreams and fictional characters. Both dreams and literature bring to the fore that which is hidden but seeks expression, such as the conundrum of fear, the propensity for destructiveness, the search for love, the search for knowledge, the search for beauty, the "will to power", and the search for the spiritual.

In short, the organising ideas of the book centre on the narrative nature of dreams: dreams as autobiographical fictions and their relationship with literature and the actual process of fiction writing.

Dreaming, generated by the process of dream thinking, is regarded as the most creative state of mind, which is digesting the primitive matter of the dream, such as sensory impressions, unbearable emotions, and thoughts without a thinker. And from this primary dream process, the psychosomatic function of dreaming, the dream mind makes images, symbols, metaphors, and autobiographical fictions. Dream thinking, in its most mature form, gives rise to new autobiographical fictions that create futures without denying the dreamer's family, cultural, and ethnic identities. Futures of the human idiom reach into imagination, innovation, and generativity.

Summary of chapters

Chapter One: Dreams and the universal design of creation

Dreaming is a creative, if not the most creative, state of mind, not unlike the fiction writer's imagination and craft that brings her world of fantasy down on to paper. Both dream creativity and the creative process governing any art form are linked with the dreamer's and the artist's internal lives. It is a world of the invisible that becomes visible if a dreamer's life is undergoing changes towards well-being, living according to the dictums of love, truthfulness, and beauty; or the world of the invisible can manifest itself in a piece of art—be it a composition, a piece of architecture, a book in your hand, or a dance performed on stage.

Dream inspiration shows this link between a vital internal life and its impact on the world of matter. Any form of art is a dream gone solid. Mozart's way of composing directly from dream states, Kafka's nocturnal preoccupation with writing, Watson's dream about the molecular structure of DNA, Auguste de Kekulé's dream about the molecular structure of benzene, Paul McCartney's dream in which the song "Yesterday" wrote itself into existence, all give evidence of the assumption made.

Dreams are governed by the universal design of creation. They follow the principles of creation inherent in the strategies of genius, quantum physics, and chaos theory. Dreams cannot be understood completely if one applies a singular model of the mind, especially theories that deal entirely with internal life, as there is, of course, the social nature of dreams, which offers a larger perspective. But we have to go further still.

I will line up strategies of genius alongside the generativity of dreams so as to make the point that anything that happens in the minds of the most creative people is linked to dreams and dream-like states of mind. The following section refers to basic laws that govern the physical world. Quantum physics, through the verification of the "God particle", the Higgs boson, has proven the very process by which our world of matter is being created. My point is that there is a parallel between the physical world and the world of the invisible. Dreams, not unlike the matter-making Higgs field, are the makers of psychic reality. Another parallel between the laws underlying the physical world and the invisible world of the psyche can be found in chaos theory. Chaos governs all dynamic systems, such as the brain, the fractal geometry of nature, the weather systems, and the formation of star constellations in deep space. The character of chaos is that nothing happens arbitrarily, but according to underlying principles of organisation. There always is a balance between order and chaos. Dreams, also a dynamic system, are governed by chaos theory. Dreams occur in the boundary area between order and chaos.

Chapter Two: The fictions of dreams

In the early twentieth century possibly the most profound methods of probing into the depths of human motivation were literature and psychoanalysis, if not philosophy. Not only did psychoanalytic thought about hidden human desire and aggression enter the world of fiction writing—Virginia Woolf, Franz Kafka, Thomas Mann, James Joyce, and the writers of the South American "Boom" movement of "magical realism" spring to mind—but literature, by its very nature of digging deep into what makes us human beings, also informed the method of psychoanalytic inquiry.

Freud, who was foremost a writer, an aesthete of the written word, gave us autobiographical fictions in his case studies, in his theories, but foremost in his personal endeavour of figuring out dreams. His life as a prolific writer started with the loss of his father and the related dreams that took him by surprise. By writing down his dreams, and allowing himself to freely associate with the dream material, he not only became a person able to think about himself but he also brought to life an entirely new discipline, psychoanalysis. One of the dream thoughts that convinced his own critical mind as to the usefulness of dreams was his fantasy of killing his own father, and also his own daughter Anna. To allow himself to think freely, with the help of dreams, about the unthinkable lurking in his own psyche, namely patricide and infanticide, he opened the door to his self-analysis and the very foundation stone of psychoanalysis.

Chapter Three: Dreams, literature, and fiction writing

This is the signature section of the book. Both as a clinician working analytically with dreams and a reader of literary fiction, two seemingly divorced worlds came together. Having analysed a large number of dreams over a prolonged time period it became obvious that all dreams of an individual dreamer are interconnected, they form "omnibus" dreams along defined themes such as major early losses, the search for an unknown parent, the overcoming of debilitating depression, the search for an identity, or the working through of severe traumatisation. Such recurring themes are the content of dream narratives that are governed by the dream's inherent nature of serving memory, multi-temporality, poiesis, historical consciousness, and "infinite connectivity". Dreams occupy time and space in which the dreamer will find her identity, once autobiographical dream fictions have dug out from concealment formative life events.

To my surprise, as I was reading world literature stemming from different cultures the writerly devices used by fiction writers were not unlike the narrative devices used by dreams.

Chapter Four: The primary human drives

Dreams are expressions of human motivation. They bring into consciousness the primary human drives, and, by way of processing once unconscious motivations and human desire, dreams are instrumental in emotional maturation. The basic human drives are the conundrum of fear, the propensity for destructiveness, the search for love, the search for knowledge, the search for beauty, the "will to power", and our spiritual searches. The dynamic interplay between the human drives are the substance of building a plot, story line, and characters in the fictions of dreams.

$$F + H + L + K + B + P + S$$

The above is not an equation, nor is it a theory of everything. It is meant as a dynamic list that describes movement on a developmental time-line. Most nightmares are furnished by F and H dreams. From primitive emotions, such as hatefulness and rage, we move to the overcoming of destructiveness, arriving at the establishment of the ethical sense, which means that we are able to acknowledge that we can be destructive to ourself and other people, and take responsibility for it—a major achievement in emotional maturation. Hatred overcome can be converted into something productive, such as the healthy aggression necessary to assert the human idiom, our uniqueness as human beings, and our life force.

And from the repeated cycles of fear, and the recovery from it, we develop the capacity to tolerate uncertainty and reach into the desire for challenge. Fear on a primitive level of experience is about survival: the fear of disintegration, falling apart, as if the centre of the psyche will not hold. If digested by the process of dreaming and its import into consciousness, the fear of survival transforms into a feeling experience that is more bearable and manageable; like the anxiety that accompanies the challenges of life, in close proximity to excitement.

A sign of emotional maturity rests in the fact that we are able to endure and process difficult emotions and uncertainty, which is dependent on the primary process of dreaming, dream thinking. Dreams are not only the repository of overwhelming emotions; they are also the very process by which emotions are contained and worked upon, so that they become more manageable and are converted into emotions that are productive. The dream's underlying intention is always freedom from the tyranny of emotion.

Apart from the high frequency of nightmares, we also have plenty of sexual dreams. They rarely mean *one* thing. They are as much about physical desire as they are concerned with the way we tend to make links with ourselves and other people. Dreams are an incitement to love, with the hidden agenda that love is *the* vehicle for change. Once touched by love, we will never be the same again. And, in that sense, love is devastating.

Dreams of climbing up the celestial ladder of self-improvement land us with a responsibility for emotional understanding, and its main driving force, which is the search for knowledge. Dreams make such demands on us that we should know better who we are, and our true nature. Such knowledge is linked with the longing for finding our identity in the context of the family constellation. Where do we come from? What is the origin of our being? Which is our foundation myth? Are we able to think how we came about in the minds of our parents?

And, again stirred by the process of dream thinking, we move on to another level of development, which is the search for beauty. The attributes of beauty are truthfulness, consciousness, and meaning. One of the first truths to be found in human development is the child's awareness that she is able to harbour good *and* bad feelings toward the same person. In adult life the realisation that one has the capacity for destructiveness is key not only to developing an ethical sense but also to finding mature love.

The "will to power" has nothing to do with power over other people, the abuse of a position of authority, nor is there any resemblance with the tyranny of violence. True power is to be emotionally connected, to do things from the perspective of the heart, and to be engaged in soul life—a life that has become meaningful by serving other people. But the will to power also has other attributes, and is about the intentional, wilful engagement with a fundamental human project, giving one's life a purposeful shape; such as overcoming adversity or physical disability, not giving in to setbacks, rising again from the unmade bed of bouts of depression, seeing financial bankruptcy as a starting point for renewal, or seeing loss as an ultimate gain. In short, using the will to power as a resource for the overcoming of impasse and the demands life makes on us.

Spiritual searches have to do with soul life, *Seelenleben*, a term Freud used to describe the psyche. The spiritual is the realisation that part of the human condition is that we are suffering and that there is suffering in the world, leading to quiet contemplation and thoughtfulness, and the resolve to do something about it, which ultimately leads to the view that we are all interconnected, that nothing happens in isolation, and thus we cannot shy away from social responsibility. This experience of infinite connectivity renders suffering in the world *our* suffering, *our* concern, and requires our participation in the addressing and reversal of inequalities through the employment of compassion and loving kindness.

Chapter Five: The father of modern dream analysis

Freud is one of the most thought about and researched exponents of influential thought in the twentieth century, not so much with regard to psychoanalysis as a treatment method but to psychoanalysis as a contribution to cultural history.

In this section I will recount how Freud discovered dreams as a means of self-discovery, following on from the death of his father, which set off a flurry of dreams about the nature of their relationship and its painful loss. Freud's foundation myth was personal to him but also relevant to the way the profession of psychoanalysis would proceed from one initial dream. I will also discuss Freud's master specimen dream, "Irma's injection", which became the foundation dream of psychoanalysis, at once establishing dreams as a way of understanding the unconscious and foretelling the development of psychoanalytic thought.

Chapter Six: Sleep research

We cannot do away with the results of sleep research that has come up with findings relevant to the psychology of dreams. Dreaming was established as an autonomous state of mind, or state of consciousness, only in the late 1950s, when rapid eye movement (REM) was discovered by the French school of Jouvet, and the American school of Aserinsky and Kleitman. Significantly, REM states show that the brain is in a heightened state of arousal, not unlike sexual and aggressive states of mind. In the main, the right brain hemisphere shows high cortical arousal, which is the seat of imagination, intuition, and creative thinking. On waking up from dreams we show physical signs of sexual arousal, clitoral engorgement in females and penile erection in males.

In order to sharpen the argument for the usefulness of the dream in digesting the demands of body and mind, I am using for our discussion counterfactuals such as the evacuation theory of dreaming, which assumes that there is nothing more to dreaming than the uncluttering of the mind. Another counterfactual is the effects of severe sleep deprivation on physical and psychic well-being.

Chapter Seven: A brief history of dream consciousness

This is not about resuscitating the ancient body of dream knowledge but we do want to know about the legs upon which we are currently standing. As Rodin put it succinctly, it is important to remain devoted to the masters before you.

Notions about the occurrence of dreams and dream interpretation of prehistoric and ancient dreamers still have a bearing on modern-day understanding. Prehistoric cosmology, going back some 40,000 years, entertained the ideas of a divine dream source and of the prophetic nature of dreams. Such notions became contentious at the time of the ancient dreamers, some 2,500 years ago. The proponents of the "naturalistic" approach—in the main Hippocrates, Aristotle, Lucretius, Cicero, and Artemidorus—located the source of the dream inside the dreamer's mind and embodied self.

In this section I will examine some of the oldest preserved texts on dreams, such as Artemidorus' *Oneirocritica* (second century AD), Freud's favourite ancient dream theorist, and dream books by Aristotle (circa fourth century BC), the grandfather of modern dream theory.

Chapter Eight: The ancient deities of dreams

In Graeco-Roman mythology, Asclepius, Apollo, and Neptune were seen as the major deities of dreams, worshipped at a large number of dream temples, which offered dreamers time for respite and cures for physical ailments. In an attempt to extract psychological meaning from the deities of dreams I will explore ancient knowledge and compare it with contemporary dream thought. Apollo, for instance, was seen as the redeemer of family curses, the bringer of consciousness, and rational thought. Asclepius demanded a close union with the dreamer in rituals before going to sleep, called dream incubation, and in return would show himself in dreams and announce procedures and remedies necessary for the cure not only of physical illnesses but also of infertility and impotence.

CHAPTER ONE

Dreams and the universal design of creation

reaming can be better understood if we leave aside
psychoanalytic thinking for the time being and bring into the
equation other models of understanding the world. It is my
belief that some of the laws that govern physical reality can illuminate
the understanding of aspects of immaterial, invisible reality such as the
psyche and its main proponent, dream life.

The universe of matter possesses an internal order, as does the universe of the mind. The dynamical systems of the material world, such
as brain function, weather systems, and the formation of planetary constellations, are governed by chaos and principles that order chaos. The
same is true for the dynamical system of the mind with its emotional
underpinning. The process of dreaming creates order out of the emotional chaos of the mind. Dreaming can be understood as operating on
the boundary area between order and chaos.

Another law that governs physical reality is that under certain conditions matter can be created out of fast-moving particles. The process of
dreaming seems to resemble nature's inherent capacity as the maker of
matter. The matter of the dream consists of images, symbols, metaphor,
and autobiographical fictions, and through the process of dream thinking the psyche creates thoughts that can be thought about, and ideas

1

that serve emotional understanding and become pivotal conceptions, leading to meaningful fictions about the dreamer's historicity and identity.

* * *

Before we venture into the parallel universes of the strategies of genius, chaos theory, and quantum physics we need to let the fictions of dreams speak for themselves. I wish to make the point that the body and the mind are connected, in order to prepare the ground for a type of thinking that does not draw a clear demarcation line between the physical world and the world of the psyche, and does not preclude the idea that all worlds we live in are governed by the same laws.

Dreams and chronic fatigue syndrome

Some twenty years ago I was asked to run an analytic group in a GP surgery for sufferers of "chronic fatigue syndrome" (CFS). The two-year project was funded by what was then the primary care trust. The group, of eight, displayed the following symptoms: long spells of exhaustion, inertia, a sense of isolation, physical neglect, anxiety, sexual impotence, and a daily struggle to do the most basic chores, such as going out food shopping, cleaning the flat, doing the washing-up. The most common physical trigger for the onset of the condition was a persistent viral infection.

The group members produced dreams in keeping with the syndrome. One patient was chased by a fire-spitting dragon but had leaden legs and could not escape. Another patient dreamt he was thrown into a cement mixer that was emptied out into the concrete foundations of a skyscraper. He slowly went under the grey mass, dying a slow death of suffocation before the concrete set. Another patient dreamt she was a statue made out of marble, admired by onlookers but not able to make herself understood from inside her solid grave.

The dream images revealed, at first sight, somatic states of being, of bodily paralysis and petrification, which was reflected in the group climate, an altogether draining experience. To sit with one patient who is stuck physically is challenging but to be with eight patients who are giving in to heaviness and deadness is somewhat unbearable. Frequently I dozed off, to the amusement and annoyance of my patients, who saw one of their own primary symptoms being displayed in public. Any kind of illness makes this demand to join in with sameness.

The group was mentally animated at times but always operated at a slow-burn tempo, held down by the heightened gravitas of lethargy. Time was dragging, tearing at one's insides. There was nothing one could do apart from be with the group's comatose emotional state; truly an underwordly place of death and dying from which there is no escape. The only thing that passed for communication was long lists of symptoms, ailments, and days spent wasting time.

Except for the sudden eruption of one of the patients who felt so exhausted that he had to sit on the floor. Duncan got up, sat on the sofa, and started to have a go at the others, in the high-pitched voice of a mezzo-soprano.

> You lazy sods! We've been coming here for six months, and nothing's happening. Always the same boring stories. I'm down already, you're pulling me down even more.

The group was stunned by the resurrection of one of its own. Duncan sounded like a preacher on a mission. Or more like a dragon spitting fire, as was the case in his dream. Yvonne, always on the verge of melancholy sadness, dared to question the preacher man. Her words seemed to give in to a downward curvature of gravity before they arrived flatly.

> What do you want us to do?

> Why don't you ask him?

Duncan pointed at me, as if slapping me across the face.

The group had conjured a wake-up call for the sleeping beauty of "chronic fatigue", which had been like surrendering to an anaesthetic, as if the aesthetic of aliveness was long gone. The frozen emotional state of the group was melting right in front of our eyes. Talk of physical ailments gave way to talking about the despair of being locked into somatic states of depression.

The patient who had woken the group from its slumber talked about the malignancy of his depressive feelings, about not being able to have a life, not being able to work, and struggling to be in a relationship. Others joined in with the current of emotion, making a plea for the human condition and for the suffering in the world. The woman with the marble statue dream, Yvonne, started to talk about the sadism of her father, a drunkard who had terrorised her family of origin with his violent outbursts. She was the one who first dared to speak up when the group's preacher man had started on his tirade, spitting the dragon's fire and lighting the flame of aliveness.

Yvonne behaved as she had done in her family, where, with mixed results, it was she who placated her father, witnessing his red-hot rage cool down to a simmer or him going off into another round of violence. That was the risk. And the great cost was the loss of her childhood innocence. Yvonne's only way out was to develop a childhood depression, which was an impasse, and after a long period of time of her torment not being relieved by a parental figure, she started to somatise, struck down by one viral infection after the other.

Matthew, the patient with the cement dream, rose out of inertia by saying that he could identify with Yvonne's terror. Although he was a stunning man, he did not feel manly inside. From as early as four years old he had wanted to be a girl, when he started crossdressing, using his mother's make-up and wigs, mixing only with girls. When his father found out he beat him heavily.

I will make a man out of you! You pervert!

Matthew carried on regardless, with the clandestine support of his mother, who rather liked having a girl.

At regular intervals he stoically went through the ritual of beatings that seemed to have given his father sexual pleasure. Matthew was not to be moved, but, emotionally speaking, he died of suffocation, as if sinking into liquid cement. He was desperate to leave home in order to live his dream, which he managed to do at the age of sixteen when his uncle took him in, in London, where he was able to find a peer group of like-minded people. The skyscraper dream of adulthood had returned to the foundations of a more liberated life. The skyscraper represented the skyline of London. The suffocation in cement expressed his feeling of still being cemented in, having to live in a male body.

Duncan, the group's awakener, chipped in, saying that as a child he too was not able to follow his dream. He had been an outstanding footballer in the under-fifteens, where he was spotted by a second-division football club and offered a contract. His father, who previously had taken him to every single match, giving a convincing impression of support and dedication to the cause, changed tack and refused to give his permission, which meant that Duncan was not allowed to move on his own to the Midlands to join the club's youth development scheme. Following this disappointment he gave up football altogether, and disappeared into deliberately wrecking his body with alcohol and drugs.

The climate in the group had changed. It had moved, from the enclosure of a purely physical narrative and identification, to the beginnings of talking about things embedded in the body, never released before into the conscious mind, nor available to be thought about. During the first six months the group had remained in a cryptic place, a bodily grave, an underworldly claustrum from which it had seemed there was no escape.

It became obvious that the condition that was diagnosed medically as purely physical was, in fact, psychosomatic, whereby emotional conflict had found refuge in the body; a depression of the body, as it were. From the somatisation of internal conflict the group went on to develop a culture in which unbearable feelings could be expressed and thought about. The actual issue was not fatigue but depression. The group evolving out of the physical realm did not, however, take a linear course of development. Naturally it followed chaos theory, always oscillating between bodily identification and emotional understanding, not unlike the nature of light, at once particle and wave.

Yvonne was not content any longer to recoil from life, as she had done in the feeble attempt to fend off her father's violence, which she had taken inside like a malignant growth, expecting it to resurface at any time. Freeing herself from out of the marble statue of the dream, she discovered the power of assertion, urged on by Duncan, who became increasingly angry with the father of his childhood for having ruined his footballing career, in turn starting to own his dream, in which he was chased by a fire-spitting dragon, unable, being leaden-footed to escape.

As the lead weight of "chronic fatigue" lessened, his fire-spitting self gained momentum, and he reconnected more and more with the life force that had gone underground. But he also recognised that he had lived on the illusion that football would have spared him from the depression that had seized him in early childhood when his mother left the family. In the final furlong of the group Duncan also understood that his father might have been envious of his footballing talent, determined to scoop it out from him, with the intention of ruining the possibility of a career.

When Matthew announced in the group that he had consulted a psychiatrist with the aim of going through with a sex change, Yvonne lost her composure.

Why do you want your willy cut off? The problem is you hate your body! The way your father hated you for being so girlish.

If there had been such a thing, the hair on the back of the group's head would have stood on end. Matthew was mortally offended, performing a girlish impression of indignation and sulking. Yvonne had, in his mind, metamorphosed into his emasculating father.

Just before time was running out and the group was approaching its two-year life span, Matthew started to come round to the idea that his problem was not being enclosed in a man's body but self-hatred fuelled by his sadistic father. In fact, on an emotional level, his father had already emasculated him. In his mind there were no pudenda left anyway. And Yvonne, who flourished on finding her power as a woman, remained solidly by Matthew's side, speaking the unspeakable. In the end he never went through with a sex-change operation, preferring to remain living in a man's body, a handsome man's body for that matter, but feeling like a woman in the privacy of his mind.

* * *

Having mapped out aspects of body–mind continuity through a case study of a psychosomatic condition and its inherent dream life, we have seen that the mind has a tendency to create somatic conditions, symptoms, as it were, of unresolved emotional conflict. And somatic conditions, once established and fortified by stubbornly held theories (*my body is the culprit, my body lets me down*), have an impact on mood and emotional well-being. It is striking, if not mind-boggling, how the way the mind and the body intelligently invent psychopathologies and illnesses, an aesthetic of despair, as it were, in order to avoid the actual crux of the matter; which means that we are inherently steering away from truthfulness and thoughts that seem too unbearable to be conceived of and experienced, except for in dreams, mainly in the shape of nightmares, which remind us of the daemons of the night.

The nightmarish dreams Duncan, Yvonne, and Matthew displayed at the beginning of treatment were in keeping with purely physical notions of, and identifications with, "chronic fatigue". And yet, within the dilemma of physical enclosure and depression lay its own solution, namely depression of an emotional nature and its origin in unbearable emotional conflict. Duncan's persecutory dragon had become a companion of assertion, Yvonne's enclosure in marble had led to her finding the fluidity of emotional life, and Matthew, once imprisoned in a cemented notion of unwanted masculinity, realised he could live in a man's body but feel feminine inside.

We are now moving on from the mind–body unity that can express a person's fear of redemption to the other side of the human scale. Instead of creating an illness, the mind creates a fundamental human project; the mind at its most potent location on the mind–matter continuum. The study of strategies of genius shows the ways in which geniuses approach and realise their creative projects, from the world of ideas to their manifestation in the real world. And it is the process of dreaming proper and of conscious dreaming in waking life that is the source of these strategies of genius.

Dreams and the strategies of genius

> All this fires my soul, and, provided I am not disturbed, my subject enlarges itself, becomes methodized and defined, and the whole, though it be long, stands almost complete and finished in my mind, so that I can survey it, like a fine picture or a beautiful statue, at a glance. Nor do I hear in my imagination the parts successively, but I hear them, as it were, all at once. What a delight this is I cannot tell. All this inventing, this producing, takes place in a pleasing lively dream. (Mozart, 1878; Sadie, 2006)

Mozart who composed entire orchestral pieces in his mind and then put the music down on paper with few corrections, gave credit to the source of his inspiration, which was dream inspiration; musical dreams, gone solid in the shape of notes. Composition for him was an aesthetic experience during which he utilised the method of conscious dreaming in waking life. Robert Dilts, who, in *Strategies of Genius* (1994), studied the creative patterns of geniuses such as Aristotle, Mozart, and Einstein, found some ten principles underpinning their productive projects.

i.   Geniuses tend to have a dominant visual sense (being able to see things in pictures),

ii.   they use numerous links between the senses (synaesthesia),

iii. they are able to hold multiple perspectives on their works of creation,

iv.   they manage to switch between perceptual positions (me, you, and observer),

v.   they are able to think simultaneously about the abstract and the concrete (ideas and their practical realization),

vi.   they maintain feedback loops between the concrete and the abstract,

vii. they show a balance of the cognitive functions (dreaming and reality), dreaming their dreams into solid existence,

viii. they ask basic questions,

ix.   they use metaphors and analogies,

x.   and they have a mission beyond individual identity. (Ibid., pp. 277–283)

Have you got the making of a genius? If you analysed a large number of dreams, you would come to the conclusion that they contain all the ingredients of genius. In fact, the underlying process of dream activity, that is, dream thinking, is the very source from which human genius springs. Not surprising, really. Dreams are the stuff we are made of.

Does that mean that we're all geniuses? Of course not. The only difference between geniuses and us ordinary mortals is that geniuses are able to use the full range of the strategies of genius inherent in the process of dreaming. Geniuses are waking dreamers, they dream their dreams into existence, using all the skills available from lucid dreaming. They are able to re-enter a creative dream at will, and come out of it with the gift of the dream, which is dream inspiration. Not only that. They are able to convert the dream into something visible, which involves reality testing and the ability to put ideas into tangible form, reaching, at its peak, a consortium of the practical, the aesthetic, and the universal design of creation.

Only a handful of us can claim to be geniuses but the aesthetic of dreams allows us to strive for genius in small pockets of our lives. We do have the potential of genius in niche areas of experience. The fact remains we *are* geniuses by ways of dreaming, in the same way that we are sexually potent both in our dreams and during somatic states of dreaming that are closely linked with the physiology of sexual arousal.

We are now talking about the possibility of something we *are* not but are *striving* to be, in an attempt to widen the scope of perception and the possibility of change. The impotent man might dream about rampant sexual encounters, feeling sexy, attractive, and immensely potent. A single mother living in poverty dreams that she is rich beyond measure, raking in money and fame by writing a bestseller. A dreamer whose singing makes the whole family, including cat and dog, cringe with embarrassment dreams about singing a solo part in a Wagnerian opera in front of hundreds of people, eliciting delirious applause. A mouse of a man dreams that he is the alpha lion of a sizeable group of lions, lionesses, and cubs. Such dreams are not necessarily compensatory, nor signs of positive inflation, as the Jungians would have it, nor symptoms of omnipotence, as the Kleinians would have it, but put into place by the dream mind as a reminder of what is possible. Dreams construct possible worlds. They get us away, for one hour and forty minutes per night, from the tedium of ordinary life, run on the tramlines of habit.

But there are pockets of emotional life, under the authorship of dreaming, that give expression to the genius of ordinariness, such as mourning, humour, play, and subject immersion. Grieving is a creative state of mind, as it takes seriously what the individual has lost, but also, in the process of mourning something is built inside whilst the ties are severed from that which is lost. This is a paradox that leads to an aesthetic substance, something good and robust that stems from experiences of a once loved person. Humour is a universal outlet for life's oddities, blunders, and paradoxes. In the main, life doesn't make sense. Laughter does away with the illusion that we know what life is about. It disarms even our fear of mortality. Humour is the weapon of holy men, great men, but also of ordinary people who realise the need for nonsense. Humour rebels against the constraints of being boxed into stereotypes, running on the tramlines of habit, and the mindless aspects of tradition, the stuffy cul-de-sac of suffocation.

When we play with reality, with possible worlds and outlandish ideas, we are in the adult's domain of revisiting the freedom of children's play. Children play themselves into reality. They play on the endless shores of imagination and fantasy (Winnicott, 1967). So should we, as adults, when we allow ourselves to take a break from the demands of everyday life so that we can return to the grind of adulthood fortified with the memory of having danced again on the sandy beaches of childhood.

Now to the real thing. Pure genius. Mozart was fortunate enough to be able to see the entirety of a new composition right in front of his eyes as if it were a painting or a statue, which would indicate the dominance of his visual sense. It was Aristotle who said that

> To the thinking soul, images serve as if they were contents of perception … just as it were seeing, it calculates and deliberates. (Ibid., p. 278)

Geniuses tend to use all of their senses and develop numerous links between them, which is called synaesthesia. Mozart experienced a sensory feast—called *Schmaus* in Viennese—during the process of composing: he sensed the music in his body, he saw the compositions taking shape in his head, and he even "tasted" musical notes as if they were ingredients of a gourmet meal, like "putting together morsels to create a meal" (Dilts, 1994, p. 282). A sense organ was not destined to do just one thing, it nudged into the ground of other senses, translating the neighbouring sense into a surprising novelty. Mozart's sensory *Schmaus* is also reflected in the concept of *convivium* (discussed later in Chapter Four), which is a "feasting together", a Renaissance idea of a conference of scholarly minds coming together to feast on food, wine, and ideas.

Mozart also entered the ground of metaphor, where images of food and food preparation stood for the process of composition. In his vivid imagination he had become an alchemist, overseeing, in his musical laboratory, cooking processes that led to a culinary triumph.

Stanford, a metaphor theorist, wrote in the 1930s that

> the essence of metaphor is that a word undergoes a change or extension of meaning. (Cox & Theilgaard, 1987, p. 95)

Mozart believed that after a spell of musical subject immersion his symphonies would write themselves, they became autonomous entities, and self-creating. The latter is a dream function, which means that if you instruct your dream world with a certain project, a wish, or an idea, what the ancient dreamers called "dream incubation", it will mull it over and come up with an answer, an end product, a piece of art, or an opus Dei.

Geniuses are able to ask basic questions, and persist with it. For Mozart, music consisted in an ongoing enquiry as to whether "two notes loved each other". Composition was the result of aesthetic questioning about the actual relationship between a couple of notes, which he extended into ever-increasing configurations, leading to orchestral pieces. Listening to Mozart, be it piano concertos, violin sonatas, string quartets, operas, or symphonies, one is always aware of the sensory impact of his music, which is full of relatedness, one note liking the other, and so on, until it becomes an act of love of the human condition.

Geniuses are on a mission beyond individual identity. Einstein's mission was no less than to try to enter the mind of the universe. He writes:

> I want to know how God created this world. I am not interested in this or that phenomenon, in the spectrum of this or that element; I want to know his thoughts; the rest are details. (Einstein, 1956, p. 98)

What Einstein eventually found in establishing the general theory of relativity were astonishing facts about the space–time continuum, doing away with Newton's static model of physics: the curvature of space and time, the aesthetic geometry of the universe, and the crucial fact that symmetry is at the heart of fundamental laws of nature.

Mozart, from an early age, was wisely guided by his father Leopold, a musician himself, to play musical instruments and to compose. Music became young Mozart's mission, beyond individual identity, and was never superseded by anything else, not even his marriage, nor his friendship with his sister, nor by any claim to courtly positions, such as being the Kapellmeister to the Austro-Hungarian Emperor. Instead, he wanted to reach into the musical sphere of God's creation.

The psychoanalyst Winnicott said that an artist needs to own a sense of ruthlessness in order to pursue her art (1956b). Mozart, being ruthlessly immersed in his composing, shared this one thing with Freud: that both men created their masterpieces following the deaths of their fathers. They also employed dreams and dream-like states of mind to pursue, in the words of Sartre, their respective "fundamental human project". Freud's edifice to his father was *The Interpretation of Dreams*; Mozart's edifice to his father was the *Requiem*. Their respective missions, beyond those of individual identity, had their roots in a major loss and the ensuing grieving process.

Dreams and quantum physics

Fifty years ago, Professor Peter Higgs, a theoretical quantum physicist, predicted that there is an invisible energy field that fills the vacuum throughout the observable universe (Baggott, 2012). Without this field we would not exist. His theory has enormous implications. At the beginning of the universe, at the time of the Big Bang, the smallest building blocks of matter, from which all else is made, were in danger of forever rushing around at the speed of light, had it not been for the presence of this energy field that facilitated the formation of matter.

The smallest particles, protons and photons, not to mention quarks, would never otherwise have come together to make stars, planets, and the solid world as we know it. The Higgs field is a maker of matter, a facilitating environment in which the formation of the visible world has occurred. Without it the universe would have collapsed into itself, fragmented forever like a psychotic mind.

In this way there is a connection, if only metaphorically, with dream states. What happens in the universe also happens inside the universe of the mind. Renaissance philosopher Marsilio Ficino talked about "a whole universe" inside the mind. The physical universe possesses an internal order, and so does the psyche. The universal design of creation does not just belong to the material world we live in, it also belongs to the world of the invisible, which is our dream world. Without the process of dreaming, the particles of the mind, such as fragmented emotion, the overload of sensory stimuli, the vast sea of language, the libraries of memory, and cognition, would all be dashing about at a dizzying speed, aimlessly creating a world of manic incoherence. The absence of dreaming, as can be witnessed during the course of a rare illness, "fatal familial insomnia" (FFI), will lead to states of utter physical exhaustion and mental fragmentation, and ultimately death. Thus a healthy dream function serves physical restoration and mental stability.

The process of dreaming as the maker of internal life is comparable to the Higgs field, which is the maker of visible reality. The process of dreaming creates a field in which, taken from the chaos of sensory overload, fragmented emotions, and senseless thoughts, the components and structures of the psyche, are being formed, such as the ability to think, to make sense of our emotional world, and to find meaning in a world that requires meaning to be made.

The most astonishing aspect of the eventual experimental verification of the Higgs boson was the way in which it came about, which was originally an idea in the mind of Peter Higgs (and other teams), put down on paper through highly complicated mathematical formulations. Mathematics at such a high altitude, based on lucid dreaming, had come up with proof of external reality. Thus, from the invisibility of ideas, expressed in elegant and aesthetic mathematical theorems, the foundation stone was laid for experimental physics. The actual verification of the existence of the Higgs boson occurred in experiments at the Large Hadron Collider (LHC), built by the European Organization for Nuclear Research (CERN), near Geneva, Switzerland, and was confirmed in July 2012 with "five-sigma confidence". As good as true.

The so-called "God particle", a term coined by Leon Lederman (1993) and despised by Higgs, who is prone to humility, was found, through the recreation of conditions that have not existed since just after the Big Bang, by smashing together protons at very high speed. The Higgs boson is a subatomic particle that gives indirect evidence of the Higgs field, which makes particles form into matter. The Higgs boson is a clustering in the Higgs field, a particle gone fat, as it were, and, after the collision, slows down and decays. Mass in the Standard Model of physics is nothing other than the interaction between small particles and the Higgs field, giving them depth and causing them to slow down. This resistance to acceleration is what we call mass. The photographic evidence of the particle collisions and the ultra-brief occurrence of the Higgs boson is as beautiful to look at as are the mathematical equations, in themselves pieces of art, that led to its discovery in the first place.

In the language of dreams we could say that the process of dreaming resembles the Higgs field, and the dream mind's nocturnal issuing of dreams resembles the occurrence of the Higgs boson, the fat God-sent particle. To the extent that the Higgs boson gives evidence of the invisible Higgs field, so dreams give evidence of a field in which something is being created at the core of the psyche. Dreams, despite the fact that they are immaterial by nature, enter the area in-between the material and the immaterial on the grounds of their representation in the dreamer's mind. Such imprints are, in the main, visual, cinematographic, highly sensual, packed with epic fictions, plot lines, cryptic language, and metaphor. In this boundary area of the world we live in, between physical reality and fantasy life, dreams leave traces of something wondrous and mysterious occurring deep inside.

In the "Higgs field of dreaming" something is being created out of the unintegration and chaos of the psyche. Such particles of the mind are sensory impressions, raw emotions, and scattered thoughts that then take on a more material reality, a fattening of ideas, as it were. The dream has matter: a building of substance out of the invisible and the corporal thinness of fantasy and imagination. Thoughts underlying dreams will accrue mass and substance so as to become markers in the chaos of the mind. The material substance of dreams can easily be felt following nightmares, sexual dreams, or dreams of sensory impact, that is, kinaesthetic dreams. And, if the dreamer is prepared to take her dream life seriously, she will be living life as directed by her invisible companion, who is in a position to give advice, providing thoughts that make sense of unconscious reality, and offer truthfulness around which the foundations of the psyche will be built.

Such as: the insight that one might be suffering from the loss of a significant person during childhood; that it is not the abused child that is mad but the abusive circumstances of volatile family life; that from early on one had the sense of not belonging to the family of origin, nor to this world on an existential level, so that the task of internal work and dream analysis is to find a foothold in this world, to join the human race, as it were. In the overcoming of human suffering we will eventually find solace, beauty, and the gift of connectedness with other people. Such building stones might also be referred to as what the ancient Greeks called *omphaloi*, sacred places that hold the centre of the world. If the centre of the individual holds, organising ideas that have sprung from dream life will be the makers of that person's futures, free from the tyranny of emotional torment.

Dreams and chaos theory

What is happening inside our mind is rather unpredictable. The self is a fluid possibility. On getting up in the morning we are never quite sure who is turning up from the mysterious world of sleep and dreams. Is it the person who enjoys the morning sunshine? Is it, perhaps, the grumpy old man, the *Morgenmuffel*, who knows exactly what a waste of time this day is going to be? Or is it the one drowned by a nightmare that cannot be shaken off, the way tar and feathers stick together. Or is it the eternal optimist showing up, hopping out of bed with a long shopping list of things to do?

The psyche follows the laws of chaos theory. We are not unlike the weather, forever changing, unpredictable, at once stormy and arrested in inertia, at once climbing the heights of a hot summer's day and conjuring up the dark clouds of a rain-sodden one. If truth be told, at times we are fed up with living as an emotional being and wish to take a break from the enslavement of emotion as much as we want to escape our maritime climate.

Chaos theory studies the laws of dynamical systems; its applications are meteorology, physics, engineering, economics, and biology. In the 1880s, Henri Poincaré, an early proponent of chaos theory, found that the trajectory of particles was not linear, as expected, but in unpredictable curvatures. The movement of the smallest parts of what makes up the physical world behaved in a rather wild and eccentric way. So, if the particles that make the world and our bodies follow the laws of chaos, it would not be surprising that our emotional world, which springs from the physical world, should also follow the laws of chaos. Dreams, which are the repositories of our emotions, are governed by chaos.

Edward Lorenz, who in the 1960s studied the chaotic nature of the weather, tried to simulate weather conditions through complex mathematical formulas. He found that weather prediction was highly dependent on "initial conditions". The smallest changes to the initial weather conditions had a large impact on the long-term outcome, only allowing for predictions a week ahead. Lorenz's definition of chaos is as follows:

> Chaos: When the present determines the future, but the approximate present does not approximately determine the future. (In Briggs, 1992)

If we apply his thinking about the weather to emotional chaos then we might conclude that if we are not fully aware of our emotional insertion in reality at any given time, we will not know where our emotions might be taking us. In other words, in order to become the authors, if not the masters, of our emotions we need to learn about and be mindful of the "initial condition", which means reading our emotions with a high degree of sensitivity, so that we don't end up in a chaotic, out of control, emotional storm. Or, on the evidence of a storm brewing, we might spare the people around us and take ourselves away into the privacy of the mind. In this way the emotional weatherman takes pride in his forecasts and in his human generosity, namely, warning others in the vicinity of impending misery and terror. Latest weather news just in: Make a runner if you can!

Freud, who had a sobering view of the human condition, famously used a metaphor for the conscious and the unconscious parts of the psyche, the "ego" and the "id". The rider, donning the colours of the ego, sits on horseback, which is none other than the id of raw emotion and instinct. This rider does not belong to the refined Viennese riding school, taking a Lippizzaner through the controlled and beautiful motions of dressage; instead the rider is always on the verge of losing control of the huge beast beneath his bottom, pelvis, and inside legs. In other words, Freud was intrinsically a proponent of chaos theory, never forgetting that what we call culture stems from the primitive emotion of cave man. Freud was never that convinced of his own premise that "where id was, ego shall be", that we will forever be brutes driven by instinct.

Lorenz's weather simulations have another application to the world of emotion. A basic psychoanalytic view of the patient in the consulting room is that the human fault-lines we see in front of us in the present are somehow determined by the emotional environment of the patient's early life. What analysts rely on is the "carrying over" of unresolved issues from the past, also called transference, played out in the present by means of memory, dreams, fantasies, and triggers in present life that bring up the daemons of the past. All of this relies on the imprecision of past emotional experience, which strictly follows chaos theory. It is not an exact science.

Knowing this conundrum, we clinicians still fall into the trap of believing everything the patient tells us. The patient at the outset of analysis always tends to "lie" about the past; not lying exactly, but not knowing very much about the "initial conditions" of her emotional foundations that stem from the original family constellation. In the process of peeling back layer after layer of early childhood memories the patient is able to make sense of her suffering in the present, to link the beginning with the end, and to demystify some of the perceived assumptions and morbid myths of family fictions, such as the cliché of happy family life, promises of love eternal, and affection, that have been sprinkled on the lush summer lawn of belongingness.

Despite their chaotic nature, dreams are still the most reliable source of memory. At the root of the dream's hallucinatory representations of reality always lies a dream thought, as sharp and precise as can be. Freud pointed out that dreams are "mnesic", meaning holding memory. Dreams wander on the time line of past, present, and future with ease, bringing up events, if not moments, that have shaped our lives and in which the doors of perception opened with lucidity and allowed the future to come in. The dream's knack of being multi-temporal shows that dreams are not unlike vast libraries that hold the books of family history, the histories of previous generations, and the knowledge of humankind.

* * *

In one of my dreams seminars a student reported a dream in which she came across a scruffy old man, bearded, smelly, living rough on the streets of London. He stood in her way, demanding not money nor booze but her attention. *Look at me closely!*, was his plea. Repulsed by what she had seen, she did not even try to contemplate what the man might stand for, as if his old man's stench still lingered in her nostrils. By disowning the dream and the bearded man like faeces of the mind, she invited the seminar group's associations.

They, by contrast, liked the dream, and formed a relationship with the old man in fantasy, playing with possible worlds. One student thought the old man was not just old, he was ancient. Another one, a musician by trade, heard the old man's words as if spoken in a different language. The dreamer, reluctantly, returned to her dream life, which issued another instalment. The old man showed up again. But this time he was not unkempt but dressed smartly in a black robe, a chequered shawl in black and white around his neck, his hair long, black, and shiny, a cap on his head, saying something in Yiddish.

The seminar group got excited, and encouraged her to do a family search. The dreamer was adamant she was not Jewish nor that she had any Jewish ancestors—*I'm Church of England*—again being dismissive, treating the dream's information with the reserved air of an ice queen. But she could not fend off her curiosity. When she rang her mother who lived in the States she heard to her astonishment that some hundred years ago her ancestors living in Latvia had converted from Judaism to Christianity, which did not help during the pogroms. The memory of hatred is long. Most of the extended family were wiped out, first by the Russians, then by the Nazis. One of the family, her grandfather, managed to escape to England. The old man in the dream, it turned out, was an influential man in the Latvian Jewish community, in his position as chief rabbi, but had become a controversial figure by preaching religious conversion. The dreamer, by way of dreams, had found her ancestral history, and her ethnic and cultural identity. Not long after the gift of the dream she announced in the group

I'm Jewish. I always was Jewish. I better do something about it.

The dream, a nightmare at first sight, had turned out to be a godsend.

* * *

Lorenz, who researched chaos in weather conditions, found that, surprisingly, there are organising fields underlying chaos. For instance, an aircraft on landing in a storm would experience turbulence, which, in fact, is caused by the tips of its own wings interacting with the density of the flow of air. There is a critical point beyond which a dynamic system creates turbulence. It is created by a "strange attractor". At the centre of the turbulence, not unlike at the centre of a tornado, there is a field that creates the vortex. The patterns of chaos, observed in weather conditions on a small as well as a large scale, can also be found in the patterns in which entire galaxies of stars are being created, again in the overall shape of a spiral or vortex. Without "strange attractors" the weather would be desperately chaotic and without any patterns. What can be seen on the television screen, when the weatherwoman is selling with a smile yet another low-pressure vortex spiralling across the British isles, is the intervention of "strange attractors" shaping total chaos up into organised chaos.

The neuroscientist Paul Rapp discovered that the brain is governed by chaos. In experiments he observed brain waves through an EEG monitor. The person observed had two tasks to perform, one of which was to close her eyes and rest, the other to solve a complicated arithmetical problem (Briggs, 1992, p. 31). Looking at the brain waves created, Rapp noticed that the chaotic activity of the brain was attracted to specific regions of the plotting space in each of the two states. The fractal geometry of the quiescent state of mind showed low waves, whereas the brain waves of heightened cortical activity were more energetic and expansive. In short, there is a "strange attractor" for the mind when it is resting and a "strange attractor" for the mind doing a maths problem.

From sleep research we know that during dreaming the brain is in a heightened state of arousal (Gawler, 1987, p. 201), not unlike during states of aggression or sexual stimulation. The mind is doing overtime, labouring away at digesting a large influx of sensory impressions, fragmented emotions, and thoughtless thoughts. If we link up Rapp's findings that there are "strange attractors" for different states of mind, we can assume that there is also one for REM states. This "strange attractor" for dream states might demonstrate the high mental energy that is summoned up in parts of the brain during dreaming. So dreaming, not unlike the brain's activity during problem-solving, has to do with the ordering of the chaos inherent in the brain and in the mind.

The "strange attractor of dreaming" is pulling together themes out of the overload of sensory impressions, fragmented feelings, and thoughts in search of an author. The "strange attractor" performs a function not dissimilar to a fiction writer who, out of the richness of vocabulary, the traditions of storytelling, and the vast libraries of literature shapes his own stories, plots, characters, and ideas.

Psychoanalyst Bion springs to mind who, in his theory of thinking, talks about the "alpha function" that the mother performs to help her baby overcome unbearable somatic states and primitive emotions (1962a). She becomes a container for the baby's distress so that the baby learns to go through the cycles of terror and relief herself. The onus of mother's containing function is on the recovery from unbearable emotion. She performs her alpha function best when she gives in to reverie, that is, to dream states. In Bion's theory of thinking this function, which depends on the mother's state of mind, her receptivity and openness to the baby's demands, is the foundation stone for the developing mind in which unbearable emotions can be thought about, leading to emotional understanding, emotional intelligence, and the development of an ethical sense. The latter is concerned with a discerning attitude towards good and bad, the knowledge that one is capable of being loving *and* hateful toward the same person, which leads to a sense of remorse and a wish to make reparation.

Thus, mother performing the alpha function, which centres on her ability to dream in the baby's presence, becomes a "strange attractor" for the baby's chaotic internal world made up mainly of primitive states of dreaming, bringing cohesion to an unintegrated mind. The "strange attractor of dreaming" underlies the mother's role of introducing peaceful states of mind to the baby.

* * *

Benoit Mandelbrot, a mathematician, is the inventor of the "theory of roughness". He observed that many of the geometrical patterns of nature are chaotic and cannot be described by linear mathematical models. In *Les objects fractals: forme, hasard et dimension* (1975) (later revised, enlarged, translated, and published in 1982 as *The Fractal Geometry of Nature*), Mandelbrot introduced the term "fractal" to suggest a geometry that focuses on broken, wrinkled, and uneven shapes. Fractal is derived from the Latin *fractus*, meaning broken or shattered. We come across fractal patterns everywhere we look: trees, mountains, a rugged coast line, a weather system, the shapes of a river delta, the spacing of stars in the night sky. But also on a smaller scale nature seems to be ordered by fractals: the intricate veins of an autumn leaf are not dissimilar to the branching of the circulatory and bronchial systems.

The patterns of chaos are nothing other than the records or imprints of ever-changing dynamical systems, like the turbulence of waves or of cyclical weather fronts leaving their traces. Fractals tell the story of the roughness of nature, its inherent energy, and its dynamical changes and transformations.

There appears to be a similarity between the notion of the fractal geometry of nature and the ancient Japanese aesthetic of the rough, *wabi-sabi*, which describes the beauty of things imperfect, impermanent, incomplete, of things humble and modest, and of things unconventional. The spiritual values of the aesthetic of the rough is that truth comes from the observation of nature, especially its murky, overlooked, and uneven details, and that beauty can be coaxed out of ugliness. In metaphysical terms, *wabi-sabi* suggests that the universe is in constant motion towards, or away from, potential, when going through the cycles of destruction and construction, nothingness and fullness.

There seems to be a fractal geometry inherent in dreams. The predominant form in which dreams present themselves is the visual sense, but dreams also make themselves known through the vehicle of synaesthesia, the merging of all the senses, and their translation from one mode to another: smell turns into sound, sound turns into the kinaesthetic, taste turns into the visual, touch turns into sound, etc. Such sensory material is shown against the screen of consciousness, except for the stuff of twilight, being just beneath the waterline of perception, in-between the many worlds we live in, opaque and mysterious in its nature.

There is nothing Hollywoodish about dreams; they are not polished, nor are they vulgar and hollow. Dreams are never the finished product; they take a lifetime to mature. Nor are they accomplished, or coherent. They follow an aesthetic of the rough. Having said that, they are the product of considerable work already invested by the "Higgs field of dreaming" and the "strange attractors of dreaming", in short, the process of dream thinking. Dreams are the makers of things essential to consciousness.

At first sight, dreams appear to be broken, however convincing their epic narrative, their sparkling images, or the elegant delivery of their cryptic syntax. There is an aspect of the presentational mode of dreams that comes straight from the Shakespearian madhouse, the royal court of internal life. Anything is possible, as it is in the broken mind, the sinister mind, the mind capable of infanticide, patricide, or matricide.

* * *

Within the fractal nature of the world there are principles that seem to order chaos. Fractal scaling shows similarities of detail on many different scales. For instance, if your camera zooms into a vine-covered wall, each magnification reveals new detail that repeats the same patterns discovered at larger scales. In the language of fractal geometry the vine is an object that exists between dimensions. Another characteristic that accompanies fractal scaling is self-similarity. This means that the shapes seen on a large scale seem to repeat themselves on a smaller scale. Have a closer look at your organic vegetable box. You might find the visual feast of a Romanesco cauliflower. The colours are a mix of light bilious green and yellow, its shape a reminder of the raggedy shape of the back of Australian dragons, and, on a larger scale, its reflection is in the Sydney Opera House with its dragon-shaped roof ridge.

Such self-similarity was produced by the use of powerful computers. Scientists and mathematicians working on fractal geometry realised that if they programmed the computers with fairly simple nonlinear equations they were able to display on the screens art of stunning beauty. The trick with the simulation of nature's aesthetic was to rerun the same equation and to feed back its results. Nature, as we know, is full of repetitions and feedback loops, and in that way it is no different from one of the primary strategies of genius (Dilts, 1994a), and its origin in dream life.

The Mandelbrot set, with its reiteration of the equation, shows an explosion of self-similarity on all scales, the same shapes occurring in different sizes in spider-like images. The mind-bending fact about being able to reproduce not only nature but also its chaotic propensity was superseded by the realisation that nature is governed by mathematical principles, even if its recapturing is in another paradigm. Chaos and order always remain twinned areas of experience. Not only that. Art, following on from the images produced in the boundary area of the Mandelbrot set, is organised by tight mathematical principles, the world of ideas, and the craft of its physical realisation. The Greeks had two terms for art, one of which was *techné*, meaning the technical aspects of any art form, the ways of realising ideas in a practical, skilful manner. You can't be a Rodin without knowing how to cast a sculpture, or without knowing the properties of metal.

* * *

The question is: are dreams following the laws of "fractal scaling" and "self-similarity"? If we take scale and self-similarity as a measurement for dreams then we need to link it up with form and emotional impact. There are recurring dreams, in the main, nightmares, that seem to follow the dreamer around. This can easily be for a lifetime. Laura is a case in point. She had lost both of her parents in a car crash, which she survived aged seven. Not only had her actual life turned into a nightmare but her dream life, unsurprisingly, issued one instalment of torment after another. In one dream she was going under, drowning in huge tidal waves, in another she was suffocating to death in narrow underground caves, never reaching the light of day. Always the same dreams, from the age of seven. As if the couple of nightmares had replaced the parental couple.

There was little redemption in her life, as her relatives were unwilling to step in and take her in. So she ended up in care homes, one after the other, where, not only was she not given solace and emotional containment for her grief to be able work itself through, but she was cruelly treated both by staff and by other children. Not that she was unable to be devious, rebellious, and indeed abusive herself. Laura rescued her lost cause by retreating into the deepest recess of her heart, so that the flame of love was not extinguished, without giving anything of her suffering away to the outside world, giving a convincing impression of an ice princess and then, in her late teens, an ice queen. Her glacial states of mind were accompanied, in the privacy of her mind, by the repetitive duet of nightmares. In an eerily beautiful sense they had become her companions. At times she thought that was all she had.

During the course of treatment the severity of her dreams lessened, to the extent that she was able to melt the glacier that was her heart. The dreams still carried on in a modified form. The drowning dream turned into dreams about swimming, floating on the surface of the water, lying on her back; the turbulence of the waves made way for softer waves lashing the sandy beach. In real life she was terrified of water, a terrible swimmer, always on the verge of rising anxiety. However, the anxiety turned into excitement, and to the sheer physical joy of being in the sea.

The suffocation dream in narrow caves turned into the spaciousness of an underworld cave system of ancient times, not unlike the Lascaux caves that host prehistoric wall paintings. All of her senses opened in this cathedral-like space. She heard the laughter of Asclepius, the deity of dreams; she saw his wife, Psyche, ride by on horseback, followed by a herd of bulls, their hooves making the ground shudder. Laura had become a huntress of bison that easily fed her family of origin, her lost family who visited her in the forbidden dormitory. On a bed of dreams she lay in-between her parents, who held her, talked to her, and gave her the freedom to let them go, so that she could get on with life instead of pining her loss. In the caves she also came across Herbie, her dog, who was as loyal as he was daft. He looked bloated. *What have I done to him?* She had, in fact, violently stuffed down his throat a huge amount of custard. *Poor creature*, she thought in the dream.

In the sessions Laura realised that she had made her dog, who was clumsy and always up to something naughty, into her confidante in the absence of close friends. She remembered the custard from childhood, crucially from the time before her parents' death. They had doted on her and had a knack of celebrating almost anything, just to make a fuss. Laura realised that, following the death of her parents, she had frozen, and, being severely depressed, there was no sense of direction, and a deadness touched everything like a layer of dust. All she had was the deadness of dead parents. As she started to mourn their loss, some twenty years after the actual loss, the cave dream of suffocation had turned into dreams that showed her aliveness as a child in the presence of loving parents. She also had to learn to take back her idealisation of them (Asclepius and Psyche in the dream), to make them into ordinary people with human faults. Having felt dehumanised as a child, it was now her task as an adult to humanise herself and her parents.

What is my point? I want to demonstrate that the fractal geometry of nature also applies to the world of dreams, and, in tandem with it, the ordering qualities of chaos, namely "fractal scaling" and "self-similarity". The shape of nightmares has a different impact on the dreamer along the timeline of life. In her early life Laura's nightmares were just overwhelming and devastating. Later on in life they still showed up with vehemence. The themes of loss, petrification, and deadness still remained but on a less catastrophic scale. The "fractal scaling of dreams" is nothing less than the same shapes of dreams showing up throughout the lifetime of a dreamer, the scale of its emotional impact shifting from enormous to bearable.

The "self-similarity of dreams" is their lifelong thread of themes spun around the same issues. *Once an orphan, always an orphan*, Laura used to say. But in her loneliness she had found a capacity for solitude, that is, being able to enjoy her own company, Herbie at her feet, smelly and with bad breath. At twenty-seven she was ready to allow other people into her heart, but in her case the propensity for being loved will always entail the theme of terrible loss. The effects of a human catastrophe will always radiate into the dreamer's life, even if it has subsequently shifted into something at the polar opposite of the original conundrum. There is no doubt that a loss is also a gain, but the gain is always imbued with the scent of loss. Behind Laura's frosty exterior and barely hidden fragility, no one had ever thought it possible that she had inside her a vast cave of riches that would enable her to stay afloat on the sea of life.

* * *

How do the findings of chaos theory and quantum physics have bearing on the world of dreams? Are we entitled to transfer universal designs of creation from one world to the other, from the physical to the invisible? The answer lies in the question as to whether or not there is indeed a demarcation line between the physical world and the world of the mind. There might, at least, be a close enough connection between the two states of being that they have a significant and mutual impact on each other. This is a dilemma that can be resolved with the notion of continuity.

There is continuity in emotional maturation from the physical to the emotional. The infant springs from a one-body universe with mother during nine months of intra-uterine life. At the caesura of birth the baby is still enclosed and contained in a symbiotic unity with mother that now displays two bodies, but internally the baby experiences no distinction. Babies, at the onset of life, live in an enclosed world that is all about sensory experience of the bodily self and the gratification of needs.

From mother's repeated containment and transformations of the baby's unbearable physical and emotional states springs the development of an infant capable of realising the difference between herself and her mother, and, gradually, of taking back from the mother her own feeling world. An infant that claims authorship of her own feelings is gradually able to endure the fear of separation (a lifelong conundrum, never fully resolved), the angst connected with her own destructive propensity, and the possibility of reparation; she is now equipped to take the first steps towards loving another, and not exclusively the self, and to do this in full view of the world.

Having looked at how a person capable of emotional experience emerges from the shared bodily experience with mother, it is equally important to consider the impact of the emotional self on the physical self. We are talking about psychosomatics, and the impact of mood on physical health.

* * *

One of my patients, Madonna, had separated from her husband. A major relationship had come to an end. In the aftermath of separation, instead of being able to engage in healthy mourning, she developed physical symptoms. Her affliction of the soul had no outlet and transmuted into a severe somatic illness. Matters of the heart had affected her heart. She suffered from palpitations, arrhythmic heartbeat, was out of breath, and could barely leave her house. Madonna was a sporty woman, being identified with a body that was in superb working order and an instrument of sheer joy when she did her long distance running. Her symptoms were so scary she ended up under observation in hospital. But, surprisingly, none of the heart specialists could find any concrete evidence of a heart condition, which made her feel a fraud.

In her analysis she realised that the separation from her husband had set off historical worries and anxieties, if not fear. In early childhood she and her sister had witnessed her mother commit suicide in the family home. Both of them had been in the playroom when they heard a loud bang. Their mother had shot herself with a sawn-off shotgun. Madonna kept her younger sister at bay when she opened the bathroom door and saw the bloody carnage, unable to recognise her mother. She had blown off parts of her head.

Madonna was seven at the time, her sister five. Their father, a banker of repute, changed his work schedule to part-time so that he could look after his daughters, sold the family home, and moved to another town where his sister's family lived. Madonna's aunt, a feisty lady who gave out robust love to five kids of her own, turned out to be a godsend to the motherless children, but there was no way the birth mother could be replaced. Suffering from a manic-depressive illness, Madonna's mother had had spells of good enough mothering but, during periods of severe depression, she locked herself away from the children, or, when present, disappeared in a heavy black cloud of inertia.

During Madonna's childhood, in the aftermath of her mother's death, there was not enough emotional holding to enable her to enter into a healthy mourning process. What she did instead was to develop one physical ailment after the other. She became a somatiser of emotional conflict. During her teens her body became her friend. In school she excelled at sport, with her long legs, high muscle tone, and an ability to study sports tactics, getting relief from and, at the same time, running away from her emotional torment. By the time her marriage fell to pieces there was nowhere else to go. Her first refuge was her body, which, as she developed a heart condition, became the source of even greater torment.

Earlier, I made the point that the infant in her development moves out of the bodily universe into an emotional one, which is about the desomatisation of the psyche. At times of great emotional conflict during adulthood we tend to go into reverse development, and one's physical health appears to play a crucial part once again.

* * *

In conclusion, observing the laws of cosmology, making a closer inspection of the world of small particles, then looking at the function of the brain, and linking it with the laws of internal life, does not seem to be that far-fetched. All dynamical systems follow the laws of chaos but they are also organised by ordering principles. The fact that "strange attractors" are to be found in deep space, in weather systems, and in the brain alike would indicate that one of nature's basic designs of creation is to bring order to chaos, which also is the function of dreams. The psyche is governed by chaos, as are dreams as the primary function of the mind. During REM states, with their high cortical activity, the dream mind creates order out of an overwhelming array of sensory impressions, unintegrated emotions, and thoughts. Its transformations bring structure and coherence to internal life, and, if the dreamer is willing to put a little effort in, peace of mind.

Spread out through deep space, the invisible "Higgs field", which is the maker of mass and the world of matter, finds a replica in the universe of the mind. Dreams are the makers of psychic structures. The process of dreaming, with its primary function of making psychic reality, of building the psyche from within, gives shape to the smallest particles of the mind, which are sensory impressions, fragmented emotions, and aimless thoughts, and, from the mind's fragmentation and chaos, makes images, symbols, metaphors, and autobiographical fictions. This is the matter of the mind.

The process of dreaming is centred on the growth of knowledge, in the sense of self-understanding and self-improvement. In this way dreams take us closer to the understanding of existential questions such as: Who am I? Where do I come from? What is my foundation myth? How do I relate to myself and other people? What is the purpose of my being in this world? What is my art? What is my contribution to humankind? What is my fundamental human project? Which worthwhile futures am I going to build?

And towards the end and at the end: Will I be able to grow old gracefully? Will I be generous to the younger generation, passing on wisdom and a collection of stories needing to be told? Will I be able die well, in peace with myself and the world, leaving behind a legacy of love and respect? The process of dreaming, not unlike the invisible Higgs field, is the maker of ideas and self-reflection, the maker of themes around which our lives are centred. And in that way the "Higgs field of dreams" brings gravitas and substance to our internal lives. Ideas shape the internal and the external worlds.

* * *

From the neighbouring disciplines of chaos theory and quantum physics we have informed the following characteristics of dream life:

1. The psyche, like all dynamic systems, follows chaos theory, as do dreams, which are the regents of unconscious life.

2. Dreams follow the "theory of roughness" in dynamic systems. Their "fractal geometry" is a succinct reminder that internal life is ragged, uneven, broken, shattered, turbulent, chaotic, etc.
3. Where there is chaos there are ordering principles. Chaos and order are twins, and in a relationship of mutual impact.
4. Dreams bring order to a chaotic mind that is crowded by sensory impressions, unintegrated emotions, and heedless thoughts. Dreams behave not unlike "strange attractors", which bring order to dynamic systems such as the weather or the brain.
5. Dreams create gravitas and solidity out of the chaos of the mind. Dreams behave not unlike the invisible "Higgs field", which is the maker of mass and matter in the universe. The process of dream thinking takes the "particles" of the mind and makes from them images, symbols, metaphors, and autobiographical fictions that are the "matter" of the dream. And by further processing the matter of the dream, ideas and conceptions will occur that will remain unifying and central to the dreamer's life.

CHAPTER TWO

The fictions of dreams

"There can be no doubt that the connections between our typical dreams and fairy tales and the material of other kinds of creative writing are neither few nor accidental. It sometimes happens that the sharp eye of a creative writer has an analytic realization of the process of transformation of which he is habitually no more than the tool."

—Freud, 1908

Dreams are the makers of fiction. They are the authors of autobiographical fictions, to be more precise. The fictions of dreams tell the stories of the dreamer's life history. Not only that: the storytelling also includes family stories passed down over many generations, and reaches into the stories told about the family clan's insertion into its ethnic and cultural identity.

Dreams walk easily on the timeline of past, present, and future, and engage in the narratives that have made the person, not so much in terms of chronological details, recording long lists of professional achievement or material success, but in terms of formative life events. These are not only events of beauty that have opened the heart and touched the soul but also destructive events that have left behind devastation and suffering. Beauty and the Beast revealed. Dreams bring up the hidden stuff of one's life history, in order to heal old wounds, in the same way the body has an inherent capacity to heal a bleeding, open wound, or a broken leg.

The fictions of dreams are directed by the poetic nature of the psyche. Poiesis means "to call something into existence that was not there before" but had always been. It is part of the dream's poetic purpose to restore the dreamer's connection with the beauty of the world, which has to do with living life under the aegis of consciousness, truthfulness, and meaning.

Case study: Katja

Before we go into the world of ideas behind the notion of dream fictions shall we allow dreams to speak for themselves? The following case study might give you a flavour of how dream analysis is done in the sanctity of the consulting room. The fictions of dreams will not only demonstrate how dream life informs the dreamer's internal life but also the way dreams make a meaningful link with the social world in which the person lives.

Katja, one of my patients, feels miserable for a number of days, if not a couple of weeks, being unable to get away from morbid thoughts, such as feeling worthless, without a sense of direction, not having achieved anything in life, despite being an eminent artist, able to exhibit, and hold court, in major galleries. Her dream mind, showing mercy, sends her a number of messages. The dreamer, stubborn as she is, does not even contemplate paying attention to her dreams, only vaguely aware that there have been some bothersome events going on in the bedroom at night—it could have been her husband snoring, his clumsy knee kicking her backside, or a wasp buzzing over her head, coming in uninvited during a hot summer's night.

Psyche, who presides over the dream mind, by now a little irritated, not understanding why her valuable dreams have been batted off like an annoying wasp, ups the stakes by sending the dreamer a nightmare. The dreamer wakes and screams, disoriented, as if emerging from beneath the waterline, short of breath, exhausted. *Darling, what's up?* Before his words reach her, her husband rolls over, resuming what he does best at night, namely snoring, barely short of ignoring her.

Katja brings her nightmare reluctantly to the consulting room, offloading it on to me, as if ridding herself of leprosy. I try to give an impression of calm and solidity, not saying very much, whilst she throws words at me like missiles, trying to disturb my peace of mind, which she hates. Her words are delivered in a deep, husky voice, as if Marlene Dietrich has entered the space between us.

You never get bloody involved! Nothing to do with you! You piss me off!

It is as if her nightmare is mine, in a reversal typical of a raging child. Underneath her ranting, I think, she has a wish to be held and contained.

In the dream she is lying in bed, no older than five, enjoying the sense of warmth, her vivid mind going on a journey into outer space. In the company of friends, riding on magic sticks from one island to another, it could easily be paradise. All of a sudden the bedroom door creaks open, spoiling the illusion. In comes a hooded figure with a large butcher's knife. She senses his bad breath wafting over her face, his heavy breathing holding her down, his pungent smell wiping out her sense of herself. His eyes glow red with lust. He is about to stab her. Had she not learned to ride on a magic stick he would have killed her. Pursued by the brute intruder she tries to escape but knows she cannot. She wakes in a sweat, screaming. As usual her husband holds her, and softly speaks to her, being used to this flurry of nightmares. *Get off me! Get off me!* She does not take easily to Jack's kindness. In fact, still caught in the haze of the dream she mistakes him for the abuser.

Her fictions of dreams has taken her right into the epicentre of her life story, namely the sexual abuse. Dreams, on a mundane physical level, help the dreamer to digest experiences during the daytime, and bring order to the chaos of the mind. An excess of sensory impressions, raw emotions, and scattered thoughts are being worked upon so that the dreamer finds physical restoration but also peace of mind. In the absence of sleep and dreaming we would become demented and die.

On a deeper level, on the level of dream thinking, the dream mind is processing emotional maturation, and, by doing so, enters the vast libraries of dream books stored in its memory, books of dreams that chronicle the dreamer's family history, knowledge of previous generations, and cultural identity. Not unlike the body's inherent capacity for healing wounds, the psyche has an inherent tendency to heal old emotional wounds, such as experiences of loss, separation, and traumatisation. The process of dream thinking serves to overcome emotional suffering, but it heals like with like. You can only overcome something that is unbearable if you know about it through the lucidity of dreams.

This was precisely her dilemma: the need to travel long journeys between the torment of the little girl being abused by her own father and her success as an artist, lapping up the limelight, if not revelling in her material affluence.

Deep down I'm impoverished. And I hate myself. And I hate my body.

Katja could swing, from one moment to another, from hilarity to despair, and from stubborn misery back to enjoyment. A trigger that easily set her off was men staring at her in a certain way.

These fuckers want to undress me with their eyes.

She was an attractive woman, so it was no surprise that men feasted on her appearance. She was always intent on holding the gaze. Saying hello to her when opening the front door was not unlike being netted by the leisurely eyes of a panther. At the time of her therapy she was unaware of her own seductiveness.

The fact that she challenged herself deeply, as an artist, in the relationship with her husband, and in the analysis, made things worse. This is the paradox of internal maturation: the more you reach into the beauty of life, the more you come into your own, the more you will invite a backlash of an envious self-attack. Envy is one of the fault-lines of the human condition. We seem to be destined to spoil the good. We are not able to look beauty in the eye unscathed, which at first sight does not make sense. But it is easier to lead a life of misery than a life of happiness. The emergence of beauty, happiness, contentment into one's life, and the prospect of being loved, is always unsettling, if you're lucky, but, most likely, is devastating. It has to do with the propensity for change, because we do not want to change, at all costs. Anything that rattles the cage of habit and convention is experienced as painful.

Katja experienced the daemon of envy in her marriage. Knowing about her flaws she was hell-bent on holding down a relationship. Sex was a disaster, so they had to find other ways of intimacy, such as endlessly talking to each other, not unlike pursuing the perpetual conversation of friendship. And caring for each other, producing luscious meals, doing sporty things together, indulging in their large appetite for cinema. Best of all, they learnt to be thoughtful about each other's needs. Instead of having sex they discovered the bliss of Eros, the gentle touch, giving each other massages, cuddling at every opportunity like teenage lovers. But was it enough?

Come night-time everything changed. A terrible beauty was born, as if the sun of day had never existed, giving way to something perilous and sinister that might happen at any time. The moon illuminating the bedroom had a contorted face, its mouth parted with devilish laughter. The mockery of the insane. The dense triumph of insanity over sanity. This anti-moon could have been her. What frightened Katja most was her impulse to kill her husband during intercourse, especially after orgasm. Why should she destroy the best she had? Why the urge to kill off beauty? With great difficulty she brought herself to talk about her seemingly bizarre urges.

I'm a pervert. I feel violence in the place of love.

She did. But the corruption had happened to her, at the hands of her father, who had mistaken violence for love.

Back now to the idea of dream thinking that I have described in the introduction as one of the organising ideas of this book. Dream thinking is a process of metabolising unconscious, if not traumatic, thoughts at the epicentre of dreaming. Katja's most unbearable thought was not that she had been sexually abused by her father, which was bad enough, but that she was capable of violence in the face of sexual embrace. In that sense her dreams were relentless, preventing her from the unthinkable. Once she had started to endure her most secret thoughts, leaving her ashamed and guilty, she was given more to endure, which was the possibility of healing.

Every nightmare encapsulates solutions to its own predicament: despair entails hope, devastation entails the grains of a new beginning. From the ruins of earthquakes and tsunami we build new life. Every nightmare carries a seedling of transformation. Every poison is a cure. The solution lies in the problem.

One rainy morning she came in, shaking her blond locks in a tightly controlled display of femininity, looking puzzled. Not that she was easily confused.

Would you believe it! I had a dream about Marilyn Monroe!

In the dream Katja had attended a photoshoot. In fact, she was behind the camera taking shots of Marilyn Monroe lounging naked on a bed, giving convincing impersonations of a sex goddess were it not that, from time to time, she disappeared behind a partition, vomiting and crying her eyes out. Katja had turned into Marilyn giving advice to Katja. Saying,

Don't wash after sex. Don't wear knickers after. Enjoy the scent of woman.

Katja was fuming, not understanding that the dream had offered her a path towards a more abuse-free experience of sexuality. Until now her body had been her enemy. She had never forgiven herself for being part of the abuse, as if, as a child, she had had choice. However, on the level of bodily stimulation she *had* taken part. There is no way around it. That is the Achilles tendon of sexual abuse. And, as a result, later on in life, it is violent phantasies that turn you on and are the cause of considerable shame and guilt.

I'm not like her! She was a dumb blonde who sold her body to men!

I thought to myself, "Your dumb blonde was able to read James Joyce's *Ullysses* or was she not?" but allowed her a good deal of the session to parade the human fault-lines of her foe. The enemy, the foe, the opposing figure in dreams is always a part of the self wishing to be overheard and recognised. Eventually, I dared to ask Katja's indignant self,

Don't you think you might not like her too much because, she, like you, was sexually abused?

And before I was able to add to the list,

And she, like you, had a father who disowned her. And she, like you, had lost a mother to mental illness,

she was on her feet shouting nervous abuse at me, producing nothing more than hot air, storming off in a huff.

That day I had to say *Time's up* without an audience, conversing with an absence, as I sat in my comfy leather chair, swivelling round for a short while. However, she eventually came round to the idea of hating the hated, namely her hating the abused and abandoned child in Marilyn Monroe, thus hating her own abused and abandoned child. Again, a case of the dream thinking the impossible, the unwanted, the taboo, making sense of emotional experience, not to mention the timely authorship of the fictions of dreams that had conjured up a protagonist to display the characteristics of the dreamer's own troubled life.

But what about the smell? she ruminated in the following session, having recovered from her outburst. I had remembered, from sessions a few years ago, that she had referred to Jack, to the time of falling in love with him, which was all about bodily delights, and rampant sex, before bodily memories of the abuse had hit the depths and before it stirred the surface of conscious thought. In the face of love she had slipped from one icy layer to another, until she was freefalling into the abyss. The centre did not hold. Just before arriving at purgatory she had said with blind conviction,

I love the smell of his neck and his hair, even the sweat in his armpits is sweet. And the smell of his breath is divine.

By contrast, when she was able to remember more clearly what her father had inflicted on her she began vomiting, even during sessions, not unlike Monroe in the dream, who was raped at the age of eleven. Katja had sensory memories of marked detail.

He was all over me. Disgusting. His bad breath. And the tomcat stench of his male sweat.

Katja was not able to see her father and herself in one single frame, in one single picture, which was too unbearable. What she did manage to see was her own sexuality, the temptress. She came to understand the photoshoot of Monroe in the dream as her own guilt over being a sexual being. She was baffled by her own sexual power as a woman, which was considerable. It does not come as a surprise that Freud talked about the "boiling heat" of transference in the consulting room. It had taken her a long time to differentiate between normal sexual development and violent premature sexualisation. She had even poked her nose into Freud's sexual theories, in part to comprehend her predicament, in part to better me—Freud, who she had previously dismissed from a feminist perspective as "an old fart who only had sex on his mind, and did not understand women, did he?" A thinly disguised hint at me, no doubt.

Again, being able to think the unthinkable she made way for mourning the losses of the small girl who had been on the receiving end of the corruption of love. One day she came into a session looking radiant, a big smile on her face.

Look at me! How do I look?

As a man you do not dare to answer such a question directly; you offer platitudes, and you dare not say nothing either. As an analyst, walking on even more dangerous ground, you are bound to monastic silence. The rule of abstinence. *I've done it again!* She merrily goes on,

And I followed Marilyn's advice. The smell of lovemaking on you, nothing better than that.

She has had the glorious idea that she should engage in lovemaking during the day. The nights were still in the grip of daemons, but she did not care, knowing that she had just started out on reconstruction. *Newcastle wasn't built in a day*, she used to say, her thoughts wandering up north, where she came from.

Freud's autobiographical fictions

In this section I will show some of the ideas behind the notion that dreams are autobiographical fictions. The Freudian psyche will be described as a poetry-making organ. The very source of creative writing, as was the case for Kafka, originates in dream states. And in that way fictions are always autobiographical. Even theories of the mind, such as psychoanalysis, are autobiographical fictions, as can be seen in Freud's theories, formed from the raw material of him being an assimilated Jew in Vienna at the turn of the nineteenth century.

In the early twentieth century the two most prevalent ways of illuminating the depths of human motivation were literature and psychoanalysis, not to mention the contribution of philosophy, which lies outside the limits of our discussion. Not only did psychoanalytic thought about hidden human desire and aggression enter the world of fiction writing (Kafka, Thomas Mann, and James Joyce spring to mind) but literature, by its very nature of digging deep into what makes us human beings, also informed the method of psychoanalytic enquiry. In truth, it was a reciprocal relationship. When, on the occasion of the celebration of his seventieth birthday, Freud was hailed as "the discoverer of the unconscious", he rejected the idea by saying:

> "The poets and philosophers before me discovered the unconscious. What I discovered was the scientific method by which the unconscious can be studied." (In Trilling, 1950, p. 34)

He had followed a humble principle of seeking human knowledge and discovery, which is, in the words of sculptor Auguste Rodin, to remain devoted to the masters who come before you.

When he established his dual instinct theory of sexuality and aggression, Freud referred to Schiller (1759–1805), a poet and philosopher in the Romantic tradition, who famously wrote the ballad "Ode to Joy" (*An die Freude*), which Beethoven set to music in his Ninth Symphony. Schiller, who collaborated with Goethe, proposed two fundamental human motivations: that we should be driven by "hunger and love". From there, Freud developed his earlier model that we are driven by self-preservation and libido (sexual desire), before he eventually proposed the duality of Eros and Thanatos, the life and death instincts, in *Beyond the Pleasure Principle* (1923).

From Goethe (1749–1832), one of the classic German writers in the Romantic tradition, the author of *Faust* and *The Sorrows of Young Werther*, Freud took the notion of sublimation. Goethe had introduced the term *sublimieren* into German, which referred to raw feelings in need of refinement. Its Latin origin, *sublimitas*, means "loftiness", "height". Sublimation as the essential factor in artistic creativity was a proposition first put forward by Plato in the *Symposium*.

Freud himself was a master of the written word. We have to remind ourselves that Freud's genius lay foremost in his literary ability, his love of language (Schoenau, 1968). He was a writer first, then a theorist, then a clinician. If you read Freud's work in its German original you will notice the sheer poetic fluency of his language, which is simple, down-to-earth and yet as evocative as only poetic language can be. In 1930 he won the Goethe Prize for Literature, Germany's equivalent of the Booker or the Pulitzer, for the poetic use of language in his psychoanalytic writing (Clark, 1980). Too ill to receive the prize himself, cancer of the jaw having become his companion, his dutiful daughter and later heiress to his throne, Anna, was sent to Frankfurt to collect it.

In typical Freudian manner, he was fairly ambivalent about the prize: for one, he appreciated the temptation of a "closer connection with Goethe", like himself a writer of prose and a natural scientist; on the other hand he was disappointed about the lack of appreciation of his work, saying that "at any time of life such recognition has neither much practical value nor great emotional significance. For a reconciliation with my contemporaries it is pretty late; and that psychoanalysis will win through long after my time I have never doubted" (ibid., p. 481).

The Strachey translation of the Standard Edition was unable to convey in English Freud's writing craft and left a bias in the reception of Freudian ideas in English-speaking countries because of its unimaginative and misleading rendering of key concepts. Bruno Bettelheim, in *Freud and Man's Soul* (1983), provides such evidence of Strachey's act of linguistic ruination of Freud's beautiful style of writing and world of ideas. What the translation failed to convey was the complexity of Freud's thought, even though his was a somewhat bizarre epistemology. He managed to straddle the sobering scientific and the imaginative poetic, to mention just two of his paradigms of understanding the psyche: Freud the scientist, part of the analytical rationalism of the Enlightenment; and Freud the prose writer, part of the world of imagination, dreams, and the high sensibility of Romanticism with its organising idea of hidden things.

To make things more complicated, Freud was also a biologist of the mind, giving due recognition to his background as a neurologist. His theories always revolved around the idea of the individual being involved in an instinctual and bodily experience. His was a sobering view of culture, namely of the struggle to free ourselves from the ancient cave of raw emotion.

Bettelheim mentions that the key concept of Freud's work, namely the concept of the "psyche", which he called *Seelenleben* (the "life of the soul"), was rendered as "mind", which takes a Romanticist notion and glosses it over with a rationalist veneer, arriving at a different paradigm of the mind, namely a scientific, quantitative point of view. The term "soul" springs from the Greek *psukhe* or psyche, meaning breath of life. Psyche, in Greek mythology, was the beloved of Eros (Cupid), the god of love. In using the terms psyche and soul, Freud placed his view of the unconscious on a much wider conceptual framework. The term mind, by contrast, is closely associated with memory and rational thought. Mind is never the psyche, nor the soul.

Another of Strachey's faux pas was the rendering of "*Deutung*" as "interpretation". Freud took the word *Deutung* from the Romantic writing tradition that implied an artful, intuitive apprehension of the hidden thing in nature and human nature. The Romanticists borrowed *Deutung* from the Renaissance discipline of astrology, meaning the stargazer's finger pointing at celestial movement, as if to say that meaning lies up there in the sky, in an entity outside of the individual, close to the ancient notion of the divine nature of dreams. *Deutung*, for the astrologer, meant to make a connection between the movement and positions of the stars and what it meant for the internal life of human beings, making a link between our physical insertion in the world and its symbolic meaning. One of its assumptions was that the moon and the sun have an impact on the fluctuations of mood.

What is inherent in the title of Freud's masterpiece *Traumdeutung* (*The Interpretation of Dreams*) is the implication that we only arrive at the actual meaning of dreams by hinting at it, by remaining in a cloud of uncertainty and letting the dreamer do the work of understanding. "Interpretation" always implies that the interpreter alone holds knowledge, a fact Freud observed when he studied one of the oldest preserved dream books from 200 CE, Artemidorus' *Oneirocritica*, coming to the conclusion that dream analysis cannot be done without the dreamer (Harris-McCoy, 2012).

A poetry-making organ

In the knowledge that Freud was wearing at least two different theoretical hats, being at once the rationalist and the poet, we can now turn to Trilling's assertion that the Freudian psyche is a "poetry-making organ".

> For all the mental systems, the Freudian psychology is the one which makes poetry indigenous to the very constitution of the mind. Indeed the mind, as Freud sees it, is in the greater part of its tendency a poetry-making organ ... It was left to Freud to discover how, in a scientific age, we still feel and think in figurative formations, and to create, what psychoanalysis is, a science of tropes, metaphor and its variants ... (Trilling, 1950, pp. 52–53)

As we shall see in Chapter Five, the origin of Freud's investigation into the psyche was the death of his father and his subsequent dreams, which he used to great effect in his self-analysis, leading to the inception of his major work on dreams. This always remained his favourite book, in spite of the fact that the theories he became best known for—the sexual and aggressive instincts, for example—were developed later in his life; dreams, in Freudian Romantic eyes, are at the very centre of psychic life, are poetry-making. If we take the different genres of fiction writing—poetry, short stories, novellas, and longer fiction—there is good reason to believe that all fiction stems from poetry, the most dense, stripped down, and figurative form of writing.

The word "poiesis" goes back to Plato, meaning "to call something into existence that was not there before". This calling forth of the unknown became a crucial idea in the literature of Romanticism, and in Freud's schema of the unconscious, with its perception of the hidden element in human nature and of the opposition between the hidden and the visible.

> What is *The Interpretation of Dreams* if not a formulation of the laws
> and logic of poetry? (Phillips, 2002, p. 9)

The philosopher Heidegger supplied us with a notion akin to poiesis, which he called "a bringing-forth out of concealment". Kafka, for instance, brought to the fore in his writing his own internal struggle with guilt and punishment, his fear of his father, and his immersion into the world of dreams. Jonathan Franzen, a contemporary American fiction writer best-known for *The Corrections*, who researched the source of Kafka's writing, came to the conclusion that literature as we know it originates in dreams and dream-like states of mind (2012). Writing fiction is always autobiographical, according to Franzen; it is born out of the writer's personal struggle with his or her identity, and a total engagement with the story of his or her own life.

Franzen goes on to say that

> Kafka devoted his whole life as a writer to describing his personal
> struggle with his family, with women, with his Jewish heritage,
> with moral law, with his unconscious, with his sense of guilt, and
> with the modern world. Kafka's work, which grows out of the

nighttime *dreamworld* in Kafka's brain, is more autobiographical than any realistic retelling of his daytime experiences at the office or with his family or with a prostitute could have been. *What is fiction, after all, if not a kind of purposeful dreaming?* The writer works to create a dream that is vivid and has meaning, so that the reader can then vividly dream it and experience meaning. *And work like Kafka's, which seems to proceed directly from dream, is therefore an exceptionally pure form of autobiography.* (Franzen, 2012, p. 129, my emphasis)

The South African writer J. M. Coetzee said that "All autobiography is storytelling, all writing is autobiographical" (Kannemeyer, 2013). The fictions of dreams are forms of storytelling, closely observing the biography of the dreamer, not so much the facts and chronology as the organising themes of a lifetime, such as loss, the search for beauty, or the overcoming of devastating life events.

* * *

Freud, on completing a new theory, would always question that theory's value but he would go even further and describe it, in its essential characteristic, as fictional; it would be modified by the development of thinking about psychoanalysis and what lies inside the psyche, and that these revisions would be made by someone who is subjective and biased by his own life history. So even a theory of the mind, such as psychoanalysis, is fictional and biographical.

As a Jew, at the turn of the nineteenth century, Freud was concerned with the anti-Semitic climate in the Austro-Hungarian Empire, which paid lip service to Jewish assimilation but did not, in reality, deliver it. Freud, it seems, converted some of the prejudices against the Jews into a science. He tackled fundamental human taboos, such as the early sexual development of infants and human violence, viewing them as part of human nature.

Gossip is one of the most potent forms of communication. Jews in Europe had been on the receiving end of defamation that had been circulating since mediaeval times. In Viennese society gossip defined Jews as "dirty", that is, sexually deviant, and it was rumoured that they abducted the children of nonbelievers in order to slaughter them in the name of religion. Thus, Freud's theories had their origins in his biography as a Jew. He thought that if all of us were sexual beings and had violent impulses, then the Jews were only part of a wider picture, and therefore might be exempt from further scapegoating.

* * *

In summary we can assume that the fictions of dreams take the material of autobiography, the dynamic forces of our internal and social lives, and make from it an art form. Dreams are autobiographical fictions. The mythological author of such fictions is Psyche, in cohort with the other deities of dreams, Asclepius, Apollo, Neptune, and Morpheus (see Chapter Eight). It is the psyche-soul that presides over the process of dream thinking. Dream thinking goes through the factual and chronological details of a dreamer's life and brings out of concealment and to the fore, coherent themes and organising ideas in fictional form, linking the beginning with the end. Such nocturnal fictions are to be read by the dreamer so that they can become a companion in self-improvement, taking the dreamer, via the "royal road", towards contentment and happiness, as the fictions of dreams touch down on the solid ground of everyday life.

Case study: Matt

The following fictions of dreams will show that dreams are, at times, strikingly accurate in the delivery of information that has a bearing on the dreamer's internal development and result in a change of perspective in his view of family history. What emerges out of the concealment of the psyche frequently does not appear plausible. Dreaming and dream analysis is not a course in miracles, but dream life can be wondrous, and touched by beauty.

Matt, one of my patients, dreamt of being in a hotel in New York's Manhattan. His room number was 111749. He was adamant the dream location was Manhattan, as it had become one of his favourite places to travel to. After contemplating the cryptic number for a number of sessions he gave up but had another dream about a bird; it must have been a bird of prey, perched on a rock, flapping its wings, talking to him in American. *The bird had seven wings. Strange,* Matt went on to say.

Matt had never known his biological father, nor was his mother willing to disclose to him who his father was. Matt was happy with his step-father, who was kind and took him fully on board as if he were his own son. But a sense of yearning, a sense of searching always remained in the depths of Matt's mind. Part of his searching was his love of travelling to New York City, and there Manhattan stood out when he found himself wandering the streets, from shop to shop, from one architectural monument to another, as if driven by a memory of the future, and a bizarre recognition of the place, as if to say *I've been here before*. He pined for something he did not know existed. Following on from his sojourns in New York he was frequently visited by dreams about barren spaces, emptied of people and aliveness.

Matt was a sewage engineer, always joking about being a *shit engineer*, but longing to be a pilot. In his early twenties he applied to be a fighter pilot and went through rigorous testing by the RAF. *I wanted to earn my wings.* It was discovered that he had a heart defect and was suffering from vertigo, so he could not fulfil his life's dream. His actual dreams left him puzzled but he stepped up his quest for his father, asking his mother pertinent questions. She did not want to go there, wanting to avoid mortification and shame. But Matt's stepfather was prepared to say what he knew: his wife, Matt's mother, had been an air stewardess, having had an affair with an American pilot, who had turned his back on her as soon as she had told him that she was pregnant with his child.

It makes sense now. The bird was him flying.

Matt was excited but also angry and hurt. The return of the good had in its wake a return of the original pain over the apprehension of an absence, a loss that had made him melancholy even though he was unaware of its source.

Matt was given his father's name and address, and eventually found him. Retired by now, living in New York's Manhattan, with his wife. His other children had left home by now. At first uncomfortable about the sin of his past turning up on his doorstep, he invited his son in. He had fathered two more children by other woman before he settled down with his wife. His wife and four children, outraged by his secrets coming to light, took him to court over his past promiscuity and lack of responsibility. Part of the family's peace deal was to ask him to search for and make contact with his other two children, an offer he could not refuse.

Matt's father took him out on his small aircraft, flying along the Hudson River towards the sea, then all the way up north along the east coast to Martha's Vineyard, to his little hideaway, his beach hut, with the intention of going fishing with his son. On the way there he handed the controls over to Matt, who was chuffed, and told his son stories of his flying career: how he had to overcome his fear of flying despite loving it; how he had suffered from vertigo; how he had flown a plane with four hundred people on board, drunk, hardly able to bring the aircraft down; how much he was addicted to sex but unable to commit; how he had loved being the captain of a large bird in the air, enjoying the majestic views over the varying landscapes of the world; how, once, he thought his time was up when one of the engines caught fire, meaning he had to do an emergency landing, giving a good impression of staying in control.

So you are the father of seven children, Dad?

I'm afraid so, Matthew.

Matt thought of the dream of a bird of prey with seven wings, of his father having been a sexual predator. Now he is alongside his father, but senses the other six children crowding in on the place he has found. He was the oldest of them but felt like a little boy inside, wishing to have father all to himself.

He really liked his father calling him Matthew. No one had called him Matthew before, but his father doing so felt like returning to something unexpectedly familiar—his melancholy self, his old craving for something unknown. Also he loved the slow, almost sluggish, drone of his father's American bass voice. Just before landing the plane his father told him his date of birth.

November 17th 1949. I'm ancient and a bloody Scorpio. And behaving like one too.

Matt, hardly able to concentrate on bringing the aircraft down, cried out,

Bloody hell! The room number! 111749!

The fiction of dreams had brought out of concealment Matt's most disturbing but most precious thoughts. Who is my father? Where do I come from? He had been drawn to his foundation myth. In it lay his identity as a young man. Paradoxically, the more he enjoyed contact with his long-lost father the more he was able to mourn him, to mourn, that is, the childhood father whom he had been unable to mourn historically because of his mother's attitude towards her own past. Instead, Matt had developed a childhood depression, not of a clinical kind but taking the form of melancholy mood swings and contemplation, forever pining but not finding.

Matt had big dark eyes that contained many absences, eyes that had witnessed many small deaths. In the analysis he realised that he himself had killed off his biological father so as not to feel the pain of absence. In the place of father he had established inside a darkness, if not a deadness. Now his dreams sprang to life with the longing for father, the little boy in him catching up with the years of repressed searching. In turn, the more he mourned his historical father, the more the adult father became his companion and friend. Flying up to Martha's Vineyard to go fishing would remain the private domain of father and son. Needless to say, his once accentuated dependency on me dissipated once he had the real thing in his life. And soon he was ready to fire me.

CHAPTER THREE

Dreams, literature, and fiction writing

There is an irresistible affinity between the fictions of dreams and fiction writing. Dreams dazzle us by their vivid and succinct images, symbols, and metaphors, which come upon us when we are asleep. One might be tempted, given the dream's constant supply of images, to call dreaming a nocturnal cinematographic event. However, given that there is no such thing as a single dream, that dreams are all interconnected through memory, time, and historicity, their true nature is that of storytelling. It is the storyline that holds dreams together. And from the storylines of dreams, thinking occurs about matters of the human condition.

Dreams are autobiographical fictions, they are the narrators of the dreamer's life history, her insertion in transgenerational family themes, and her ethnic and cultural identity. In that sense dreams are psycho-social depositories and makers, they internalise the social context in which we live, and through the socialisation of its interiority they become the makers of an ever-changing perception of external reality.

As we have already addressed in the previous chapter on Jonathan Franzen's dream theory of fiction writing, dreams and dream states are the source of immersive fiction writing, and, because of the dream's interiority, novel writing always remains autobiographical. Writing is to take the capital of real life and make it into an art form by authorising it. French writer Patrick Modiano explicitly refers to dream states as the origin of the creative writing process. Not only that. He writes in a memorial mode that is, equally, the dream's main driving force.

Literature is a solid dream, which means that fictions originate in the writer's autobiographical and cultural context and her capacity for putting down on paper her world of imagination during states of lucid dreaming and dream thinking. The writer's lucid dreams, gone solid, evoke in the reader her own dream images, dream-like states of mind, and allows her to enter a world of imagination, so that reading becomes a truly immersive experience in which the characters become the lenses through which the reader reads her own mind and moves through the barriers of a restricted self to a horizon of greater possibilities.

To close the circle of connectivity, not only do dream states, and their attendant writerly devices, impact on the creative process of fiction writing but writerly devices, as we find them in literature, inform dream life and a theory of dreams. It is a reciprocal relationship between the processes of dreaming and fiction writing.

The parallel universes of dreaming and fiction writing tend to employ the same writerly devices: memory (Freud, Patrick Modiano), multi-temporality (Gabriel Garcia Márquez), poiesis (Freud, Lionel Trilling, Kafka, Ted Hughes, Colm Tóibín), historical consciousness (Charles Stewart, Irene Némirovsky), and "infinite connectivity" (Patrick White).

The autobiographical fictions of dreams

Dreams are storytellers on three different levels: they tell the dreamer's individual life history; they recount the hidden themes of family history, going back generations; and they tell the stories of ethnic and cultural identity.

Family history

The following dream shows that dreams have a tendency of walking back on the timeline into the dreamer's family history. They bring out of concealment the unthinkable, the forgotten, the not-talked-about aspects of family life, in order to restore the person's sense of identity. Identity here means to link the beginning with the end, in order to live life more fully in the conscious gaze of self-reflection. We give in to emotional deadness if we are not in touch with the hidden stuff of our life histories. That does not necessarily mean the shying away, or dissociation, from past traumatic events; it also entails transformative experiences and things of beauty.

One of my group patients, Maria, had a dream in which a man threw puppies high in the air with the intention of killing them. One of them died, another one just about survived, limping off, terrified. Trying to make sense of the dream, Maria pondered the word *dog*. The group was quick to remind her of her *dogged* attitude to her work as an academic but also to friendship and marriage. Everything was a labour, everything deeply felt. A dream never stands alone, and she remembered other dreams, of a sexual nature, in which dogs played a part. The confluence of the sexual and of violence led her to assume that the dream was about her father, which took her right back to childhood. She came from a large family that was under the irrational rule of her father. Not without kindness or love, a charismatic man, he had violent outbursts, especially with his older sons. Maria, being the youngest, was spared from his eruptions but she grew up in an atmosphere of impending threat.

The two of them had a profound emotional connection but there was a sense that her father struggled with his erotic desire for his daughter, which came to an impasse when she entered puberty. He abruptly turned away from her, being unable to cope with her nascent sexuality. In the group a phrase peeled off from dream contemplation: *He was a dog of a man*. The dream fiction of the dog had opened up an avenue of understanding the crux of her relationship with her father, namely his violence—which had a devastating impact on Maria's brothers—but also his instinctual sexuality, which he was hardly able to keep under wraps. Following on from the dream, Maria had to deal with her anger and contempt for a father who was not without love and generosity but who struggled to contain both his aggression and his sexuality. Maria thought the puppy who had survived in the dream, limping away, was her; limping in relation to finding a good man in her life, a man assertive but not violent, a man sexual but not intrusive.

Transgenerational themes

In one of my analytic groups some of the patients had most baffling dreams; dreams that did not make sense, in the same way that pockets of their private lives did not make sense. In the main, highly successful professionals with fairly intact family lives, the patients suffered from inexplicable bouts of depression, depersonalisation, malignant despair, and dissociation from feelings. The nightmares were triggered by one group member whose explicit dreams resonated in the group, leading to an avalanche of somewhat unbearable dreams by a number of dreamers. The communal dreams told the stories of large numbers of people incarcerated, held in camps made of low wooden buildings, starved to death, some beaten to death, others stripped naked, pushed into confined spaces, to be gassed. There were scenes of mass graves, mass executions, of bodies piled up, waiting to be incinerated. The dream narratives had arrived at a critical mass.

These initial fictions of dreams moved from a monologue of interiority to a dialogue amongst group members, and, eventually, to a discourse that meant that the patients were able to think what the dreams might mean. As if emerging from the haze of distant memory, patients used language akin to experiences of humiliation and self degradation.

I'm unworthy of living. I'm rotten to the core. I'm dirty and repulsive.

One patient even fell into rudimentary German, saying *Ich bin ein Unmensch,* which means

I'm not a human being. I'm a monster.

With trepidation, in the group's public domain, in the presence of other people, patients allowed themselves to say the unthinkable, the unsayable, the hidden self concepts that, despite good enough lives, had been held deep down, and, at times, had surfaced far too close to the line of consciousness, threatening to encroach on well-designed lives.

Despite the fact that a good number of dreams had arrived at evidencing the extremes of human cruelty and that the dreamers' associations showed high levels of self-loathing and self-hatred, the dreamers tended not to take ownership of their own dreams nor of their notions about themselves.

It feels as if the dreams I've had are not my dreams. And the words which come from down below are not mine, they are as if spoken by somebody else in a foreign language.

This dissociation from dream life and negative thoughts went hand in hand with a deep-seated sense of self-alienation. It was as if Kafka or Camus were given a voice of human detachment, the latter saying

Forever I will be an alien to myself.

Some patients also talked about something more literal, more physical, as if something of unknown origin had implanted itself on the somatic level of being, gesturing towards the heart or the belly.

There is something inside me like a cancerous growth.

It took considerable time for the group's dialogue about bizarre notions of self-alienation to enter another level of consciousness. The group's eventual discourse of emotional understanding, which originated in obscure dream narratives, leading to secondary fictions without authorship being claimed, came to the fore through the searches of one of the patients into her own family history. A secular Jew, she found out from a distant relative that both her parents were Holocaust survivors. She stormed off into rages

Why on earth did you never tell me?

—asking her parents pertinent questions, who, from the perspective of survival and a hard-won but fragile equilibrium, answered,

Why should we have? We wanted to protect you. In truth, we have told you but we didn't want to talk about it.

In fact she *had* known but failed to connect emotionally with what it had meant to her parents and the unconscious impact it had had on her own internal life. Her parents, as survivors, understandably wanted to move on and carve out a life away from the ruinous time in the camps. Little did they know that by doing so they would unconsciously pass on the emotional terrors of survival, such as unspeakable fear, upsurges of hatefulness, confused states of mind, emotional dissociation, and a sense of depersonalisation and alienation from the self (Rheinschmiedt, 1998).

The group patients were second generation holocaust survivors, suffering from "survivor syndrome transmission" (Slipp, 1990). The initially reluctant dream life of the patients, once embedded in a developing group culture of open discourse, became the vehicle of working through severe states of traumatisation. Dreams serve de-traumatisation.

The pockets of inexplicable "traumatic introjects" no longer lived autonomous, unrelated internal lives but became essential ingredients in the patients' understanding of their transgenerational histories (Schuetzenberger, 1998). Part of the recovery from their parents' unredeemed emotional legacies was to get in touch with the feeling nature of having been "used" as receptacles for the unwanted, the forgotten, the not-talked-about terror of the camps. Separation was needed, and a healthy amount of aggression was called upon to let go of something so alien to the self.

> Feeling so devastated does not belong to me, I have to hand it back to my parents' generation.

Following wave after wave of angry and hateful feelings toward the perpetrators of unconscious transmission, the next phase of recovery meant engaging with mourning. A childhood so crowded with internal alien traumatic objects was a childhood not had. Apocalyptic nightmares were described; they began at an early age—sometimes from two to three years of age—and turned into recurring dreams that told the terror of the previous generation, pushing aside the nightmares and dreams of beauty that belong to ordinary infantile development. The process of healthy mourning over a lost childhood became the entry point to the patients' new-found feeling worlds rather than them being possessed by alien emotions that had not been theirs in the first place. *Ich bin doch ein Mensch,* a phrase often used by Jews in the extermination camps, now became rewritten by the second generation with an altogether different meaning. *I am, after all, a human being.* The edited narrative refers to the possibility of a life freed from the burden of an enforced past; steps can be taken to rediscover the voice of the little child who was never given a voice, a free space to play in, and to be engrossed in a fantasy world of infinite possibilities.

Historical consciousness

Dreams can be reminders of the distant past and of social and ethnic identity. Dreams as the carriers of historical consciousness make the point that history is not necessarily history of things past but of history still lived in and experienced in the present. We do not exist without owning our varied histories.

Case study: Zlatan

I have had the privilege of working with an immigrant from the war-torn Balkans of the mid-1990s. In the truest sense of the phrase, it was a matter of learning from the patient. It gave me a first-hand insight into the civil war in former Yugoslavia, and the level of traumatisation war time can inflict on individuals, their families, and the communities in which they live. Zlatan was pensive, a man of few words, always on the verge of tears; he was tall but seemed shrunken, coiled up on himself, head lowered, hardly any eye contact, his jet-black hair standing up in a brush, as if designed by chaos theory. Zlatan's broken English amused and frustrated him in equal measure. He had left his country of origin after the hospital in which he worked had been laid to rubble by shell fire, him being one of a handful of survivors. As was often the case, if words failed him, his dark-brown eyes would seem to disappear inside, away from the present moment, from this world. A sense of despair and terror, an invisible density of human suffering, made itself felt in the stillness of the consulting room. After repeatedly going through the cycles of silence, which in his mind were taken over by shellfire, explosions, falling walls and ceilings, cries of despair, smell of burning flesh, he only managed to say,

Don't know what to say.

What is there to say in the face of utter human destruction?

Not only had he lost his workplace, his colleagues, and the patients he had cared for as a doctor but also, only six months earlier, his entire family: his wife and three young children. Their house had been in the line of fire. This was a loss that, in his eyes, could never be redeemed. After the obliteration of the hospital he walked and walked, aimlessly, not knowing where it would take him. He was beyond the fear of death;

numb, petrified, ice cold. Nothing would rattle him any longer, not even death. As it was, he wanted nothing more than death to come.

He was found unconscious, dehydrated, and starving by the NATO peace-keeping forces. On his flight from war he eventually found refuge in England, left with nothing except a small photograph of his family he had kept in his wallet, and a dried flower which his youngest daughter had given him days before she died. In order to work as a doctor again he had to learn a new language and had to retake medical exams. Zlatan did not mind, knowing that to help others would eventually help him to build a new life from the rubble of the old. When he started working in the analysis, he said, *There is nothing left of me.* And, indeed, there was a thinness of being. The long working hours in hospital kept him busy but did not alleviate the suffering of his unquiet mind, waking up in the middle of the night by nightmares, broken out in sweat, too frightened to switch on the light, in fear of a sniper in waiting.

I hate the night. I hate dreams.

Not surprisingly, the first period of dreaming in the analysis was dominated by dreams about the war, the burnt-out family home, the burnt-out hospital. He never dreamt of people. His dreams were crowded with ruins, skeletons of buildings, fallen high-rises, empty streets, gun-fire, heavy artillery, shells flying, breaking the spine of the city, black smoke rising, tanks moving slowly, deadly, through the thinly held triumph of destruction. There was no escape from the inferno. There was no redemption. He realised that the more he told the stories of his dreams, the more he was able to go through everyday life unscathed, unharmed by his volatile internal images. His was a double life. The kind and knowledgeable doctor available to patients, nurses, and office staff, and the private man, hardly able to breathe, in fear of savage images coming up from nowhere, uninvited, tormenting his broken soul. Despite his eyes welling up and his contorted face showing his internal struggle, he remained cut-off from his feeling nature. *I'm dead inside*, he would say, as if to reassure himself that he still existed, although he did not live, not in the way he had lived with his family before the civil war, a life of ordinary beauty.

His depressive side, the deadness inside, the weight of emotional burden, made itself felt in the consulting room. Not infrequently, Zlatan, usually a patient totally committed to the cause of working things through, with a considerable work ethic, could not keep his eyes open, his speech slurred, his head swaying in slow motion, jerking, then dropping, giving in to drowsiness. On waking up he was startled, embarrassed, trying to apologise,

I'm working too much. I'm always tired,

knowing very well that the primary reason for his wish to fall asleep lay in the unbearable nature of his feelings, the cumulative trauma so great it dragged him asleep. The drowsiness that emanated from him like invisible waves also went straight into my bodily self like an unconscious infection. If it was not him dozing off, it was me going off into "gaga land". This somatic floor of experience is typical for the initial phase of an analysis when projective identification predominates. The patient, instead of owning his unwanted feeling world, puts it into the analyst for safekeeping. It is a ridding from the self of unbearable somatic states, primitive emotions, and thoughts that cannot be thought about.

Given time, Zlatan became more relaxed about falling asleep during sessions, and he also started to notice that he had an impact on me in an unconscious way, saying, *I've sent you to sleep again*. This going in and out of drowsiness became a learning ground. He understood that if he allowed himself to go into a dream-like state of not knowing, he would come out of it with a thought, a memory perhaps, something tangible that made him understand an emotional conundrum. Bion (1962a) taught us precisely that: that this process of dream-diving and dream immersion, and the resultant little gem of a thought, called the selected fact, was imperative in getting at unconscious motivation and memory.

In hospital, when calling patients and their children from the waiting room, Zlatan was never quite sure whether or not he had just seen one of his children playing on the floor, or just hopping away out of sight, singing a familiar song. His wife he saw everywhere: in hospital corridors, on the way home on the bus, on the green outside his flat, in the house opposite, as if she was looking through the bay window, waiting for him to come home. Zlatan's first reprieve came in a dream a good two years into his analysis. He was sitting at the kitchen table having breakfast on his own. It was a darkened room, a smell of neglect and deprivation in the air, an altogether claustrophobic place that made him breathe heavily. The scene changed to the kitchen-diner of his former family home. The room was lit with sunshine, the patio doors stood open to the garden. He looked out into the garden and saw his three small children playing. As he turned his head back he saw his wife sitting opposite him, looking at him with serenity and calm. She held his gaze, then smiled but did not utter a word. Only the excited sounds of kids playing outside and quarrelling broke the silence.

The dark, confined space in the dream represented an internal claustrum, a place of deadness. In the face of severe traumatisation—which in Zlatan's case was a matter of cumulative trauma—his means of survival had been to dissociate from his feeling nature. His once buoyant emotional life no longer vibrates with excitement and openness but has shrunk to a densely restricted space, an experience of one-pointedness and singularity, cemented and bunkered in. Not only that. The dreamer is breathless, which would indicate the absence of the soul. The word "psyche" originates from the Greek word *psukhe*, which stands for breath, the breath of life, the life of the soul. In the dream, all life had gone, and with it the life of the soul, followed by the sudden appearance of light.

This epiphany dream shows that if you are prepared to look suffering directly in the eye redeeming features might arise. The dream showed not only Zlatan's despair but also his spiritual searches. The dead are only dead, they are not gone. He started to realise that in order to come to terms with trauma he had to stay in touch with his emotions of devastation and loss, and be prepared for the cycles of cold dissociation and tempestuous feeling to repeat themselves again and again.

Zlatan was disturbed in the sessions following the dream, happy to have seen his family in a dream but full of rage at their having been taken away from him. When I say that he has had a healing dream, an epiphany dream, he loses his temper.

You're telling me fancy shit. Fucking epiphany.

He made the last word sound like *eebeez-fanny*. He was right, I was doing my fancy thinking rather than allowing him to be. A time of raw emotion had erupted. In hospital he had learned the sophisticated vocabulary of the medical profession but behind the smart suit and the stethoscope lay his base self, which had assimilated a less refined repertoire of words. At the time, I actively encouraged him to revert to his native tongue, swearing and all, vis-à-vis unbearable emotion.

Paradoxically, just behind the jargon of aggression, rage, and hatefulness tender words, spoken for his wife and children, lay in wait. And just to name them, not by proper name but by their role—his *supruga* (wife) and *deca* (children)—was enough, not to bring them back to life but into his heart and emotional self. From a heart that had been broken and dissociated from, he now had glimpses of his former self.

A close observer of the unfolding civil war, Zlatan, on hearing about the peace negotiations, instinctually understood the Serb faction's long-held theories of being the victims of history. He told me in minute detail of the Croats' collaboration with the Nazis during World War Two and their campaign of exterminating a large number of Serbs. To make things more complicated he was the son of a Serbian father and a Croatian mother. So within the family of origin there lay an ethnic divide. On rare occasions when his parents had got angry with each other, they quickly referred to unfinished historical business, his father calling his mother a *Croatian traitor*, and his mother pouncing back with *srpski govno*, meaning something like *You Serbian shit*. Time had collapsed. However, family peace talks happened rapidly, both parents making up and rejoicing in their solid and loving relationship, setting the tone for their five sons' growing capacity for appreciating difference and forgiveness across ethnic division and internal divides.

As he embarked into quieter emotional waters, Zlatan returned to the epiphany dream, which had been a watershed, not only for the reopening of his feeling world but also for our working relationship. Now, in comes humour. At times, the deeper the traumatisation goes, the more humour comes out of concealment if the patient is able to do the work of restoration. Humour is, no doubt, a creative state of mind, redemptive in its intention, able to lift the person out of the tramlines of habit and to offer a perspective of renewal. We cracked up with laughter when he referred back to his getting angry with me and not noticing at the time that he had used a sexually charged word, something like "Ebe's fanny", instead of "epiphany".

Once Zlatan was more able to endure his internal daemons and multiple losses he was then given more to endure. His dreams did not stop bringing back the loss of his wife and family into his internal life and sobering consciousness; again and again, relentlessly, so that he learned the lesson of grieving, of letting go, of embarking on a new life but never forgetting. One small marker of moving along the bumpy road of recovery was when he dreamt that his daughter had given him a fresh flower from their garden, a bright red geranium, her favourite flower, delivered with a cheeky *Love you Dad* through the gaps of her teeth. Zlatan cried in the session, showing me the dried flower from his wallet. *It was the flower of the dream.* It was as if "the god of small things" had arrived and given him back aspects of her original aliveness, her love for the colour red. Before she died she had lived fully, red hot temper and all. The geranium she had given him had been intended as reparation for her most recent anger tantrum: a sweet peace offering.

Another trigger for his unconscious life happened just after a peace deal was signed in Bosnia-Herzegovina in 1996. He heard news of his family of origin. Both his father and mother had survived the civil war. However, two of his brothers had been killed in action. Now his dreams, as if collapsed in time, took him right back to his extended family's losses during World War Two. It struck him now that there had been a considerable impact on his parents' internal lives; they had, periodically, been absent-minded and dissociated from their feelings, especially his father who was prone to living in an ice-cold sea of emotion and then erupting into hot tantrums of anger. His parents' initial attempt at getting married—an inter-ethnic marriage between a Croat and Serb—was opposed by both strands of the clan. It was as if the massacre of thousands of Serbs by Nazi-collaborating Croats, the fascist Ushtashi, had occurred only the day before.

Zlatan remembered that he has had recurring dreams about war—clearly during his teenage years, and more opaquely in his early life—dreams embedded in the social unconscious both of his parents and of the ethnic group in which they lived, fuelled by stories told by elders who had survived the atrocities. Songs, legends, poems, oral fictions of all kinds had resulted from the blood of history. It became a collectively held fixed point, a form of identity, one of victimisation and never-ending lament and chronic mourning. If people do not mourn healthily, that is, let the past be the past and restore, inside, qualities and memories of the thing lost, they are prone to repetition, to going over and over the same ground of conflict and grievances, as if arrested in time—in trauma time, that is—and, by doing so, they establish a collectively held belief of victimisation that does not hold up to the scrutiny of history.

World War Two was not the only historical time of great intensity and ethnic impact. As if time had collapsed yet again, the Serb community had kept alive the Battle of Kosovo, some six hundred years earlier, which had led to the occupation of Serb-held territories by the

Ottoman Turks, who imposed Islamic rule on the region for hundreds of years. Defeat and subjugation had become an integral part of the Serb community's beleaguered psyche, adding yet another layer to a self-sustaining myth of victimisation. Zlatan's father, an ardent Serb nationalist, rode on this wave of primitive thought—the Serbs as the victims, the Muslims as the aggressors, which was, of course, in sharp contrast to his own marriage to a Croat and his views on ethnic diversity.

He was proud when he realised that his son had recurring dreams not only about World War Two but also about the Battle of Kosovo in 1389. In his dreams, fortified by songs of Kosovo and heroic lyric tales about Prince Lazar—the Serb leader at the time, who fought against his Ottoman foe, the Turkish sultan Marat I—young Zlatan had created fictions that bore close historical resemblance to actual events at the time. Without Zlatan asking for it, he was held out by nationalist Serbs in his community as some kind of bearer of historical consciousness.

In his late teenage years, when he realised this appropriation of his most private self, he rebelled openly against his father and his nationalist friends; this later led him to the decision to move with his young family into a Muslim-dominated area of Sarajevo in the knowledge that they are not, and will not be, the aggressor as portrayed by his own clan. The stubbornly held view of Muslims as the aggressor, he thought, was an easy option to take to escape not only the complexities of history but, more importantly, the conundrum of human aggression that, in this case, was being violently projected out and into another ethnic group. The struggle with destructive impulses is part of the human condition, and, if it can be recognised, is integral to human maturation and the development of the ethical sense. Zlatan, by being pushed to the brink of extinction as a person, had learned that he had to take responsibility for his own destructive fantasies and intentions. And, in the face of violence and loss, he had become a raging man, but it was a rage he was prepared to saddle with compassion so that it could be integrated. He found it refreshing to realise that he loved hating himself and the world; a good foundation stone from which to make amends and transform the god of fury into a life force in the service of the community.

During this time of intense learning Zlatan had repeated dreams about crows. Crows flying across sombre skies, landing on grave stones, crowing tales about death, dying, and destruction. Flocks of crows were gathering high up in tree tops, and in a chorus of contempt they were mocking the God of Love and praising the God of Darkness. Zlatan had always had a passion for storytelling and fiction, but most of all poetry. During these dark times he found affinity with Ted Hughes' poetry, especially the 1970 collection *Crow*. In its words he found a resemblance to his loss of faith, his most private apostasy. Had he not, as a Christian Serb, firmly believed in the power of love and compassion? However, two human catastrophes later, he had lost faith and wondered if the ruling principle of this world was nothing but death and destruction.

From time to time Zlatan brought with him a slim volume of poetry, designed in black, reading poems from it, with a strong Serbian accent. He knew that the crow poems were Hughes' own way of putting into words the suicide of his first wife, Sylvia Plath, and only six years later the suicide of his partner, Assia, who had also killed their daughter, Shura. His poetry gave voice not to the power of love but to the power of human destructiveness, not shying away from his own disillusionment in himself, namely his unholy giving in to the "daemon of phallic energy". Zlatan, in a different way, was disillusioned in himself, thinking that he had been unable to protect his own family from the savagery of war. He read from Hughes' poem "Crow hears fate knock on the door" (Hughes, 1970). The poem expounds a prophecy, mockingly delivered, about the surrender of the vitality of personhood to an altogether darker alliance: the forces of death, destruction, and fatedness. Taken over by the triumph of destructiveness, what remains of a person is cold dissociation, looking out at the world from a sinister place, "from a buried cell of bloody blackness" (ibid., p. 12), deeply hidden inside, a place of one-pointedness, deadly quiet, and inhumane detachment. Taken over by fatedness, there appears to be nothing left in the person but the voice of a sombre and ruinous prophecy, as if the fate of utter destruction cannot and will not be escaped, no voice of redemption heard.

Never having conceived of himself as being destructive, Zlatan had now joined the human race and its primary struggle—that between love and destructiveness. The outcome uncertain, he allowed himself to experience hateful thoughts without acting on them. *I live in a heart of darkness*, he would say poetically. And by doing so, he began to integrate the good and the bad in himself.

Post-war, more and more information became available to Zlatan about the circumstances of his family's perishing. They had lived in an affluent quarter of Sarajevo, mainly occupied by Muslim Bosnian Serbs. It was the Serbs, his own ethnic group, who had pounded the district with artillery fire from positions high above the city. The dreams that followed paradoxically returned to the historical consciousness embedded in his community of origin. He had vivid repetitions of the kind of dreams he had had as a teenager, which were about the massacre of his own people during the Second World War. It was as if the old bloodlines had again opened up the blood of history. Such an historical fixation on extermination and victimisation was deeply embedded in him. Needless to say that he also had recurring dreams about the Battle of Kosovo, the source of the Serbs' anachronistic and divisive notion of being victimised.

By confronting the personal traumas of having survived the shelling of the hospital he had worked in and the loss of his family, the doors of history opened and he walked down the timeline of dreams that reminded him of the cumulative traumas of his parents' generation and of traumas of the distant past that had affected his ethnic group. In order to become a person in his own right, to find freedom from the tyranny of emotion that did not belong to him, he had to find ways of separating: not only from the transmission of parental trauma but also from historical consciousness that had become inflammatory to racial hatred, taken by the Serb leaders during the Yugoslav civil war as justification to engage in massacres against Bosnian Muslims.

Vamık Volkan, a professor of psychiatry specialising in international relations, reported in *Blood Lines: From Ethnic Pride to Ethnic Terrorism* (1997), that former president Jimmy Carter had led a delegation of peace negotiators in Bosnia-Herzegovina with the aim of getting the Bosnian Serbs back to the negotiating table. Later, convicted war criminals Radovan Karadži and Ratko Mladi, taking part in the negotiations, rapidly and furiously went into historical grievances about World War Two massacres against the Serbs and, to everyone's surprise, the Battle of Kosovo of 1389. In their minds they had done nothing wrong when inciting genocide against Muslim Serbs in Srebrenica and other killing fields. Hannah Arendt, the German-Jewish philosopher, following the trial of Adolf Eichmann in Israel, controversially described the notion of "the banality of evil" (Arendt, 2007, p. 470). There is no depth to the thinking of perpetrators of such calibre. There is no moral conscience. There is nothing that would indicate any form of humanity towards other people. All that counts is the sadistic triumph of eliminating life.

For Zlatan, to recover not only from cumulative personal trauma but also deeply held racist notions of his own Serbian tribe, he had to become an independent person, with a mind of his own, countering the weight of history. His sense of depersonalisation held out for a good five years in his analysis. A not uncommon phrase he used was that he is a *working machine, nothing more,* gladly eating up some seventy working hours per week, if he had to.

His landlady, who lived in the flat upstairs, regularly invited him for luscious *Kaffee und Kuchen,* which she had lovingly baked, and for delicious east-European cuisine. She was from the Sudetenland, a German-speaking part of the present-day Czech Republic, a Jewish wartime immigrant. She suggested he did not clean his own flat.

"Young man! You're working such long hours already!" Her cleaning lady could easily step in. Not only was he a *working machine* but also, in his own words, a *cleaning machine*; desperately trying to clean up the blood of his family, the blood spilled in the hospital in Sarajevo, and with it the blood of history.

Without him initially understanding its meaning, his dream world issued a prophetic dream. As so often before, he re-entered a previous dream, the one in which he sat in dark solitude at the kitchen table, then being joined by his wife, children, and an experience of illumination. This time, the dream had a variation of theme up its sleeve. As the sunshine lit up the darkened room, he found himself sitting opposite not only his wife but also her friend, a blonde woman who was in deep conversation with his wife but also keeping an eye on the children playing outside in the garden. Neither of them took any notice of him. They nattered endlessly, as if to keep up a perpetual conversation of friendship. Eventually his wife gave her friend a present. It was the light blue jacket she had worn on their wedding day.

Zlatan, forever perplexed by his own dreams, had no concept of his attraction as a man: tall, handsome, dark eyes, designer stubble, sonorous voice, always dressed elegantly, his wild brush of hair adding another dimension of male splendour, if not of vulnerability. He loved people from a distance but, following the human tragedy of the loss of his entire family, he was not interested in amorous pursuits. The only person who was able to get anywhere near him was a colleague, a consultant anaesthetist from Canada. They confided in each other, spent breaks together, and also met outside of working hours—a rarity, given the inhumanely long hours Zlatan used to work. Two years after the dream about his wife and her friend, he realised he was deeply attracted to his friend. When she also declared her love for him, Zlatan fell into a deep depression, was unable to go to work, in short, he fell to pieces. A paradox of the human condition: when beauty comes along with its consort, love, it can be a devastating experience. Now, prepared to open his heart again, the actual feelings of his past traumas came to the fore. He experienced what Yeats described when he wrote: "A terrible beauty is born" (Yeats, 1992, p. 228). There was love again, but also deep despair.

During his breakdown we increased the number of sessions for a six-month period. There was not very much talking. It was all about emotionally re-experiencing events that were, in truth, nothing other than unbearable, unthinkable, beyond human comprehension. Time dragged heavily. Memories came back, tormenting images, furnished by a flurry of dreams that were about disintegration, falling apart, falling through the centre of his being. This process of regression took its own course, in the way a physical illness does. Once, out of the blur of fear, rage, and despair, a lucid phrase appeared in the consulting room. *I hope you know what you're doing,* he said. How did I know?

In the knowledge that he had grown up with elders prone to story-telling, I told him a story, a parable of sorts. A decade ago, during the final leg of the famous Sydney to Hobart yacht race, a storm had built up, making waves over thirty feet high. The sails were lowered, then taken in; most of the crew went below deck, the few men on deck tied themselves to safety ropes so that they would not be swept overboard. The ocean-going yacht, some fifty feet long, was battered in the storm for hours, skipper and crew desperately holding on, scared and shaken. Through the violent spray of the swell the skipper saw an enormous wave approaching, a black wall of water. Deadpan, he said, "Don't worry, mates! We're going under but we'll come up again." Zlatan cracked up with laughter.

The captain was bluffing. How did he know?

In the face of the storm the skipper had remembered previous storms and what happened when freak waves hit the yacht. They went under for what must have felt like an eternity. In fact, they sailed right through the belly of the wave, did a full 360-degree overhead turn, but remained unscathed, spat up to the surface by a furious sea. The mast broken, the crew's hearts were pounding with shock that gave way to quiet excitement. All of them had survived, whereas other crews had lost men overboard, and a number of other vessels had sunk and their crews perished, later to be found floating lifelessly hundreds of miles away.

Redemptive features of Zlatan's controlled breakdown were that the hospital were not disagreeable to him taking time off from work, that he increasingly trusted me guiding him through the tempest of his raw feelings, mockingly calling me *skipper*, but, most importantly, Charlene, his friend, then lover, stood by him. She was unperturbed by the burden and the uncertain outcome of his collapse; instead she welcomed the reopening of his heart and the retrieval of his soul. If truth were told, she had had her own experience of long-term psychoanalysis back in Canada, so she had an inkling of the nature of the work, with its inherent ups and downs. One evening, when she came over to his flat to check on him, the storm of his raw feelings hit her without mercy. She had let herself in and found him fast asleep on the coach in front of the television, which was blaring out platitudes. She ruffled his brush of hair and kissed him on the forehead. On waking up he jumped up and yelled at her, *Get out! Get out!* staring at her as if she was a ghost. An apparition? The devil incarnate?

The next day, during the session, he realised why he had responded in such an irrational, crazy manner. An image had hit the depths before it had risen and stirred the surface. Charlene had worn a light-blue jacket, not unlike the jacket of the dream, some two years ago, the one his wife had worn on their wedding day, the one she had passed on, in the dream, to her friend. It now sank in that his wife, in a prophetic dream, had given him permission to move on in life, and passed on her mantle to another woman.

Writerly devices in dreams and literature

Dreams serve memory. As mentioned earlier, dreams are autobiographical fictions that bring memories up from the dreamer's personal history, transgenerational themes of the family clan, and the latter's insertion in social and cultural history. Freud made the point that dreams are embedded in memory, they are "mnesic", if not "hypermnesic", that is, excessively in pursuit of memory:

Early memories which the subject had completely forgotten, but the truth of which can be objectively confirmed, not infrequently occur with startling fidelity even in the manifest content. (Freud, 1900)

Patrick Modiano's memorial mode

French writer Patrick Modiano, who was unexpectedly awarded the 2014 Nobel Prize for Literature, hardly known outside of France, writes in a style that deals with broken memory. Most of his books gravitate towards the time of the German occupation of France during World War Two. Modiano's fiction, such as *Suspended Sentences* (2015b) or *Dora Bruder* (2015a) are not easy reads; they are about the corrupted or broken life histories of elusive, unknowable characters who refuse interiority, ending up close to a sense of depersonalisation. The structures of the stories are maintained by neurotically detailed observation of dates, times, and locations. Not only that. Modiano seems to write the same book over and over, with recurring characters, locations, obscured memories, and no redemptive features of a reconciliation with a time sought for, but seemingly lost forever.

> I often have the impression that the book I've just finished isn't satisfied, that it rejects me because I haven't successfully completed it. Because there is no going back, I'm forced to begin a new book, so that I can finally complete the previous one These repetitions have a hypnotic quality, like a litany The repetition may stem from the fact that I'm troubled by a period of my life that resurfaced endlessly in my mind. (Muhlstein, 2014, p. 42)

What Modiano is really talking about is that in his mind he is for ever re-entering a recurring dream, if not a nightmare. The recurring dream is closely autobiographical and goes back to 1945, when he was born, and the time of the occupation. His father, a half-Jew, was a reckless black-market racketeer with Gestapo connections. Refusing to wear the yellow Star of David, he was arrested and about to be deported when his Nazi friends intervened and set him free. His collaboration saved his life but also morally compromised him. On the maternal side, things were not much better. Modiano described his mother as having an "arid" heart, being barren, dry, sober, without any obvious signs of enjoying motherhood. Both his father and his mother showed little interest in him as a child; he was left alone for long periods, and placed in a series of boarding schools where his "only oxygen was reading" (ibid.).

The other redeeming feature of his teenage years was writing. Aged fifteen, he was introduced to his mother's friend, the charismatic and innovative writer Raymond Queneau, whose *Zazie dans le Métro* became a cult book following its publication in 1959. Queneau was instrumental in fostering Modiano's nascent writing career, recommending his first book manuscript to Gallimard, who published *La Place de L'Etoile*—*étoile* being an allusion to the Jewish star—in 1967 when Modiano was only twenty three.

Referring to his father's shady past and his mother's barren heart, he said: "That's the soil—or the manure—from which I sprang" (ibid., p. 42). Not unlike Kafka, his pining for his father became a lifelong obsession. In all of his novels there is a narrator whose biography closely resembles Modiano's, making his writing spin toward the autobiographical.

> In contemplating what his art might be, he is forever searching for a father he never had. It was neither a vocation nor a particular gift that pushed me to write, but quite simply the enigma posed by a man I had no chance of finding again, and by all those questions that would never have an answer. (Thirlwell, 2014)

Case study: Thomas

Modiano's inability to mourn his absent father can be put in the context of one of my patient's search for *his* father. Thomas's father had died young of a heart attack when Thomas was only eight years old. He sought solace from his mother, but she had a breakdown, was hospitalised, and was absent for a few months whilst he stayed with his much older brother. He was not allowed to see his father's body nor attend the funeral. At the time, Thomas, struggled, in the absence of a holding environment, to grieve for the loss of his father, an inability that carried on throughout his life. To go back, in his mind, to that formative year had been too traumatic, always remembering a time of relentless deadness and depression. However, inherent in the problem always lies the solution: his *annus horribilis* turned out to be the making of his later developmental life.

> There is always one moment in one's past when the door opens and lets the future in. (Greene, 1940)

In the analysis Thomas had a crucial dream in which he pushed a large red balloon up his dog's anus, making it blow up out of all proportion. My patient was initially concerned about doing him harm but quickly reverted to thinking about not taking the dream image too literally, instead looking for the underlying dream thought. He remembered that his dog, who had been his companion for a good ten years in his twenties, had become a receptacle of his love, trust, and companionship, more so than any human being. A true soul companion. An animal consort. The red balloon Thomas linked with childhood games with his father, opening a historical door to other memories of his father that predated his death. In his dreams his father had sprung to life. He recalled the intimacy and closeness with his father, his father as a solid anchor in his early life.

Thomas's previous inability to mourn had obscured the aliveness of eight years spent together. Now that his dream life had initiated his belated process of mourning, his father showed up on a daily basis. In St Augustine's words, the dead are only dead, they are not gone. And by embarking on conversations with his father, Thomas had found a companion in his internal life; a companion who had, in fact, always been there but, because of his unbearable feelings of loss, Thomas had been unable to recognise.

* * *

What is my point here? I'm not saying that if Modiano had been properly psychoanalysed he would not have made art out of his very private searches for the past and the impossibility of memory. There is more to it. It is the weight of history. Born right at the end of the war, with his father's unholy insertion into the moral dilemmas of war-time violence and survival as a Jew, Modiano became one of the few people who held the consciousness of history. Perhaps history had implanted itself into an individual so that he would become a mouthpiece of the moral dilemmas of war-time collaboration and its attendant phenomenon of broken, fragmented memory. That Modiano was not able to healthily mourn the loss of his father might have been a personal issue but he was born into a turbulent time of recovery from severe traumatisation. The greater the traumatisation, the more powerful are the psychic mechanisms—such as dissociation from a feeling memory and the inability to mourn—put in place in order not to remember.

Modiano's almost neurotic concentration on the occupation made him become the nation's memory—the nation's fractured memory, to be precise; in this way we can better understand why his fiction has never reached wider acceptance or appreciation, either abroad or in France, particularly given France's not so splendid post-war track record of coming to terms with collaboration.

> It is the fragments of forgetfulness that most fascinate me. [For me] to write is to dream of being able to go back ... As if I could pass through the mirror of time and fix the past. (Muhlstein, 2014, p. 44)

The quotation demonstrates his style of writing, that is, the memorial mode; in his own words "literature's main engine is often memory", broken memory, for that matter. But it also shows a leaning towards dreams and dream-like states of mind employed in the process of writing. His theories of writing are full of references to the world of dreams. Talking about the writerly composition of fleeting impressions of characters, their elusiveness, and unintegration, he says that he "did so as if in a dream".

> It's like in the morning when you try to recall your dream from the night before, but all that's left are scraps that dissolve before you can put them together. (Ibid.)

Again, Modiano's fiction is not about memory as such but the arduous and painstaking *process* of memory. In his novel *Rue des Boutiques obscures*, which won him the Prix Goncourt in 1978, he goes fully into the impasse of memory, namely amnesia. The main character, a detective, who has lost his memory through a traumatic event, is desperately searching for the person who might be him: searching, searching but never finding. In his masterpiece, *Dora Bruder* (2015a), Modiano weaves together his research into the life of a perished Jewish teenager during the war, his own memories of the locations in Paris the girl had lived in, and a poetic reconstruction of what her life might have been like.

The idea for the novel came to him whilst he was leafing through old newspaper articles about the time of the occupation. There was an entry for 31 December 1942: "Dora Bruder, 15 years old, disappeared". With the assistance of Serge Klarsfeld who, ten years earlier, in his *Mémorial de la Déportation des Juifs de France* had painstakingly collected all the names of the 80,000 Jews who had perished, Modiano assembled a skeleton of information about Dora Bruder. In the end it became as much a search for his own father, who emerged out of dream-like images of distorted memory. He had, after all, reassembled out of the ruins of early life a semblance of father: *Habemus papam* ("We have a father")—an expression used by the Vatican when the white smoke rises above the chimney stacks of the Sistine Chapel, announcing the new pope to the world.

Dreams are expressions of multi-temporality. Dreams walk easily on the timeline of past, present, and future, and by doing so they are the arbiters of historical consciousness, which is the awareness of the individual not only as embedded in the soil of family history but also immersed in the strong currents of history.

We have already established the Freudian notion that dreams are "mnesic", that they serve memory, especially events that lie hidden in the dreamer's infantile past. The present finds equal expression in dreams, as they are the receptacle of day residues, a notion Freud used to describe the way in which everyday events seem to find their way into the making of a dream. Not only that. Sensory impressions, raw emotions, and thoughts without a thinker, all of which originate in present-day life, also provide the dream's internal workshop with basic material, if not clutter, from which the dream mind forms images, symbols, and metaphors. And by way of further processing through dream thinking the dream produces thoughts that serve the dreamer's self-understanding and a lifetime's narrative.

The dream is also at home in the future. Prehistoric and ancient conceptions of dreaming underline the prophetic nature of dreams. Prophecy remains a contemporary notion that can be detected at crucial moments in one's life, such as embarking on a new vocational project, at the crossroads of marriage, starting a family with a baby coming into this world, or being driven by a new creative venture. At such formative times dreams will come up that show the stuff that lies ahead, inherent in the new task to be undertaken. These prophetic dreams can be as mundane as a dream on New Year's Day that shows images and symbols of a new chapter in one's life, a chapter as yet unwritten and yet anticipated in dreams. It is inherent in the human condition that we tend to create futures; not only dreams that resemble wishes and longings—if not illusions—waiting to be fulfilled, but also tangible work projects in progress coming to fruition. And that includes the human projects of committed relationships, fatherhood, motherhood, or lasting friendship.

Dreams do away with linear, chronological time. The consensus of neuroscience is that dreaming is predominantly governed by the right brain hemisphere, which is the source of intuitive connections, giving rise to thinking in images, seeing the larger whole of things, attributing meaning to events, in short, the polarity of rational thought and linear, detailed, and factual thinking. Applied to the experience of time, dreams align themselves on the side of cyclical or circular time in which the experience of past, present, and future is simultaneous rather than strictly chronologically ordered. Historian Charles Stewart said that

> [c]hronology is the historian's way of making sure that everything
> does not happen at the same time. (2012, p. 1)

The nature of dreams is that *everything* happens at the same time. Dream time is always simultaneous, and being in dream time means that internally we are of all ages. We know from the baffling and provocative contents of dreams that claiming to be an adult, living fully in the present, is a reality but equally an illusion, as we harbour inside, at all times, memories of the foetus, the new-born baby, the toddler, the youngster, the teenager, the young man, the adult, the middle-aged man, and the man of old age. As Charles Stewart says, "dreaming violates the historical separation of past and present." And, by doing so, dreams are the makers of historical consciousness in which we experience the continuity of time, which also means that there is no such thing as a single dream. All dreams are interconnected, they are *omnibus* dreams. Any dream that occurs in the present has a historical link to previous clusters of dreams, going right back to the beginning of life. This thought, taken further, also shows that, through dreaming, we are able to reconnect not only with our own life history but with transgenerational themes, and themes going right back through the history of mankind.

A final thought: Frank Kermode (2000), a professor of literature, critic, and Shakespearean scholar, once said that "[m]en die because they cannot join the beginning with the end".

What he meant was that to live fully we have to link the beginning with the end, that is, to make sense of our human idiom and identity by engaging with our own historicity. We stand on the shoulders of past events that need to be connected to how we are in the present. Dreaming, always in the service of moving out of emotional stuckness, fossilisation, and deadness, leads the way in making us join the beginning with the end in order to become a more rounded person.

Multi-temporality in the writings of Garcia Márquez

The Colombian writer Gabriel Garcia Márquez (1928–2014), best known for his masterpiece *One Hundred Years of Solitude* (1967), belonged to the "Boom" circle of Latin American writers. This literary movement, with its heyday in the 1960s, the Peruvian author Mario Vargas Llosa in its ranks, set in motion a new style of writing in South America, greatly inspired by the modernism of James Joyce, Virginia Woolf, and William Faulkner. It was a move towards the interiority of characters, a non-linear, cyclical notion of time with the simultaneous occurrence of past, present, and future, and stream of consciousness writing that thrived on, and portrayed, altered states of consciousness. Garcia Márquez's own version of the "Boomers" new literary venture was described as "magical realism", a tag he disliked. Instead he preferred to use the term "sorrowful realism", which underlines some of his main characters' melancholy moods: in search of a beloved one in the case of Florentino's lifelong pining for his childhood sweetheart in *Love in the Time of Cholera*; or, in *The General in his Labyrinth*, Simon Bolivar's search for the life of power and status he has lost, now in the service of the revolution, the continent's liberation from the Spanish, during his final days drifting down the Magdalena River, recovering memories.

There is no doubt about the origin of magical realism. Márquez, brought up by his grandparents, was exposed to his grandfather's gory stories about the violence then erupting all over Colombia. Márquez, as a child, witnessed atrocities committed against striking banana-plant workers, and he once saw a woman, inconsolable and despairing, picking up and cradling the severed head of her husband, following a lethal machete fight. His grandmother was blind, living in an internal world but one rich in poetry and fantastical stories in the tradition of the indigenous people of the Caribbean. She supplied the infant Márquez with the seeds of magical thinking that saw the spirit world of the Taino omnipresent in the material world. The Taino worshiped and evoked their ancestors in rituals, not unlike the indigenous peoples of Australia with their practices of "dreamtime".

When the young Márquez came across Kafka's *Metamorphosis*, it was, in Graham Greene's phrase, a moment when the portal to the future opened. On reading this most bizarre fantastical and dream-like story of self-alienation, he instinctively knew he was going to be a writer. He must also have intuitively sensed the inner world from which Kafka's writing sprang. Kafka had, indeed, lived in a nocturnal world of dreams, imagination, and obscure lucidity, more so than in concrete reality. One of his diary entries at the beginning of World War One reads, deadpan: "Today, declaration of war. Gone for a swim in the afternoon."

Garcia Márquez is one of the exceptions to the rule that post-Nobel Prize writing is often accompanied by a drying up of inspiration, in tandem with a watering down of the writerly craft. His best work came after the 1982 Nobel Prize and *One Hundred Years of Solitude*, which had launched his writing career. He was fond of *Love in the Time of Cholera* (1985) throughout his life—"My best. The novel that was written from my gut." It is a love story in old age, a celebration of late-flowering love and of the late triumph of romance. There is possibly no equal in world literature that elevates old age to such a status of new-found beauty, erotic courtship, and, in its finality, arrives at profoundly spiritual experiences in the face of mortality.

The protagonists, Florentino and Fermina, are on a steamboat travelling up the Magdalena River, reunited after fifty years of separation, going back to their teenage years. When asked by the captain, "For how long the journey?", Florentino answers, "For the rest of our lives", which is a hint at conscious dying but is also Márquez playing with time, evoking in the reader images of an old couple going on and on, reaching into that rare experience of living fully in the moment. Even after death their souls continue upstream, slowly and consciously. Always calling upon cyclical time, the curvature of time, and its simultaneity, in which the beginning of the story is woven into its ending, Márquez portrays the notion that, as we move towards old age, so we revisit states of childhood and the sensuality of its rich flavours. Márquez creates a paradigm in the mind of the reader, an archetype of old age aliveness and lushness of experience. *If they can reach old age happiness, I can do it as well.* To be living old age gracefully and with intent, is a rare thing indeed. Márquez has created, in literature, an endearing and everlasting image.

There is a term in art history, *Altersstil* (Kellman, 2005, p. 329), that expresses the style of ageing masters, old-age creativity, and a late blossoming of creative art. Goethe (1749–1832) is a case in point. He spent thirty-three years on his major work, *Dr. Faustus*, right up to the end of his life, aged eighty-three. Jewish American novelist Henry Roth (1906–1995) wrote his first masterpiece, *Call it Sleep*, in 1934. Subsequently, his writing craft went underground for some sixty years—as he was occupied running a chicken farm—then re-emerged late in life just before his death with the publication of another master-piece, *Mercy of a Rude Stream*, in 1994.

* * *

Márquez has given his characters, in the final furlong of their lives, a new *raison d'etre*, a meaning which lies in the consummation of a love interrupted, a love that is now becoming a love eternal, extending a cliché into something real and lived in.

> Love is not love
> Which alters when it alteration finds
> (Shakespeare, Sonnet 116, in Vendler, 1997, p. 487)

This is how Shakespeare describes enduring love, love which does not change in its essence, even in the face of adversity and major life changes, in short, a love "That looks at tempests and is never shaken". Most of Garcia Márquez's novel is taken up by the tempest of unful-filled love, love broken apart because Florentino does not fit the bill of a good enough future husband. Fermina is taken away from the passion-ate currents of teenage love, placed far away with relatives, and returns to be married to another man, a medical doctor. Both lovers continue to live in the realm of sweet memory and fantasies of a love that can never be broken. Florentino hangs on to the memory of her "beautiful panther eyes", that, over the course of fifty years of separation, becomes a fleeting, dream-like image that wraps itself around him as the gentle touch of her arms, her husky voice, and her female scent used to. At the time of first love, during his teenage years, her panther eyes had opened a door to the future but also the future had pounced on him, taking him prisoner in a sense of unbroken temporality.

In dream theory, powerful animals, such as panthers, and big cats in general, represent what Nietzsche called the "will to power". It constitutes one of the basic human drives: living life fully according to one's strengths and talents; being driven towards finding one's own authority and place in the world, with the aim of making a contribution to the lives of others; and not being defeated by the trials of life. As the Black American writer Maya Angelou says, "While one may encounter many defeats, one must not be defeated" (1993).

Both Florentino and Fermina never were defeated. She found solace in running a household for a man who did not love or understand her; his primary love was medicine, and his parrot. Florentino, meanwhile, gave himself to the pleasures of dirty love, hiring a room in a brothel, meticulously recording his carnal pleasures in his diary. With typical irony, Márquez—playing on what he knew of the sexual appetites both of his father, who fathered no fewer than thirteen children, and his womanising grandfather, both described as, among other things, "fornicators"—gives Florentino absolution by saying that through the excesses of the bodily self he has learned invaluable lessons about love eternal; the fornicator as a student of love, as it were, "whose heart has more rooms than a whore-house". During Florentino's education through carnality he always returns to the singularity of his life's search: the woman he really loved. In order to maintain contact, if only in his mind, he not only gives in to reminiscing about her panther eyes but also writes letter after letter, hundreds of them, which are never posted but are, by way of dream-like apprehension, received.

By way of another Márquezian irony, Fermina's husband dies falling off a ladder as he tries to rescue his beloved parrot from high up in a tree. Now the door has opened once again for the original lovers to be reunited on a boat journey upstream. Florentino's uncle is given the final word, saying that life obliges human beings "over and over again to give birth to themselves". So close to death and yet so alive. A suitable epilogue to late-flowering love.

* * *

In *The General and His Labyrinth* (1989) Márquez's inclination to write in cyclical time, where in one phrase the present might be overlaid with reminiscences from the past and fantasies about the future, is at its most apparent. The story takes us through the last calamitous fortnight in the life of Simon Bolivar (1783–1830). As the great historical figure is dying of tuberculosis, on his last journey sailing down the Magdalena River, away from Bogota toward the Caribbean Sea, the reader is drawn into a quality of multi-temporality: everything is happening at the same time. The curvature of time in old age and dying makes a multitude of life events appear on the stage of memory.

With a weakened body, his only remaining faculty his sharp mind, Bolivar takes stock of his turbulent life: from the heights of his old noble self as "The Liberator" of South America from the Spaniards, he is now descending into his base self, ousted from power and deserted by his comrades in arms, except for a handful of loyal followers by his side. Larger than life in his prime, the fall from grace is humiliating and sobering. His body is shrunk, at times he is too weak to eat, feverish, prone to coughing fits that tear deep into his being; in the place where once he paraded the regalia of absolute power, in the building of five new nations, the smell of old man and death cling to him.

And yet, the more his body deteriorates the more he moves into the higher realms of spiritual life. His mind still intact in a morbid body, he feels great regret over his own abuse of power in the wars of liberation from Spanish rule; given dictatorial powers by congress, it was a rule that then became his. His war of liberation had been a war of barbarism, a "war to the death" that annihilated not only the Spaniards but also local defectors from his noble cause. His was a world of contradictions. The same brutal general had freed the northern region of South America, Bolivia, Colombia, Venezuela, Ecuador, and Peru, and abolished slavery, an affront to the ruling classes from which he came.

On the journey—both real and figurative—downstream, the mind of the dying man takes him back to the beginning, to his foundation myth, which, having been born into the elite in Caracas, was an affluent beginning but, early on, was overshadowed by major losses. His father died when he was three, his mother when he was nine. If that was not enough, he had also lost his young wife, Maria Teresa, shortly after their wedding when he was in his early twenties. The loss of the great love of his life propelled Bolivar into history, into the slow-flowing, molten lava of the Latin American Revolution.

> "He who serves the revolution ploughs the sea."
> (Simon Bolivar in Márquez, 1991)

Never again did he give himself to another woman, which is not to say that he did not have a large appetite for romantic and sexual love. In fact, during his mature years, he had an eight-year liaison with the legendary Manuela Sáenz, a woman his equal in intellect, independence, and strong will. They shared the fire of intellectual debate, the passions of the body, and an appreciation of the beauty of the world.

In his blurry last days, "the General", as he is referred to in the novel, believes in an implausible dream to return to the plantation of his childhood in Venezuela, only to arrive there in feverish fantasy. In his mind he links the present with all the formative experiences of the past: of childhood abundance, of the loss of both his parents, of the loss of his young wife that made him enter history and abandon private life. Facing up to death and dying, he is reborn spiritually as a man capable of universal love and generosity, even towards his old foes. And yet, his head is crowded with contradictions and issues that never can be resolved. As he says with his last words: "How will I ever get out of this labyrinth?"

* * *

In the previous chapter we heard about Freud the prize-winning prose writer, his inclination, when donning the hat of Romanticism, to see a close link between fiction writing and dreams, and Lionel Trilling's assertion that the Freudian psyche is a "poetry-making organ" that depends so much on the comprehension of dreams with its rich source of images, symbols, metaphors, and its narrative capability. We also called upon Jonathan Franzen's theory—which he developed by studying the origin of Kafka's work and his style of writing—that fiction writing is "purposeful dreaming".

Kafka, the poet of alienation

Franz Kafka (1883–1924), one of the pioneers of Modernism, was the poet of alienation. His writing created a new style, if not genre, in world literature. "Kafkaesque" fictional reality is about the combination of the ordinary and the sinister in the human condition: the separateness of human beings, their enigmatic reality that can never be fully understood, leading lonely lives, perplexed by the complexities of the modern world, threatened by the power relations of authority, guilty over their unspeakable and dark internal wishes that never find explicit mention or expression in social life or in the pages of literature.

"We need the books that affect us like a disaster, that grieve us deeply, like the death of someone we loved more than ourselves, like being banished into forests far from everyone, like a suicide. A book must be an axe for the frozen sea inside us. That is my belief." (Kafka, in Banvillle, 2013, p. 17)

As a result of Kafka's writing in the 1910s and 1920s, literature became a more sobering place: it did not shy away from describing how the industrial revolution of the previous century had led to an increasing sense of human alienation and how mass culture in large cities pushed the individual to the periphery. By painstakingly telling stories of human separateness and of the individual's disappearance as a result of the power relations of the state, he tackled one of the existential questions that is still unbearable to the modern reader, reaching into our basic fears. What are we afraid of?

We are afraid of mortality, we are afraid of separateness, we are afraid of loss, we are afraid of insanity, we are afraid of being alive, and we are afraid of beauty. Such existential fears also lie at the root of dreaming. Why do we dream? Dreams knock at the door of our conscious mind and make the following demand: that we should confront the inherent fear of the human condition, and, in the face of fear, move on to leading a more considered and vivified life, based on humanist principles such as moral courage, the search for understanding, and critical thinking.

The same existential questions of mortality, loss, separateness, insanity, vivification, and beauty that underlie dream life are, of course, also posed by world literature. Why literature? Literature is there to ask, but not answer, pertinent existential questions. In this wider context of the imperatives of dream life and literary life, Kafka made a huge contribution to the understanding of human alienation.

In *The Trial* (1925), for instance, he takes us into the bizarre world of Joseph K. Being accused of something unfathomable, not knowing why, the main character is at the mercy of an incomprehensible power. Wandering through the labyrinths of apartment blocks, endless corridors of gloomy offices, low-ceilinged rooms that offer nothing but a sense of suffocation, Joseph K struggles with guilt over something, but he does not know what it was. There is a threat, the threat of accusation but really a threat of violence, which paralyses and exhausts him. His cause is utterly futile. Towards the end of the book, before Joseph K is condemned to death, the narrator offers a hint of relief by asking pertinent questions: "Where was the judge he had never seen? Where was the High Court he had never reached? He raised his hands and spread out all his fingers."

Kafka had, in an uncanny way, apprehended a totalitarian state. As early as the decade between 1915 and 1925 he unconsciously had an inkling of what was to come for the Jews under Nazi rule. His writing was prophetic: the Holocaust bore witness to the premonitions Kafka took from his dream life. A human paradox: being a lifelong dreamer, prone to shying away from reality, he had become a receptacle for the vast psychosocial undercurrents of his time. His dreamtime had aligned itself closely to the actual *zeitgeist* of huge social transformation and to the power struggle between good and bad that later, during the Weimar Republic and the upsurge of fascist violence, became apparent.

The Trial could also be an apt description of aspects of the post-war communist regime in East Germany, where no less than a third of the population, on the payroll of the Stasi, spied on the other two thirds; and, as the result of a collapsing economy, a considerable part of the population had to live in barren and depressing apartment blocks that had risen out of the rubble of war, and out of guilt and shame (Stach, 2013, 2015).

Primo Levi, Italian chemist, socialist, and chronicler of human malice in his book *If This is a Man* (1959), who had survived the concentration camps, was asked to translate Kafka's *The Trial* into Italian. He was so affected by the task, as he slipped back into memories of the purgatory of human destructiveness, that he became severely depressed. Since his unlikely survival, bouts of debilitating depression—which eventually, late in his life, would lead him to take his own life—had been his companion.

Kafka, the poet of alienation, himself struggled with issues of otherness and not belonging. As a German-speaking Jew in Prague, he witnessed the decline, after some seven hundred years of hegemony, of the pre-dominant German culture, and the rise of Czech culture (MacGregor, 2014). Kafka's Jewishness also put him outside of the cultural norm that shifted from the cosmopolitanism of the Austro-Hungarian Empire to blatant nationalism and resentment. Alienated from his family of origin, especially from his father, he withdrew into his most private self. And, most tormenting, at the core of his being, were his homosexual urges, which he kept hidden, even, so it seems, from himself.

The German-American critic Erich Heller described Kafka as "the creator of the most *obscure lucidity* in the history of literature" (Banville,

2013, my emphasis). In his writing there is always something that is not being said. So what is the hidden stuff in his writing? Is it informed and fuelled by his internal life? Saul Friedländer, who thought of Kafka as "the poet of his own disorder" (2013), refers to his inner torture over his homosexual fantasies, and his disgust towards women, despite the fact that he had three meaningful liaisons with women over the course of his life, keeping them at bay by correspondence rather than relating, except for the last companion, Diamant, who nursed him through his final months. He was also fascinated by violent fantasies of torture and evisceration, which went hand in hand with his self-hatred and self-disgust.

> "No one sings as purely as these who inhabit the deepest hell ...",
> "I am dirty, ..., infinitely dirty, this is why I scream so much about purity." (Kafka, in Banville, 2013)

"The poet of his own disorder" showed courage by confronting truthfully his own daemons, his human fault-lines, and elevated his struggle to an art form, the poetry of alienation. He had no illusions about the unspeakable aspects of the human condition, namely fear, aggression, hatred, and sexual repression. "My prison cell—my fortress", was how he described his most private thoughts. No doubt, there is more to Kafka than "the poet of his own disorder". He was a supreme ironist, capable of laughing at himself. Once, when reading from the first few pages of *The Trial* to his Prague friends, he laughed himself into such a state that his private show was interrupted (Banville, 2013). As we know, humour is one of the most creative states of mind, and is also the staple diet of dream life; humour that shines light on the base self rather than on elevated or illusory conceptions of the self.

> "My penchant for portraying my dreamlike inner life has rendered everything else inconsequential; my life has atrophied terribly, and does not stop atrophying." (Kafka, ibid., p. 19)

* * *

Erich Heller's term "obscure lucidity", which he uses to describe Kafka's cryptic writing style, sits well with dream theory. Dreams are both obscure and lucid. Dreams are about unmasking, peeling layer upon protective layer off the naked truth, leading out of concealment assumptions the dreamer thought impossible to own, all in the service of consciousness and self-knowledge. However, dreams engage us in a dilemma: they reveal but they also seem to obscure. In short, obscuration is one of the dream's characteristic provocations. The meaning of a dream is never straightforward, never entirely exhausted, nor is it revealed in a manner open to quickened rational thought. Images, symbols, metaphors, and narrative are not conducive to immediate comprehension, nor are they in line with conclusive thought. Dreams evoke, provoke, tease, and rapture, in order to unhinge us from the tramlines of habit and preconceived ideas. Dreams widen our horizons of imagination, creativity, and conceptual frameworks. Having inflicted on us during the night-time, when unprepared and fast asleep, an array of new images and storylines, the world of dreams releases us into a daytime of baffled rumination and sensory afterglow. What was once held in obscuration, is now open to being experienced more fully, and by ways of sensory vivification we start to emotionally comprehend core issues of our life histories.

Depending on the labours undertaken by the dreamer—it might be just a shifting positive attitude towards one's own dreams—the dream more and more reveals, but never completely satisfies, the search for knowledge. A dream can never be fully understood. It is at this stage of emotional investment that dreams become more lucid, or so it seems; it is more likely that they are experienced as more lucid as the dreamer reaches into her own lucidity of thinking and comprehension. The final answer to the decreasing obscurity and pregnant lucidity of dreams lies in the dreamer-dream relationship. What we have initially identified as the dream's obscurity is nothing less than the dreamer's own obscurity, referring to one of the conundrums of the human condition, namely the struggle to know oneself.

The dream's inherent obscurity is intentional. It asks of the dreamer pertinent questions. And it is the dreamer alone who can step up and utilise the gift of the dream. Dreams are like detective stories. Who's done it, what lies behind the visible, its obscurity being its dynamic force, is not its final purpose; it is more about getting there, the journey, the process of discovery.

This can be seen in Andrea Camilleri's formulaic but delightfully humorous detective stories, where the story lives on the main character's lucidity and warped humanity. Inspector Montalbano displays a curious, philosophical, and searching attitude towards the crime and the culprit's machinations of obscuration. In his house by a sandy beach he tends to wake from morbid dreams, and in the primeval soup of reverie he finds a single thought, an illumination of sorts. Fortified by his dream-like thinking about the fault-lines of the human condition, and in-between spending time in empty rumination by the sea, gorging himself on Sicilian cuisine, and mixing with beautiful women erotically drawn to him, he inches from obscurity to lucidity. All of a sudden it makes sense. A single thought. A single revelation: but not all is done. Not all is revealed in the mysteries of Andrea Camilleri's detective stories.

The single emergent thought is not unlike what psychoanalyst Bion calls "the selected fact". In his theory of thinking, which takes the reader from obscurity to lucidity, the raw materials of self-knowledge and understanding are sensory impressions, primitive feelings, and thoughts without a thinker. Bring on what he calls the "alpha function", which is a dream function, and such a chaotic mass of emotion and physicality turns into thinking proper, into emotional understanding and consciousness. So what we call culture, sophistication of thought, and the development of humanistic principles originates in a primeval soup of instinctual life that is then converted on to a higher plane of mental functioning through dream thinking. Dream thinking is at home in the dynamic interplay between obscurity and lucidity.

Ted Hughes and the poetry of loss

Michael Hofmann, acclaimed translator and a poet himself, places Hughes' writing on the higher echelons of the shortest fictions of all. "Hughes is at least arguably the greatest English poet since Shakespeare" (2014).

Hughes' poetry springs from his passion for nature. What some critics limply call "primitivism", the search for nature and its rich symbolism in poetic form, was for Hughes a wounded search for an original wholeness. His love for nature, for fishing and hunting, imprinted during the first seven years of his life, became a refuge from the severe depressive mood swings of his shell-shocked father. Hughes retained a lifelong passion for fishing, and had recurring dreams about lakes, streams, fishing, and fish, a world of imagination and undifferentiated-ness. He saw his dreams as "symbols of deep vital life", and by referring to spiritual traditions he said that "rivers have been gods", "water has been the soul", and "water is the ultimate life". Only in nature did he feel a deep connectedness with "the stuff of the earth", a world "which pre-dates language" from which his poetry sprang (O'Brien, 2003).

In the sense that nature became a leading backdrop, if not character, in his poetry, he can be aligned with an unlikely companion writer, namely Patrick White, the Australian novelist whose writing so much depends on place, locality, that is, Australia's vast and unforgiving outback. White uses the term "infinite connectivity", which describes man's deep insertion into nature, being ravished, but in equal measure, grounded by it. One character, Miss Hare, in *Riders in the Chariot*, finds her spiritual home, her "chariot", in fevers and madness, but in the soil of the land she finds redemption from an altogether disintegrated life. She is, in figurative terms, an earth spirit, an *Erdgeist*, speaking to herself: "The earth is wonderful. It is all we have. It has brought me back, when, otherwise I should have died" (White, 1961).

No surprise then, given Hughes' love for nature and his penchant for dream life, that he came up with a nature dream just before getting married to Sylvia Plath in 1956. The dream narrative goes: "I hooked a pike at tremendous depth. As it came up, its head filled the lake. I brought it out and its girth filled the entire lake. And I was backing up, dragging the thing out" (Hughes, 1999b). His marriage dream was prophetic of the coming together of two unquiet souls, richly gifted with artistic talent. What followed over the next six years was the strong union of two dedicated writers who inspired each other. At the root of any dream, beyond image, symbol, metaphor, and narrative, always lies a dream thought: "What lies at the bottom of the marital lake?" It was a marriage of two kindred souls but also of emotional suffering, at once a godsend and a claustrum: the godsend, the artistic inspiration; the claustrum, of an emotional nature, the confluence of Hughes' tendency to depressive bouts, possibly linked to his father's war trauma, and Plath's manic-depressive illness and sudden violent outbursts. Her suffering, in all likelihood, was linked to the loss of her father when she was aged eight. Not unlike Kafka she was a "poet of her own disorder", to use Saul Friedländer's term. Her poetry sprang from the tyranny of a malignant sadness, a claustrum, a confined space, that never entirely released her into a joyful life.

Following her suicide, Hughes was maligned, and not only by ardent feminists, as the guilty party, as if his womanising had been the only reason for Plath's demise. Thirty-five years later Hughes' testimony to his profound connection with Plath and his terrible loss was expressed in a collection of poetry, *Birthday Letters*. In the poem "Dream life", he gives an account of Plath's troubled nocturnal life (Hughes, 1998). Plath's waking life, when in the grip of her manic-depressive illness, was frequently a nightmare. So it is not surprising that during the night-time instalments of her inner life, being in the realm of Asclepius, she was overwhelmed by nightmares. "Your dreams were a sea clogged with corpses" (ibid., p. 141). Afraid of sleep, afraid of dreams, her dream life was always a descent into Hades, the underworld, an underview of the world populated with the dead of history, with unspeakable atrocities, bodily dismemberment, as if with direct access to the memory of concentration camp experience, burdened by the weight of historical consciousness. But her nocturnal descent was also a personal one, a visitation of her father's illness, his gangrenous leg, and his premature death that left her, aged eight, devastated and prone to childhood depression. Dream life, for the poet of her own disorder, was death life, a coming to terms with mortality and the curse of manic-depressive illness, a malignant sadness, emotional experiences so demanding they pushed her to the brink of the unbearable; and, yet, they became precisely the capital and driving force of her creative work, which developed to combine high technical skill with deep emotional power.

* * *

The process of mourning belongs to one of the most creative states of mind, as it reinstates inside the grieving person's psyche remnants of the person lost. It is productive, by making the mourner an internally enriched person. Images of the person lost, snippets of conversations, humour shared, unforgettable moments of happiness but also of ordinariness, sit alongside each other on the endless shore of affection; the perpetual conversation of friendship is reignited in memory, physical memories, smell, scent, the warmth of bodily embrace, and the recovery from the failures of love, all of which have become ingredients of afterlife, still consumed during quiet moments of remembrance. The dead are only dead, they are not gone, to use St Augustine's words. Naturally, such reminiscences come upon us when we give in to dream-like states of mind. Not only that. One of the dream's main functions is to facilitate the process of mourning. Dreams that brings forth the losses the dreamer might have forgotten about, or repressed, or pushed away from conscious memory, are almost as frequent as anxiety dreams, and dreams about aggression and sexuality.

Why do we dream? On an existential level, dreams deal with the fundamentals of the human condition. We dream in order to come to terms with mortality, separateness, loss, insanity, being alive, and beauty. The relationship with such existential questions is mainly one of fear, so dreams regulate our fear in the face of impending death, human separateness, losses great and small, the lure of insanity, the not so easy task of living life to the full, and the innate struggle to look beauty in the eye.

Hughes, by being dedicated to the worlds of nature, dreams, and the process of mourning, gave contemporary poetry considerable gravitas and inner strength; and through the publication of *Birthday Letters* he created a late monument to the poetic legacy of Sylvia Plath and a redeeming public statement of their profound but burdened marriage of six years, moving beyond the claustrum of his human fault-lines and her debilitating illness.

Colm Tóibín, the poet of loss

The Irish novelist Colm Tóibín, born in Dublin in 1955, is another poet of loss. His writing is broadened by the perspective he offers on his characters' social lives, as well as their inner lives. The melancholy tone of his novels has resonances with Tóibín's own biography, having lost his father at an early age, but also with issues of historical consciousness as he taps into the stream of Ireland's troubled history, mainly the exodus of people from deprivation and unemployment in the 1950s. Tóibín's novel *Brooklyn* (2009), which is about the emigration of an Irish woman to New York City, describes in a measured and quiet tone the emotional power that emanates from the loss of family and country, and the development of a somewhat tentative new beginning out of isolation and cultural difference.

In his most recent novel, *Nora Webster* (2014), Colm Tóibín ventures into what he does best, namely setting a stage for loss, bereavement, and the slow recovery from it. It is Ireland in the late 1960s. Nora Webster has lost her husband Maurice, leaving behind a set of older girls, who have by then left home, and a set of younger boys who still need looking after. The book takes the reader through Nora's and her children's gradual recovery, over some three years, from the loss of a previously contented and ordinary happy family life.

Fiercely intelligent and self-possessed, Nora pushes against the stream of narrow social expectation. Painfully slowly, she is shedding the old life by selling the family's summer house by the beach; she goes to work again, and finds solace in her own resolve by standing up to obnoxious, parochial, and unthoughtful people at work and in her boys' school. Nora is the maker of a new life, in the face of relentless grieving and having to hold it together for her four children. The paradox of grieving is that a loss is a gain: something new always makes itself known amid material and invisible aspects of the old life that has gone to pieces. Beauty enters Nora's life by means of listening to classical music, going for singing lessons, and starting up friendships with two women, one of whom is her eccentric music teacher. The perpetual conversation of friendship helps her in a final act of defiance. After three years of mourning, she throws out Maurice's clothes.

Her act of separation from the past does not mean that her husband is ousted from her life altogether. In quiet moments she gives in to tender reflection on their shared life. The culmination of the book is an epiphany dream. Maurice shows up in her bedroom, sits down, and, like in old times, they get a conversation going. Fortified by her dream she knows that her late husband will always be alongside her, not in a morbid way, hanging on to the old, but as a companion spirit. The dead are only dead, they are not gone.

Colm Tóibín, reflecting on the writerly genesis of *Nora Webster,* said that it had taken him over a decade to complete the book. The slow burner stayed with him, interspersed by the completion of the novels *Brooklyn* and *The Testament of Mary,* and two short story collections, *Mothers and Sons* and *The Empty Family.* "It seemed that in all these books I was circling the story that was Nora Webster's, working out ways of writing about family and loss and trauma," Tóibín disclosed in *The Guardian Review* (2016). Why did it take so long? It had to do with memory, autobiographical memory; he lost his father in the same year the father in *Nora Webster,* Maurice, died. Location and family circumstances, closely resembling the author's own life, issued memories that were unexpectedly sharp, with defined contours, interrupting his daily routines more than he wished. His own early life, in an agonising process of transformation, had to be rendered authorial, to be made into an art form. As an imaginative writer of prose, Tóibín had found his capital for prose writing, that is, his own life.

Memory got in the way of rapid writing. Not only that. It was also the process of mourning itself which made such demands: of self-reflection, of pausing in the middle of a busy life, of giving in to still-ness, in short, to finding the ontology of loss, that is, ways of beingness alongside mortality. In *Nora Webster* the protagonist is Nora, but there is another, who is hardly mentioned, or only appears out of memories, and yet his presence is all-encompassing, directing from beyond, as it were, earthly matters in the here and now. Against this backdrop, of the at once gone and present substance of Mauriceness, Nora finds her-self constructing a new life; against the backdrop of the early loss of his father, Colm Tóibín first dreams and then makes himself up as a writer. In his reflections on the gestation and manifestation of thought on paper, Tóibín speaks of the "battle between the night and the day" (ibid.). When he went to sleep he had a fair idea of how to take Nora Webster's story further but on waking the author of the night did not stand up to the scrutiny of early morning light, usually the bringer of truthfulness and consciousness, if not sobering reflection. Ten years on, Tóibín had made from painful memory an edifice of his father in the shape of a book. A loss, once processed, is always a gain.

Historical consciousness

Charles Stewart, in *Dreaming and Historical Consciousness in Island Greece* (2012), makes two theoretical suggestions as to the social nature of dreaming and its temporality. He asserted that "[d]reaming violates the historical separation of past and present". Dreams are multi-temporal, they represent the confluence of different times where past, present, and future occur simultaneously. Dreams do not usually run in chrono-logical, linear time; they are proponents of cyclical time.

Not only that. Dreams are the repositories and makers of history, they carry "historical consciousness". Stewart, a historian, studied the records of two time periods in the dream history of the Greek island of Naxos, specifically the village of Kronos. In 1831 farmers and shep-herds in the region started to have collective dreams in which they had visions of the Virgin Mary. The dreams revolved around a hidden icon, an image of the Panagia, which is the Greek term for the Virgin Mary, the "All-Holy" one. Rapidly, the interiority of the dreams became socialised and the property of the community, always in search of spiritual expe-rience. A farmer, digging in a cavern, found bones allegedly belonging to a family of Egyptian Christians of the Byzantine era who had taken refuge in the cave. In 1836, whilst hundreds of people watched, three icons were discovered. A cult of the Virgin Mary had come into being from which further dreams sprang. The Panagia of communal dreams instructed her followers to build a temple in her honour, but this was too much for the established Orthodox Church and for the government, which intervened and confiscated the icons.

In 1930 a second outbreak of collective dreaming occurred. In Kronos a villager rediscovered the missing icon of the Panagia, which set off the second wave of dreaming. This time the dreamers were predominantly middle-aged women and schoolchildren. The Panagia's dream instruction was to search for another icon, but the icon was never found and the community turned against the dreamers, accusing them of heresy. Thus the communal dream fever came to an unholy end.

Charles Stewart drew the following conclusions from the dream records and the social context of the dream episodes. He found evidence that during the first outbreak of collective dreaming in the 1830s there was a crisis in the mining industry that posed a threat to the islanders' livelihoods. Equally in the 1930s there was another economic crisis in the emery, that is, iron oxide, mining industry. The Great Depression had led to the total collapse of the industry. Stewart concluded that "a repeated blurring between two subterranean treasures", icons and emery, had occurred (ibid.); a confluence and a mutual relationship between the interiority of dreams and actual economic events, with a huge social impact on the community and on communal dream life. It showed that whatever happens in history will have an impact on dream life, and that dream life conjures up its own redemptive solutions to historical and economic impasse.

Historical consciousness in Irène Némirovsky

Jewish French writer Irène Némirovsky (1903–1942), wrote her final book as she was living on the pulse of history, perhaps more so than any other novelist in the history of literature. Daughter of a Tsarist Russian banker who had taken refuge in France from the Reds after the 1917 Revolution, she grew up in an affluent area in Paris. The good life, however, did not last. After their exile and the recovery from adversity, worse was to come. The Germans overran the French in six weeks, and the Blitzkrieg forced the evacuation of the population of Paris to the countryside.

Némirovsky, by now an established writer, some seventeen novels under her belt, married with two small children, joined the mass exodus of 1940, despite the fact that she had opportunities and the financial means to leave the country (Philipponnat & Lienhardt, 2010). Did she not anticipate what was to come? Maybe, maybe not. As it was, she observed with the unrelenting scrutiny only a writer can muster, the French response to Germany's invasion. In *Suite Française*, written between1941 and 1942, as history unfolded right in front of her eyes, she wrote savage depictions of French collaboration and lack of moral courage. In condemnatory words she described her countrymen as "lethargic, bowed, docile, crushed like a cattle in a storm" (Némirovsky, 2006), in a manner not dissimilar from the anti-Semitic jargon used by the Nazis.

In fact, in her overall oeuvre Jewish characters were never more than caricatures of Jews. In *L'Enfant génial* (2005), (written in 1927, but renamed *L'enfant prodige* in 1992), for instance, she describes a young aspiring writer, Ismael, a child prodigy who is discovered by a bohemian poet outside of his Jewish community but, in the end, never makes it as a writer as he disappears back into his Jewish roots and becomes a shoemaker. His unquiet soul, though, doesn't give him any reprieve. Ismael's struggle, in Némirovsky's eyes, has nothing to do with the Russian persecution of the Jews but is a result of their own doing, an "impoverished race, … fearing the light of day" (Weiss, 2007, p. 11). She describes Jewish children from poor backgrounds as "swarming vermin" and their parents as "garrulous and obsequious". Judaism, in her view, was "detrimental to literary creation", and Jewish traditions "too primitive to be followed strictly" (ibid., p. 10).

To learn this is a staggering realisation, given that she ended her life in the concentration camp of Auschwitz, dying of typhus, merely because she was a Jew. Némirovsky an anti-Semite? Born into a wealthy Jewish family up on the leafy hills of Kiev, she looked down on the poor Jews living in the quarters below. She never mixed with the lower classes of her own kind, nor did she, later on during her exile in Paris, mix with émigré Russians, nor did she write in Russian, and, most perplexing of all, in Paris she chose to surrounded herself with friends and colleagues in the publishing industry who were outspoken and vitriolic anti-Semites. One of her biographers, Jonathan Weiss, draws the conclusion that "Irene Némirovsky was an author in search of an identity" (ibid., p. 5); that is, a pure French identity, despite the fact that she was refused citizenship.

Her determined detachment from her Jewish heritage originated in the elevated social class from which she came, and her own bizarre theory of how to become a writer, washing her Jewishness out of her identity, being baptized as a Catholic in 1938; but predominantly it originated in finding ways out of the traumatisation that she had experienced as a Jew in Russia. As a baby she had narrowly survived the 1905 pogroms; she had witnessed a mock execution by the Bolsheviks at the outset of the revolution in 1917 (Raphael, 2010); and, later on in France, she witnessed the moral collapse of French society in the face of war. Another view of her attempt to shed her Jewish identity is that part of Jewish psychosocial identity has a tradition of self-mockery and self-criticism, as if to play out, as protagonist rather than victim, a pertinent social drama that in the face of the fear of annihilation could easily descend into self-hatred.

Even if, cushioned by her wealth, she dissociated from severe traumatisation, the violence and hatred in social relations had an impact on her individual psyche. At times of great historical upheaval the imprint of the social unconscious can outweigh the individual's coping mechanisms. Being an intelligent, socially aware, young woman she would have known very well that her family's wealth and class could not protect her from anti-Jewish hatred and violence, and yet she firmly believed that some eminent people with whom she had socialised before the war would step in and rescue her. By means of strongly held emotional dissociation she lived a life "above the rest", dedicated to her art, but in the end she too perished in a historic and violent tsunami.

During the crucial time following the Paris exodus of 1940, rehoused to the small village of Issy-l'Eveque, near the border of the "free zone" of the Vichy regime, Némirovsky took time to write, preferably in the surrounding woods. Despite her personal rage at the fate of ordinary people, and a sense of isolation amongst the French, despite the threat of more violence to come, she was still able to find peace and quiet in herself, able to produce a book—or a fragment of a book, as it was never completed—with a lyrical narrative glowing with life and human understanding. Its tone resonates with a profound understanding of the human condition under extreme conditions, describing not only defiant composure in the face of violation but also ordinary human failings. Parisian evacuees were depicted as panicky, self-centred, uninterested in helping out fellow travellers; one wealthy family, its car fully packed, waited and waited for their fresh laundry to arrive before they would set off, as if oblivious to the danger they were in.

Némirovsky's greatest moral achievement was the way in which she showed the humanity of individual Germans; not just a cliché of a sensitive piano-playing officer who falls for a local girl but also of ordinary soldiers who, on hearing about the war's escalation into Russia, were rudely awakened from a shallow sense of triumph and an illusion of peace, realising that it was they who were to fill the mass graves of fallen soldiers on the Russian front.

Born in Kiev in the Ukraine, Némirovsky was profoundly Russian, and her writing was inspired by Tolstoy, not lacking in intensity, or passion, or truthfulness, but never leaving behind lyricism, earthiness, and an appreciation for the beauty of the world. She paints on the bleak canvas of humanity, stating that "important events do not change a man's soul, they merely bring it into relief, and highlight what is hidden in the shadows" (Bickerton, 2006). Picasso's take on modern art springs to mind, the way he described it as "a sum of destructions". But despite sharply chronicling the sum of destructions, Némirowsky also finds a spatial prose that is able to redeem features of the human condition.

Is *Suite Française* a masterpiece, as it was posthumously declared to be? It is, without doubt good writing; a masterpiece it is not. After all, it remained a fragment, as incomplete as Némirovsky's writing career, cut short. But what really makes it a monument to historical consciousness are the circumstances of its inception and making. Her writing became a repository of the psychosocial currents of the occupation, not unlike a lyrical form of the genre of war reportage, and by writing, she herself made history. Némirovsky showed considerable moral courage by going on writing, despite being afraid and angry in equal measure. She was not bowed, docile, or crushed, as were some of her fictional characters in the way in which they dealt with the threat of annihilation. In 1942, before she was deported, she made sure that her daughters would survive, and she left behind a case with her unfinished manuscript. Her husband, Michel Epstein, whilst searching for her, was also arrested and perished in a concentration camp. Némirovsky's writing legacy, too painful for her daughters to handle, came to light some sixty years after her death, when one of them found the courage to open the case for posterity, leading to the publication of the manuscript within it.

Patrick White's "infinite connectivity"

Patrick White (1912–1990), Australian novelist, was internationally renowned for a string of masterpieces, such as *The Tree of Man* (1955),

Voss (1957), *Riders in the Chariot* (1961), *The Solid Mandala* (1966), and *The Eye of the Storm* (1973). Labelled by Australian critics as "Australia's most unreadable novelist", White returned the insult by saying about his native country, "It is possible to recycle shit" (Sutherland, 2011, p. 522). He also had the reputation of being an un-Australian writer, surprisingly so, given his ability to depict Australia's vast interior spaces and to narrate the history of its colonisation, as in *The Tree of Man*, describing the hard life of the early settlers, or in *Voss*, in which an explorer in the 1840s goes into uncharted territory, into the arid and uninhabitable interior of the outback, only to arrive at his own barren interior.

White, chronicler of historical Australia, invented characters that represent a mentality typical of his country, except perhaps that he had a leaning towards outsiders, if not outcasts, symbolising his own position in Australia during a time when there was a culture reluctant to address social issues. Patrick White, openly gay and in a long-term relationship, used his clout as a writer, the first Australian to have won the Nobel Prize for Literature, to be outspoken about gay issues, the repression of the Aborigines, and the insipid post-war ignorance about the war and the Holocaust (Schmidt, 2014, pp. 991–995).

The notion of "infinite connectivity" that Patrick White coined in his early writing, *Happy Valley* (1939), refers to a profound connection between one person and another, between a person and an object or animal or place (Gunn, 2013). It is a spiritual concept that implies that everything that belongs to this world is connected with another, the demarcation lines between me and you, and me and the world, almost an illusion. Infinite connectivity as a concept lies in close proximity to the Buddhist notion of the interdependence of all sentient beings, and to Einstein's notion of "we-consciousness". He says:

> "A human being is part of the whole called by us 'Universe', a part limited in time and space. He experiences himself, his thoughts and feelings as something separate from the rest—a kind of optical delusion of his consciousness. This delusion is a kind of prison for us, restricting us to our personal desires and to affection for a few persons nearest to us. Our task must be to free ourselves from this prison by widening our circle of compassion to embrace all living creatures and the whole of nature in its beauty." (Einstein, in Calaprice, 2011, p. 339)

* * *

Infinite connectivity is the property of dreams, or to be more precise, it originates from dreams and dream-related states of consciousness. Dreams remind us of the fluid boundary areas between self and others, self and the natural world. We are an integral part of the world in which we live, so anything that happens has to do with us and has a bearing on us. Patrick White, by making the idea of the interdependence of all beings and inanimate things a central feature of his writing, and, by doing away with the illusion of an ego superbly in control, intrinsically aligns himself with the world of dreams as an underlying concept of his work. Dreams also find a presence in his *style* of writing, which is hallucinatory, making dream fictions as it were, and evoking dream states in the reader who then dreams her own dream. White's writing is striking not only by its mastery of lyrical language, which leads to lucidity and reflection, but also by its mission to demonstrate that the boundary areas between me and you and them are fluid, as we all belong to the basic stock of humanity.

* * *

Patrick White's writing style reflects the underlying concept of infinite connectivity. The characters do not maintain their "you-out-there" position; they easily merge with the reader's "me-in-here" position through sentences that run on and in a stream of consciousness narrative in which internal reflection animates and vivifies solid reality, as if reality were made of thought.

As a reader you are taken into a character's ruminations and the interior dialogues that make her, simultaneously, different from another character and the same. The dissolution of the self goes almost unnoticed, except when the reader wakes up to the uncertain thought: Who is who? For instance, one of Whites's most derisive and reviled characters is Elizabeth Hunter in *The Eye of the Storm* (1973). A wealthy woman, dying of old age, lies in the luxurious bed of memory and belated self-reflection, as always, ruthless, obnoxious, and tyrannical, as if holding her last court, not inclined to give up her considerable powers. In her heyday she has been a seductress, a wrecker of relationships. The reader duly identifies with the lesser characters around her, such as the young night nurse who is not afraid of her employer, nursing her without fuss, while the smells of old age and defecation are not barred from close observation (Marr, 1992, pp. 492–515).

White draws us into a gravitational force of moral judgment, only to bring us back to moments of sheer beauty: the contemptuous old lady enjoys the sight of a vase, on the windowsill, filled with a huge bunch of scented roses against the first morning rays of sun, as the nurse draws open the heavy curtains. In the night, during moments of companionship with the young nurse, Elizabeth Hunter has metamorphosed, into the full range of what it is to be a human being. She remembers a severe hurricane that she survived, as a young woman on an island, by seeking shelter underground: as the storm raged outside she found peace and stillness inside herself. In the eye of the storm.

This was an experience she has never been able to share with anybody, until now, as she faces up to mortality, the loss of a flamboyant life and the abdication of beauty—beauty she has found not in the power of female seduction but in a recurring dream. As she narrates the dreams to her nocturnal companion, walking on the sea bed, she cannot help but slap an imaginary psychoanalyst by saying: "Accuse me of obscene desires." Then she relents, with: "The truth was always beautiful." She goes on to say: "What I remember in particular from each of these dreams is the light I found below—sometimes flowing around me—like water—then, on other occasions, as though emanating from myself: I was playing a single beam on objects I thought might be of interest" (White, 1973, p. 403). Now the reader is immersed in the full flow of White's teasing constructions of "infinite connectivity". "Who is who?" is no longer the question. We now know that the old woman's contemptful exterior is matched inside by a deep sense of spiritual connection with the beauty of the world. For those of us who have written the character off as abhorrent, things are made even worse, as we now realise that she is not only capable of experiencing beauty but that she also has the gift of lucid dreaming, a rarefied form of dreaming; she is aware in her dream of what she is doing, of playing with the source of light. As in her waking life, so too she seems to be in control of her dream life.

Her recurring dream is, in fact, a death dream. We are beings of light. When she was younger the dream was about the death of a robustly held ego; dreaming herself into the deep waters of universal beauty, so precious that it was never to be shared, so as not to forget the stillness in the eye of the storm. She did not die bitter. Nor without beauty.

* * *

The notion of "infinite connectivity" comes from a man and author who was deeply religious; not a church-going man, but someone who, in the privacy of his mind, believed in God, and was carried through life by faith. This is hard to believe given White's rationalist love of combat, controversy, and outspokenness, his unforgiving and robustly scathing nature, in part not unlike good old Elizabeth Hunter. When offered the Nobel Prize for Literature in 1973, he declined to go to the ceremony, saying, "I don't want to pretend to be me"; a baffling comment, because, as the people closest to him painfully experienced, he never was pretending. Instead he sent a friend, on whom one of his fictional characters was based; his envoy was a fictional character, not the real thing. His motto in life and in writing was "No compromise!" Of his parents he said, resentfully, that from an early age they had "the capacity for boring me" (Sutherland, 2011, pp. 519–522). Before the age of ten, in his isolation as a child plagued by asthma, he wrote ambitiously, and found solace in reading, both activities being frowned upon by his parents.

"Infinite connectivity" is a spiritual notion but equally based on White's deep understanding of the human condition, as can be seen in characters that are outsiders, outcasts even, and who seem to struggle with bouts of insanity and the shifting margins between reality and fantasy. Again, White's writing style reflects this precisely; it is dream-like, hallucinatory, as if the self is a fluid possibility. It is the instability of the self he knew about as a person. His Greek partner of fifty years, Manoly Lascaris, was, at times, his only firm anchor to reality, as he descended into "the deep end of the unconscious", not unlike his character Voss exploring the vast open spaces of the Australian outback.

Voss finds, before the unrelenting heat devours him, that he has lived an illusion: Australia cannot be mapped, explored, or understood, it can only be imagined (White, 1957). On his final journey into his own interiority he is sustained by the thoughts of a Platonic relationship with Laura Trevelyan. In his feverish and hallucinatory states of mind he engages in a spiritual communication with his other half, as he confides, in his diary, that "she is locked inside". As death approaches, she, in turn, senses what is to come. After his demise, Laura continues, in the public domain, to hold on to his memory as an explorer: a memorial stone is being erected in his honour. In private, the perpetual conversation of friendship between Voss and Laura carries on regardless. The dead are only dead, they are not gone.

CHAPTER FOUR

The primary human drives

The following model of the mind I found useful in the long-term work with dreaming patients. It is an attempt at mapping an internal territory of soul life, which is notoriously difficult to describe. Having said that, it is also true to say that precision and accuracy can be found, in terms of patterns and structures that dictate the apparent chaos, fluidity, and uncertainty of what the psyche is. The self is a fluid possibility. The psyche, after all, follows the laws of poetry, imagination, chaos theory and its ordering principles.

$$F + H + L + K + B + P + S$$

Dreams give expressions to our seven primary human drives: the conundrum of fear; the propensity for destructiveness; the search for love; the search for knowledge; the search for beauty; the "will to power"; and our spiritual longings.

This model of the mind owes reference to Freud's dual instinct theory, which gave exposition to two fundamental human motivations: namely, the sexual instinct and aggression (L + H). As we know, sexuality is not love but love is underpinned by sexual desire. The notion of love, surprisingly, is not an integral part of psychoanalytic theory. Instead, theorists talk about "object relations" to describe the connection between people, an unfortunate turn of phrase in as much as part of emotional maturation is that we do not end up relating to the other as an object. However, it is somewhat understandable in terms of how theory developed, as Freud saw the infant only in ways that were about instinctual gratification of her needs, with little reference to emergent relationships.

Bion, belonging to the Kleinian school of psychoanalysis, expanded on Freud by focusing on the fragmentation of the psychotic mind (F), giving rise to the idea that the deepest form of fear is the fear of falling apart, the fear of annihilation, never to return to sanity. Bion also developed a "theory of thinking", which is about emotional understanding and the growth of knowledge (K).

My concept of dream thinking is based on Bion's psychology, which gives credit to the idea that we live more rounded lives if we understand ourselves emotionally, not just in connection with daily grumpy moods and living by the script of grievances written by ordinary misery, but with the deeper level of our soul lives. In order to achieve emotional maturation we have to face up to the hidden truths in our lives: such as the early loss of a parent due to cancer leading us into childhood depression; or the trauma suffered at the hands of violent alcoholic parents resulting in being taken away from the family and placed in foster care; or sexual abuse within the family during childhood with the consequence of the collapse of ordinary emotional development, with its inherent reversal of love and hatred.

So, Bion's K, the search for knowledge, poses pertinent questions to be answered by a person who is willing to move on from the tyranny of bad feelings into the growing freedom to think on one's own behalf, to have a mind of one's own. A mind that is not clouded over by the shadows of the past, that brings with it the ultimate qualities of experiencing peace of mind and the beauty of the world.

I have added a few more ingredients to the consortium of primary human drives by proposing the notion that we cannot live without the search for beauty (B), which is about finding consciousness, truthfulness, and meaning in one's life, those foundation stones of the human aesthetic.

Keats said that "a thing of beauty is a joy for ever". The same is true for our inner lives. If we are able to find meaningful relationships, remain truthful to who we are, not blundering about over our own human fault-lines, and leave behind the cave of primitive emotional responses to conflict, then we will be living in the field of self-improvement, with the possible reward of finding beauty.

The term "will to power" (P), borrowed from Nietzschean philosophy, is about the intentional, wilful engagement with a fundamental human project, giving one's life a purposeful shape; such as the overcoming of adversity and physical disability, not giving in to setbacks, rising again from the unmade bed of depressive bouts, seeing financial bankruptcy as a starting point for renewal, and seeing losses as an ultimate gain. In short, using the will to power as a resource for the overcoming of impasse and the demands life makes on us.

The spiritual searches (S) have to do with soul life, *Seelenleben*, a term Freud used to describe the psyche. The spiritual is the realisation that it is part of the human condition that we are suffering and that there is suffering in the world, leading to quiet contemplation and thoughtfulness, and the resolve to do something about it. This leads to the realisation that we are all interconnected, that nothing happens in isolation, and thus we cannot shy away from social responsibility.

* * *

Dreams can be understood as expressions of the basic human drives. They are the dynamic forces within the psyche that make us human beings. Naturally we are complex creatures but the primary motivational forces are always the same in their tendencies, even though they are open to transformation if worked upon. For example, fear on a primitive level is the fear of survival but fear in relation to creative work is a motivational force, urging us on. The primary human drives are the basic rhythm of psychic life. Whatever we do, it boils down to seven basic drives that, according to the mental state we are in, might remain unconscious or can be made conscious and therefore modified because open to change. Dreams put the spotlight of consciousness on to our drives, and by doing so give us the opportunity to change the fabric of our being. They are the bringers of light that shines into the obscurity and cryptic nature of unconscious life.

Primary drives are like the ingredients of a chef's signature dish. One ingredient missing and the whole meal is out of sync. Cooking is an art form but it is also a technical affair. The Greeks used two terms for art, one of which was *techné*, meaning the actual graft, the technical aspect of making any creative piece of art. Fine cooking requires precision in the cooking process but also an artist, a chef, who is in charge both of the aesthetics of the culinary feast and of the selection of the right ingredients, food preparation, the application of heat, the presentation of food, and the overall execution of the dish; leading to an orchestration of the sensual and, if nothing gets burnt, an aesthetic triumph.

Renaissance philosopher Marsilio Ficino (1433–1499) used the word *convivium* to describe the coming together of the leading scholars in Europe to discuss an essential harmony between Neoplatonism and Christianity, although the Pope was not convinced of the scheme and contemplated declaring heresy. Ficino—hard-drinking monk, philosopher, medical doctor, and astrologer—was a generous host in his "Platonic Academy", up in the foothills near Florence, enjoying the spoils of Humanism.

There was plenty of food, wine, and gambling going on, to distract from the possible consequences of perilous discussions, under the watchful eye of Cosimo de' Medici's patronage. The word *convivium* means "feasting together"—on food, wine, and ideas. Friar Ficino introduced the term and concept of "Platonic love", an attraction that moves from a physical to a spiritual plane, ultimately leading the lover to the love of God. This was based on his own life experience; he was erotically attracted to one of his young disciples, but did not act on it, and transported his earthly love on to a higher plane (Ficino, 1489).

In our discussion of the primary human drives we will apply the Renaissance monk's thinking about sublimation to the idea of developmentally differing levels of human motivation. We also will apply his notion of *convivium* to the consortium of drives.

If parts of sexual love, for instance, can be elevated into spiritual longing then we can employ the same principle to the gradual development of the seven human drives. Fear of falling apart might be transformed into the anxiety and excitement typical of a new work project. Hatefulness, the destroyer of life's beauty, can be converted into the kind of aggression necessary to assert the self, to claim from the tyranny of bad feelings the freedom of the self.

Cynical, if not hateful, thinking can be transformed into the ability to think about oneself and other people from the perspective of loving kindness and belonging. The search for beauty—more often than not ending up in recoiling from the beauty in one's life, out of fear of living life in the name of success and mindfulness—can be changed to the actual pursuit of beauty, in the knowledge that we deserve to have a life directed by the attributes of beauty, which are consciousness, truthfulness, and meaning.

The "will to power", so often exploited in order to have power over people, to perpetuate inequality, can be expressed on a higher plane that is about empowering human qualities in oneself and others, and can take one's drive towards achievement into projects that serve humanity.

Our spiritual longings, frequently distorted by the daemons of dogmatism, righteousness, and fundamentalism, can be converted into sincere worship of human qualities that, in Erich Fromm's words in *The Art of Loving* (1956), have to do with universal love: the love of the world and the love of humanity. And, to add the Dalai Lama's perspective on the spiritual, the Buddhist tradition embraces the practice of loving kindness and compassion in the face of human suffering.

The primary human drives, so it seems, can be expressed either in primitive or in mature ways. They also are companions to our development through from childhood to adulthood. A baby's love is naturally self-centred, in the face of survival eagerly taking in parental love without really being aware of who the provider is, although displaying a presence that instils a sense of beauty and love in the smitten onlooker. In reality we cannot speak of the infant's authorship of her emotional world. In the beginning there is simply an experiencing self, not a thinking self. Such states of being are infantile dream states without self-reflection and self-knowledge.

Mature dreams, with their inbuilt capacity for driving us off the tramlines of habit, out of the claustrum of destructiveness, not to mention selfishness, will always remind us on what level we operate as human beings, which might come as an insult to our perceived perfections. If we are prepared to embark on the task of self-improvement with the help of our dreams then we will enter the aesthetic territory of the *convivium*, to use Marsilio Ficino's term, a feasting together of the primary human drives on a higher level of consciousness.

Instead of giving in to crippling fear (−F), enjoying the triumph of hatefulness (−H), rebuffing the possibility of being loved (−L), making lies the nourishment of the mind (−K), recoiling from the beauty of the world (−B), being seduced by the dictatorial use of power (−P), and giving our due to religious dogma and fundamentalism (−S),

$$(-F) + (-H) + (-L) + (-K) + (-B) + (-P) + (-S),$$

we could try out the anxiety and excitement that accompanies new and valuable work projects, we could surrender to being loved and receiving love, we could use the aggression inherent in our life force to assert our uniqueness as human beings, we could make truthfulness the nourishment of the mind, we could look beauty directly in the eye, we could use our "will to power" for the benefit of other people, and we could employ our spiritual searches to address the suffering and inequalities in the world.

This is precisely our moral dilemma as human beings: to go down the road of destructively expressing our primary human drives; or to use them in a productive and socially mindful manner.

The conundrum of fear

Fear is a fundamental driving force in unconscious life, and radiates widely into everyday life. We are afraid of birth, life, and death. The essentials of our existence pose this dilemma of a fearful response. We are also afraid of change, of love, of intimacy, and, in Socrates' words, we are afraid of the beauty of the world. There is very little that is out of reach of fear. And, naturally, fear plays a huge role in the establishment of defences when traumatic life events overwhelm the individual in the way a tsunami does, leaving the person in an emotionally frozen state of mind, giving in to dissociation from feelings in order to survive and get on with life in a one-dimensional way.

Primary fear, that is, fear of survival, is at the deepest level of the psyche. At times of severe crisis or dangerous situations we are compelled to go down the well-trodden, well-worn path of fear. Our relationship to fear as adults is determined by ways in which fear has been managed during childhood. Parenting requires the containment of the baby's primary states of fear. If the parents are able to contain their own fear and offer themselves as a receptacle for the baby's fear, and manage it, then the baby is able to recover from the repeated cycles of anxiety states. And, having completed cycle after cycle of tolerating fear, the infant is able to tolerate her own raw emotions later on in life. She will learn that once fear can be endured it turns into something resembling anxiety and its twin, excitement, which is a healthy driving force, and will instruct the challenges of teenage and adult life.

Just think of an actor's stage fright before the opening night of a new play; the pre-teenage student at her first day in secondary school; the last days leading up to the birth of your first child; the hours before the first date ever; the time leading up to a lecture in front of hundreds of people; etc. In these cases anxiety is a preparation for something good to come, a revving up of the senses, an acuteness of sensory perception, in order to be on one's guard. And it means a strengthening of the backbone, a mustering of one's resolve, not to speak of anxiety's most sophisticated companion, which is a heightened state of consciousness. All in the service of not messing up. Not to allow the daemon of envy to spoil the good. Doing meaningful things right.

Back to the development of fear. If the parental environment has failed the infant by not containing her primary fear, in a climate where love and emotional understanding is absent, not to speak of cruelty and violence, then the infant will get lost in the icy storms of fear. Fear will become so paramount that the infant is afraid of falling apart. In adult life the afflicted person will either be driven into high performance activity, soldiering on regardless, and dissociate from fear, or go inside and disappear in an abyss that might give rise to psychotic states of mind. This frequently tends to happen during teenage years. Another exit route from experiencing unspeakable fear is to cloak it over with anger and rage. It is easier to be angry than to be afraid. The bully, instilling fear in the other, is, himself, always afraid just beneath the waterline.

In the cauldron of overwhelming fear the person becomes more and more hateful of the self and the world, and eventually the world can only be perceived as persecutory, out to destroy her; not knowing that it is her, or the bizarre workings of her own mind, that is destroying the self and other people in fantasy, if not in reality.

A plea for nightmares

Anxiety dreams are as frequent as sexual dreams and dreams ruled by aggression. The consortium of fear, sex, and aggression is the primary emotional underpinning of the psyche. In their most primitive forms these feelings and desires serve survival and the continuity of the species. In its most mature form fear might turn into anxiety experienced when you challenge yourself or are engaged in a worthwhile work project. The sexual urge might turn into a wish to deeply relate to another human being, to embark on a union of kindred souls, or to find a marriage with deeper strata of the self, such as finding solace and peace in helping people in need, reaching into universal love. The drive fuelled by aggression might turn into something resembling the assertion of the self, into standing up for one's rights, and, once one's head is turned towards the social, standing up for inequalities being addressed in an unequal world.

Dreams, in their poetic nature, serve the function of bringing to the fore not only unresolved issues but also healthy parts of the self that have been neglected, not lived in, put on a shelf of concealment. If there are issues lurking deep inside from past experience, they will, most likely, come out in the form of nightmares.

If, by common conception, ordinary dreams are looked upon with suspicion and incomprehension, nightmares seem to be the baddies of our internal lives, the thing we do not want nor want to engage with. And yet, if we turn around and ask what they are about, the return will be an enrichment of the way we understand ourselves and the way we live. Nightmares want to be overheard and understood. In the hierarchy of dream conception, they lie securely at the bottom of the wish list. The Senoi tribe in Malaysia, who build their psychosocial life on the wisdom of dreams, tend to instruct their youngsters that nightmares are a gift, not a plague (Garfield, 1974). The instructions are to turn around and ask the attacker what he or she wants; the dreamer is asked to offer a gift to the one appearing to be frightening and menacing; the offer is of love and friendship. The Senoi's approach is one of dream control, lucid dreaming, and the integration of something that, at first sight, appears to be dark and sinister.

Paradoxically, many people tend to shy away from the joy of sexual dreams, the fictions of epic dreams, the entertainment of humorous dreams, and dreams of stunning beauty; it is as if we are sitting on a goldmine and not mining it, and, by doing so, throwing away the winning lottery ticket. Nightmares—at first sight, the ugly prince—are treated with contempt, as if something alien has made itself known in the place of our illusory sense of perfection, as if a leper has taken a seat next to the dreamer on the couch of habit. In order to do justice to dreams you always have to think in paradoxes, in polarities. Nightmares, however frightening and disturbing, might entail things of utter beauty, parts of the self that are in need of discovery and appreciation.

Nightmares are the psyche's final reminders, issued after one inviting dream after another has remained unnoticed, even been dismissed, by the indifferent dreamer. Recurring dreams and omnibus dreams (a series of dreams connected by the same theme) are the precursors of nightmares. If we do not listen to what lies in the depth of the soul we will, more often than not, be on the receiving end of a pounding by nightmares that serve the ancient temple inscription that sits on Apollo's dream shrine: *Know Thyself*. Apollo is one of the ancient Greek dream deities who stands for consciousness, alleviating family curses, the heroine's journey, and self-knowledge (Larousse, 1959).

Nightmares preceding birth and postnatal nightmares seem to be linked with the pregnant woman and the mother's processing of what is possibly the most stirring event in a person's life. Growing life inside, giving life, witnessing nascent life, as much as it is part of nature is, nonetheless, accompanied with high anxiety and triggers that set off memories of the mother's own entry point into life. Her own foundation myth will come to the fore in the shape of nightmares. How did she come into existence in her parents' minds, not just in the union of the flesh? How did the actual birth occur? What was intra-uterine life like? As it happens, the more the mother is visited by nightmares the easier the emotional transition into motherhood and the actual birth process seem to be. Dreams, in this instance, are working hard at digesting some unbearable emotions, in the main, anxiety and fear.

At their most elevated layer of mental functioning anxiety dreams accompany excitement. Physiologically speaking there seems to be little difference between the two states of mind, the one leaning and reaching into the other, as if twinned. The proximity between anxiety and excitement becomes apparent in dream material. At times we think we have had an anxiety dream but in fact it is more to do with its other half, that is, excitement, and, possibly, exhilaration. Birth dreams and dreams about babies usually have this signature of the confluence of anxiety and excitement. They are dreams that indicate we are on the verge of something new, a new beginning in one's vocational life or romantic life. The baby might represent a time of unprecedented growth, of a new idea, a new business project, a threshold experience such as going off to university, an initiation into adulthood, or into contented retirement.

The teleogical drive

We are creatures of habit, not wishing to change, despite professing the opposite. The reason is that we are afraid of what might lie ahead; moving house, change of career, the wish to get married, or moving on from a relationship that is no longer satisfactory. Anxiety dreams, in their most mature form, are indicators of new creative activity to come, driving us on towards something that becomes more fulfilling. And, at times, that means giving something up that has been outgrown and no longer serves our development.

This movement towards change is the teleological aspect of dreaming. Teleology, in its original sense, means that "nature shows signs of divine or cosmic design or purpose". In a psychological sense the teleological nature of dreaming relates to its purposiveness. Its intention is to reveal, and therefore it sets the tone for change. Dreams design futures, taking the material of everyday life and shaping it into productive potential. Paradoxically, in order to move forward we find that, at times, we need to give something up.

* * *

A patient of mine, Rosie, a successful entrepreneur, who discovered in therapy that she had been driven throughout her life to succeed, realised that the driving force behind her obsession to be successful and build herself a little empire was, indeed, an emptiness. She was rich in monetary terms but, deep inside, felt empty and impoverished by the early loss of a loving mother who had died of cancer when the patient was three. She was forever pining for her mother, but was never to find her, until, through her dreams, her mother showed herself, as if awoken from a sleeping beauty state of frozenness, and talked to her. Surprisingly, after Rosie started to mourn her mother, some forty-five years after the actual loss (it is never too late to embark on grieving), she had numerous dreams in which she found herself aimless, full of anxiety. Rosie did not do anxiety, so she was baffled by her own dreams. In one of the dreams she saw herself being handcuffed, unable to do anything. In another she was paralysed, not able to get out of bed.

Eventually she understood that she had to learn just to be, finding her own, personal ontology, that is, states of being; starting with just half an hour a day, then half a day, then a number of days. Being the head-on person she was, she prescribed herself so-called quiet time, quality time, even daring to go on a week-long meditation retreat held in silence. States of being in early life are an important link between infant and mother during which the infant learns to play freely in the presence of an unintrusive mother. And from such states, which are not unlike dream states in waking life, that is, reverie, the infant builds her own universe of fantasy and imagination—her kite flying high, safely anchored in the presence of mother.

All her life Rosie had avoided her greatest fear, namely to pause and reflect; she feared the return of the bad that was the loss of her mother. But, in reality, she had found her and a place in herself that felt more caring. She allowed herself to feel the catastrophic early loss, by which she gained. Engaging in healthy mourning always constitutes an enrichment of internal life. But the *Via Dolorosa*, the path of suffering, also requires attention, mindfulness, and hard work. Needless to say that she appointed a new chief executive for her company who did all the running around whilst she, in her own words, turned into an *enlightened slob*, allowing herself to go crazy as she pleased, turning into a couch potato, fortified by comfort food, wrapped up in a blanket, hot water bottle in her lap, dog at her feet, crying her heart out at the minutest of triggers whilst watching soaps for hours on end. "How pathetic," her old companion, the achiever at all costs, mocked her, whilst the God of Small Things replied, "Sod off. You can go now."

* * *

In summary, anxiety dreams (F dreams) serve the purpose of bringing to the fore unresolved issues from the past, illuminating human faultlines in the management of anxiety and fear. But also, anxiety dreams reach into the future, where excitement will take us into areas we did not know existed. Anxiety dreams can be hidden excitement dreams, which are creative dreams, holding inside them the seed of a life force wishing to come to the surface, like in early spring when a new shoot is bursting through the soil.

Elena Ferrante's "dissolving margins"

Elena Ferrante, in her four Neapolitan novels—*My Brilliant Friend, The Story of a New Name, Those Who Leave and Those Who Stay, The Story of the Lost Child* (2012–2015)—narrates, across 1,700 pages, the unlikely friendship of two women, Elena and Lila, spanning some fifty years from their early school days through into their sixties. Ferrante has written a *bildungsroman* on female friendship from a woman's perspective, like no other in modern literature. It is testament to enduring friendship despite the test of time. Friendship is not friendship "which alters when it alteration finds", in Shakespeare's words; it is a love "that looks on tempests and is never shaken" (Sonnet 116). It is also a reminder of the philosopher Hannah Arendt's notion of friendship, which entails the capacity to make friends with one's own human fault-lines in order to understand oneself and others better on the painful path of self-improvement. Elena lacks self-confidence, always doubting herself, always thinking that Lila is far ahead of her intellectually and as a sexual woman, being a stubborn feminist without parading the placard of feminism; always having thought that Lila had entered her whole being and made her the person she is, over time Elena concedes that it is, in fact, she who narrates the story of her friend and, in the knowledge of Lila's declaration of love, if not respect, at the outset of the story, it is she who can say, "You are my brilliant friend."

Elena and Lila's perpetual conversation of friendship never ends, even in the face of stacked-up hatred, cutting the other to pieces by ways of thinking differently, and seemingly having ended up on opposite sides of the social divide, the one staying behind in Naples, the other venturing to Pisa, Florence, and Paris. And at the very end, in her late sixties, as Lila disappears from Napoli without a trace, driven by grief and self-loathing, she is still held in her friend's mind and in her writing.

The inherent dynamic of the book lies in the fact that the author makes a rare feat of remaining unknown to the reader and the general public, not giving in to the usual publicity stunts now required by the publishing industry. This absence of autobiography (O'Rourke, 2014) makes the reader focus on one thing only, which is the written word, and at the same time leaves her wondering about how much of Ferrante's actual life experience has entered the world of fiction. The narrator carries her name, Elena, who is plundering the diaries of her best friend Lila, with which to assemble an astonishing piece of writing on Italian psychosocial history, feminism, economics, and politics in the late twentieth century.

The author's absence from public life compounds a curiosity and enquiry about the fictions constellated on the page. As the psycho-analyst Bion pointed out in his theory of thinking, thinking occurs in the absence of a thing. The first human thought, according to Bion, is the baby's rudimentary and primitive thought of "nonbreast", in the absence of mother's breast (Bion, 1962a). In the absence of the author, the reader thinks about, and expounds on, the author through the issues explored in the book. An absence shores up the author's real life behind all the fiction, the invisible made dense and more solid in a double act of fantasy. We fantasise both about the narrator Elena's stories but equally about the untold and yet unapprehended fictions that belong to the author Elena Ferrante. But in the end, the art of writing is to take the capital of real life and authorise it, make an art form out of it. Meghan O'Rourke's final words in her article express it succinctly, reiterating a phrase taken from one of Ferrante's own letters: "The mystery of literature is in some ways its difference from the person who wrote it, the unfathomable effacement of self that leads to its creation."

A further dynamic that makes the *quartetto* of books both memorable and readable is that of the unresolved issues between the main characters, issues that can never be resolved, only lived in. So, if you come from a poor, working class, impoverished, and violent background, are you doomed forever or does the problem, if it is one, entail its own solution? Elena creates from the writing capital of poverty, repression of women, and widespread violence, fictional stories that she has made available to the reading and thinking public. And, by doing so, she has claimed back her cultural identity. But it is also an act of personal revenge on her parents, who live in a world of thoughtlessness; in her view, they are nothing more than the primitive base self of human existence. The search for knowledge is an essential ingredient in Ferrante's writing, which again is duplicated in Bion's psychoanalytic theories on the growth of knowledge, that is, of emotional understanding, emotional intelligence, and the search for truth. "Truth is the nourishment of the mind, lies its poison," he says. For him the "epistemological instinct" outweighs all other ingredients of human motivation such as fear, aggression, and love (Bion, 1962a). In that sense, by placing the search for knowledge at the centre of their respective art forms, both Ferrante the writer and Bion the psychoanalytic theorist align themselves with the very centrepiece of dream theory, which is dream thinking.

However successful Elena's career as a writer has become she always carries underneath a thin skin smouldering thoughts of not being good enough, especially when, through an unhappy marriage to an academic, she climbs the heavenly ladder into the educated and sophisticated higher middle classes. Her mother-in-law, Adele, who the narrator-cum-author brutally exposes, is a paradigm of, simultaneously, benignly pseudo-mothering Elena with her young children in tow, and cutting her to pieces with words and thoughts in a single swipe of class distinction and power relations: *You do not belong to us, and never will.*

Ferrante also exposes the type of violence that usually goes unnoticed. The reader has to ponder as many forms of violence as there are different types of snow in Iceland. Lila is being beaten by her husband Stefano, the son of money shark Don Achille; both Lila and Elena as children witness their mothers being beaten by their fathers, as if it is a common diet; at one point Elena sees her friend flying out of the window, being attacked by her father; a woman gone mad by the rebuffal of love and empty promises of poetry, throws part of her already impoverished furniture out of the window into the *stradone*; and, from the distant news reports, murders are committed by Red Brigade terrorists; and so on.

But the main strands of violence are those exerted by the people in charge of the neighbourhood, that is, the ruling Camorra, and the ones exerting background violence from the loftiness of their minds. The reader has to agonise over whether the physical and sexual violence of men without education is worse than the epistemic and sexual violence of educated men. Elena's first sexual experience is of being sexually molested, then raped, by Donato Sarratore, a married railway worker and aspiring poet. Nino Sarratore follows in the footsteps of his father's unholy womanising and sexualising drive, on the way becoming first Lila's, then Elena's lover, fathering children with them but, like a raven father, discarding them, always on the lookout for the next woman to bed; as an academic, a professor of literature, in barely hidden bouts of epistemic violence, he dismantles the women close to him by ways of thinking, knowing better, and performing a convincing impression of the smartest male beauty in the land.

Lila's solution to witnessing violence en masse is a robust one; not unlike a homeopath, she treats same with same, violence with violence, but lives not entirely free from the value of knowledge. As Elena walks up the shaky steps of the middle school, Lila, unsupported by her ignorant parents, leaves school, lured by early marriage and a baby. Gifted with a brilliant mind, she publicly renounces books and knowledge, as if to slap down her friend and her expectant teachers, but secretly she goes on studying and reading, easily able to read the likes of James Joyce. In a scene that describes Lila's typical simultaneous contempt and mastery of knowledge, she is now running a shop payrolled by the local Camorra; she is sitting on a bench reading *Ulysses*, a pram parked up next to her, when her old teacher, who had favoured and admired her for her brilliant mind, appears in front of her out of the distant past.

Maestra Oliviero quizzes her in her accustomed sharpish tone about the large volume, ignoring the gift of the baby. Lila counters: "It says that our heads are full of nonsense. That we are flesh, blood, and bone. That one person has the same value as another. That we want only to eat, drink, fuck" (Ferrante, 2013, p. 381).

This phrase sums it all up. From the perspective of a refined literary critic and avid reader, well able to understand Joyce's masterpiece, she sounds vulgar, but from the perspective of her class of origin, her roots in the community, and her chosen path of engaging with ordinary life—which turns out never to be so ordinary in its vast chaos—she makes a statement that demonstrates her knowledge of Greek tragedy, seeing that Joyce's *Ulysses* is a modern version of Homer's *Odyssey*, with its central theme: Are our lives fated from the beginning or are we in control of our individual destinies? (Kiberd, 2009). More so than her friend Elena, Lila stands up for herself, seemingly unafraid of male violence and the sinister dealings of the Camorra in her rundown neighbourhood.

There were early signs of her resolve. Once, as a child, she put a knife to the throat of a Camorra son who had ripped off Elena's necklace, asking him to pick it up, fuming with rage. Marcello Solara subsequently and throughout his life admired her for her courage, trying to court her and failing to make her part of his dubious business ventures. She did run one of his shops though, but never lost her critical eye nor her personal integrity as part of the deal. She could not be owned by anybody. And in order to escape the grasp of the Solara brothers she disappears into a meat factory, working amidst the foul smell of guts, blood, and fat, courting the god of visceral ugliness and repulsion.

Another experience as a child that showed Lila's resolve and lack of fear involved Don Achille, a loan shark, feared in the neighbourhood in epic proportions. Lila and Elena play with their dolls by a grate above Don Achille's cellar. As if to test fate Lila drops Elena's doll into the cellar, and, in retaliation, Elena does the same with Lila's doll. Lila goes ahead, searching the cellar, and when they do not find their precious possessions Lila leads the long, long way up the stairs to Don Achille's flat. Elena almost dies with fear whilst Lila keeps hers under wraps, living on the adrenaline of danger. Surprisingly, the old ogre responds kindly.

Both Lila and Elena grow up in a sea of fear and violence. Elena manages to find refuge in books and in testing motherhood, while

Lila engages with her psychosocial environment by causing havoc and admiration as she designs and makes shoes, becomes a shop-keeper, a lowly worker in a meat factory, and then reinvents herself as a computer programmer, rising from the ashes of obscurity, and placing herself outside of the power relations of her neighbourhood. She is reckless, obstinate, unafraid, or so it seems, even of the violence of men, fiercely preoccupied with herself. In rare moments of self-reflection she says "It's I who hurt people", "I am beauty and the beast, good and evil", increasingly realising her considerable powers of destruction, her epistemic violence, the knives in her mind. "I have something that hurts here, behind the eyes, something is pressing. You see the knives there? I just gave them to the knife grinder. While I'm slicing salami I think how much blood there is in a person's body. If you put too much stuff in things, they break" (Ferrante, 2013, p. 144).

The narrator talks about "dissolving margins" in the mind of Lila. As she observes a cracked and crumpled copper frying pan hanging on the wall, noticing the fractured surface, she realises her own fractured mind. She has discovered an aesthetic of ugliness, the fractal geometry of the world of matter, a theory of roughness, as it were, not unlike the Japanese philosophy of *wabi-sabi*. Her fear is of going insane, of losing all of that which is her. The people around her, events, places, are crowding her head, pulsating loudly against her skull, as if the world outside has become that which is inside. "No form could ever contain Lila, and that sooner or later she would break everything again," says the narrator (Ferrante, 2012, p. 266). During such times of dissolving boundaries she experiences a fractured world, inside her mind and outside. And now it seems that her courage, her powers of seduction as a woman, and, even more so, her appetite for destructiveness, seem to be built on the shaky grounds of fragmentation.

She realises at crucial times in her life—for instance, when she leaves the volatile marriage with Stefano and rushes into building a new life with lover Nino—that she will never be able to escape the past, the violence of her early childhood, living in fear, being severely traumatised. What she does is to create a new chapter in her life with the faint hope of building a container for her fear, like coming home into the passionate love shared with Nino that in the end turns out to be illusory. On parting from Stefano, her centre does not hold. She falls apart. She goes through psychotic states of mind. "Especially at night she was afraid of waking up and finding him formless in the bed, transformed into excrescences that burst out because of too much fluid, the flesh melting and dripping, and with it everything around, the furniture, the entire apartment and she herself, his wife, broken, sucked into that stream polluted by living matter" (Ferrante, 2013, p. 356).

Elena, possibly the only one, apart from Enzo—who enters relatively late in Lila's life as a solid anchor—to know about Lila's tendency to fragmentation, observes her friend helplessly, brushed aside by a strong force of will, before Lila rises up again from formlessness, dissolving matter, the curvature of time and space, not to mention the unbounded-ness of fear. "The sky is the throne of fear": these words are spoken as she and Elena sit on a beach on the island of Ischia as young women, watching the sea at night and the beauty of the starry heavens. Elena's sense of beauty is countered by Lila's belief that there is no such thing as beauty, there is only a world made up of fear. In her aesthetic of fear she can only see in the world what is inside her. After the young women have given expression to their differing aesthetics, Lila, a married woman, goes off, spending a passionate night with Nino, a dangerous undertaking as both could be killed at her raging husband's hand. Elena, still sitting by the beach, for once reaches into her own untogetherness as fear takes over, as if her friend has implanted in her the regent of her underworld. "It is not at all beautiful, it's terrifying; along with this beach, the sea, the swarm of animal forms, I am part of universal terror; at this moment I'm the infinitesimal particle through which the fear of every thing becomes conscious of itself" (ibid., p. 289).

Elena, in the main the voice of reason, also crumbles when she becomes a mother and surprises herself by her outbursts of irrational feelings and bizarre bodily experiences during which the margins of the self dissolve. "And would my body too, one day be ruined by the emergence not only of my mother's body but my father's?" (ibid., p. 102). The closest she gets to a dissolving self is through her infatuation with Nino, which goes right back to her school years. She eventually bags him during the time when her husband, Pietro, chronically neglects her and her two daughters over his love of books. Both Elena and Nino embark on a passionate and reckless affair, and, however devastating, it enraptures her being to such an degree that she finds liberation from the newly acquired social class that is not her own, from the tyrannical aspects of motherhood, and from her humble origins, now standing alone in the world with her books, lecture tours, and the passing on of knowledge.

Elena has arrived as a fiction writer, using the rich soil of her Neapolitan upbringing; first she became known for a novel in which she described teenage sexual experience that was received in her old neighbourhood with ridicule and ignorance; then she embarked on disseminating feminist issues; and, eventually, she felt strong enough to disclose the power relations of her childhood neighbourhood that had been ruled by Camorra violence. Her unhappy marriage to Pietro ends and she returns to Napoli with her two daughters, Dede and Elsa, into the neighbourhood of her childhood, as if she has had to close a circle by linking the beginning with the end.

She lives right above Lila's flat, helping her out by childminding her young daughter. Lila, always on the edge of danger, supplies her writer friend Elena with sensitive information about the Camorra's rule of terror, drugs empire, and political bribery. Elena, because of her public profile, gets away with writing about it, but Lila pays the ultimate price. Her young daughter is abducted and killed, a fact never fully revealed, but apprehended, which leads to Lila's final descent into the "dissolving margins" of her mind. She cannot recover from the loss of her young child; she disappears without trace, to where, no one knows. In all likelihood she has disappeared not into yet another self-made incarnation but into the erasure of the self, into violent self-annihilation. In the end, you cannot escape your past.

* * *

The fear of mortality

If we ask the philosophical question, Why do we dream?, we stumble across a number of answers. In brief, there are five existential reasons why we should dream: we are longing to come to terms with loss; we are afraid of our mortality; we are afraid of our separateness as human beings; we are afraid of being struck by insanity; and we are afraid of our propensity to be fully alive. Dreams mull over such existential questions on our behalf. There are no answers; there only are attempts to come to terms with the aesthetic of the inevitable.

The central reason for dream activity is that of coming to terms with mortality. What makes us different from the animal kingdom is our knowledge and apprehension of death. We know that we are going to die. We are born, we live, we die. So simple, and, yet, so complicated. We cannot tolerate the idea of death, not helped by our Western approach to dying, which, is, in the main, one of denial. We do not talk about death, unless it hits us in unexpected ways.

Death comes in different guises. Death is all-present in our lives but eludes immediate detection. At times, death comes in the costume of melancholia, meaning the healthy side of melancholic moods. In the delightful embrace of romantic experience, we might feel sad when a special moment of intimacy is gone; rather like a stunning sunset, when a red-hot sun fills the horizon one precious minute, then is suddenly gone, never to return, or so it seems. Death comes in the guise of severe depression. The life force spent, the person goes into some kind of para-lysed, even comatose, state. Deadness rules the roost. A numbing of the feeling world. Nothing matters any longer.

The most painful experience of mortality is the loss of a loved one and the ensuing grieving process. In the case study on Zlatan (Chapter Three) we saw how long it can take to embark on the process of mourn-ing, given that we tend to dissociate from the feeling impact of loss and its devastating nature.

The propensity for destructiveness

"Two souls, alas, are housed within my breast"

—Goethe, *Faust*

I will begin with an epilogue that entails an ethical notion. One of the highest achievements in emotional, if not cultural, development is the ethical sense, to be able to differentiate right from wrong, good from bad. If, as adults, we start to take responsibility for our own actions and stop blaming other people for our own human misery, we are on the way to realising the true nature of what makes us a human being. We are forever bound up in the human conundrum between love and hatred; we are capable of either, but we prefer to see ourselves as not going down the path of destructiveness.

The ethical sense

There is a sigh of relief in the consulting room when one of my patients reaches precisely this high altitude peak of self-improvement. You would overhear, *I love to hate myself*. Or, on a more advanced level of human development, on the way to integration,

> I love my husband dearly. But lately, waking up next to him, I can't stand him. It's not his bad breath, nor his snoring. I think I hate him.

Or another person saying, in a bout of honesty,

> I've got murderous feelings when I'm in the middle of the act of lovemaking. I feel so ashamed.

All in the service of the naked truth. The shutters of normality taken off. The first step of self-improvement.

That might sound like the stuff of which disturbed human beings are made, but it is part of an internal struggle between good and bad that every one of us is going through. It is, of course, shameful to admit to unspeakable feelings, mostly so when the recipients of our aggression and hateful thoughts are the people we love the most, such as innocent children, relying on us for love but trading in rebuffal. There is no profound love without coming to terms with our destructive impulses. Once we allow ourselves to be opened by the beauty of love, all the bad stuff that has been experienced will resurface and has to be dealt with.

The foundation myth

Donald Winnicott, a psychoanalyst and paediatrician, created a furore in the 1950s when he wrote about the mental state of mothers before and after birth. He realised that giving birth and caring for a small baby is not such an entirely blissful experience (Winnicott, 1949). As women know from experience, and men do not, the physical experience of giving birth can be unbearably painful and savage, if not a danger to the mother's life. On one side there is the most beautiful experience in any person's life, the birth of a baby, the first human aesthetic; but, on the other, an emotional nightmare, especially with the first-born. For both mother and father (the one up to the task) it brings back memories of one's own birth, one's own start to life: the person's foundation myth. From the perspective of the foundation myth we ponder such questions as,

Was I wanted as a baby?
Was I made of the union of two people in the name of love?
Was the substance passed between mother and father actually love?

One of my patients, Stephanie, mentioned later in this chapter, had dreams leading up to giving birth in which she saw her mother wishing to kill her in various ways, a reality she had desperately kept away from her conscious mind, having realised that her mother suffered from a severe personality disorder. Because of such destructive behaviour her mother was admitted to a mental hospital for treatment (with her baby), under close observation. This was not an ordinary mother, nor an ordinary foundation myth entailing, as it did, the close proximity of birth and death.

The patient, understandably, was concerned about her own mothering qualities. She, in fact, turned into an ice-cold mother, struggling to emotionally connect with her baby. It took her the best part of the baby's first year to establish an emotional attachment. Further down the road the patient started to have dreams of grand houses she and her parents had lived in, happily, when she was a child. She had conjured up, in her mind, an idealised environment of her family of origin. In her analysis, at the time, she felt dirty, rotten, unworthy of being alive. She had taken, as children do, full responsibility for the destructiveness of her mother.

I'm all bad. I'm rotten to the core.

Paradoxically, such extreme feelings of self-hatred were accompanied by an increase in her mothering ability, which means that once you face your internal daemons, you are able to live a more balanced life.

* * *

A plea for the ubiquity of hatred

Back to Winnicott; and H dreams. He wrote a famous paper, in the late 1940s, about the need for the mother to hate her baby, listing some seventeen(!) reasons. This was regarded as scandalous at the time. We know that mothers (and engaged fathers) don't really act on those impulses; far from it. But the prenatal, perinatal, and postnatal experiences cause havoc with an otherwise peaceful, balanced mind. It is almost like an unconscious infection that runs its course on the borderline between the soma and the psyche. A few taster examples from Winnicott's list of maternal grievances:

> The baby is a danger to her [the mother's] body in pregnancy and in birth.
> He [the baby] is ruthless, treats her as scum, an unpaid servant, a slave.
> He is suspicious, refuses her good food, and makes her doubt herself, but eats well with his aunt. ...
> After an awful morning with him she goes out, and he smiles at a stranger, who says: "Isn't he sweet?" (Winnicott, 1949, p. 201)

For mother and father to return to some kind of sanity they have to go through the turbulence of an unquiet, tired mind. Winnicott in his theories was sensitive, almost lyrical, in describing the loving relationship that develops between mother and child. He was the arbiter of play, humour, and the necessity of creating illusion for the baby so that she can imagine that the milky flow from the universe of the breast might flow for ever, or that her preoccupations with a dreadfully dirty teddy bear will remain unchallenged. Winnicott pointed out that there is, inevitably, a pair of opposites at work, that is, the dynamic between loving and hateful feelings. We all know how the famous tantrums of the two-year-old, if not retaliated upon, help her on her way of emotional development. Being allowed to be hateful sets the tone for her capacity to tolerate unbearable feelings. *I hate you, Dad!* should afford a reply in attitude and thought such as, *I love you too*, which helps the infant in coming to terms with ambivalence and meaning that it is okay to have good and bad feelings towards the same person. This, in turn, leads to the first rudimentary form of an ethical sense.

I've got good and bad feelings. My bad feelings might harm the other.

Of course, if such unbearable feelings can be endured and contained in the parental mind, the infant is able to gradually build a containing mind herself. It is precisely this containing, transformational function of the parental mind that dreams perform every night. Dream thinking is a process in which unbearable feelings are made more bearable, and therefore dreams offer solid ground for the shaky parents to walk on. Behind a contended child is a containing parent, and behind a containing parent is the containing dream world, holding everything together.

The return of the ethical sense

Rounding off the epilogue, placed wrongly at the beginning, we have to understand that being able to say the following is a major achievement in emotional maturity.

At times, I'm aggressive.
And I'm loving.
From moment to moment
I swing from one to the other.
I'm capable of hateful thoughts.
And I return to affection,
Surfing the waves of human emotion.
I have to watch my destructive impulses
Toward myself and others.
Not to diminish the beauty of the world.

No longer in denial over our own human destructiveness, we can embrace more deeply the other half of aggression and hatred, which is love. The overcoming of hatred has love in its wake. And seen from the opposite vantage point, there is never any depth to love if our destructive impulses are not brought about, called into action, then looked at and scrutinised. The possibility of love elicits hatefulness.

* * *

Freud was the first psychologist who reflected on human aggression. In his analytic work he had come across patients who had survived World War One, shell-shocked and debilitated, and he, as a Jew, a close observer of the anti-Semitic and violent society in which he lived, started to widen his theory to include human aggression. His more complete instinct theory now included the sexual instinct, Eros, coupled with Thanatos, the wish to destroy.

At this juncture we should also mention Melanie Klein who, as a woman in a man's world of psychoanalysis, battled it out in the war years with the Freudians, at the time with Anna Freud at their helm, and the Independent Group, the Winnicottians, over issues of human motivation. The London Institute of Psychoanalysis had become the refuge of eminent psychoanalysts fleeing the Nazi regime. Klein made a significant contribution to the understanding of human aggression, documented in "The Controversial Discussions, 1943–1944" (Hinshelwood, 1989, p. 251), making us aware that the disturbed mind is capable of destroying itself, and, as a consequence, has a propensity to destroy others, by the destructive forces of envy and hatefulness.

* * *

A history of blood

We do not have to quote psychoanalysts in order to make a point, the point being that we human beings can be destructive beyond measure. If we look at the course of the history of mankind it is a history of blood, warfare, and cultural and social change based on power relations. One could say that social change and the rise and fall of civilisations mainly came about through the sword. And, progress in the humanities and sciences always runs parallel or, in fact, is a contingent part of wars. The development of modern psychology during World War Two is just one example, which gave us psychometric testing, the IQ test, and personality tests. Psychiatry, in the slip-stream of the war years, also grew into a science, developing psychotropic medicine for the treatment of mental illness, learning from shell-shocked soldiers about the broken mind, and coming up with a now widely recognised diagnostic tool box. Psychiatry, in the war years, made it its purpose not only to give sanctuary to shell-shocked servicemen but also to mend them so that they could return to the battleground.

We are tempted to talk of peace but seem to forget human nature, which is destructive beyond measure. We also seem to forget that just a few years back there was yet another war. The reality is that there is war going on right now. There is, of course, a demarcation line between warfare and genocide but it is one that, most of the time, is blurred.

Shall we list a few events in history that are difficult to align with human civilisation? The genocide by the Catholic Church during the Holy Inquisition, in the main the slaughter of outspoken women, declaring them to be witches and heretics; the genocide undertaken by the crusaders, under papal instruction; is Alexander the Great really that great, did he not walk the thin line between conqueror and mass murderer, as did Caesar, as did Napoleon?; the Holocaust, the death of six million Jews, in Hitler's Germany, the prime example in human history of barbaric and depraved behaviour; the mass slaughter of 900,000 German civilians, mainly women and children, through calculated incendiary bombings during World War Two, which was "Bomber" Harris' work, on Churchill's orders; the overall death toll of World War Two, which amounts to a staggering fifty million people, twenty-five million of which were Russians; the mass killings of his own people by communist dictator Stalin in Russia, amounting to at least fifteen million; the mass killings of his own people by communist dictator Mao in China during the Cultural Revolution, some fifty million; the mass slaughter by the Americans in Vietnam, not to speak of their recent slaughter in Iraq, in tandem with the British, all in the name of freedom and democracy. The list is long.

What conclusion do we draw from such violence and terror? It is evidence of the destructive side of human beings, plain and visible. But it needs to be put in the context of all other human endeavours. Mainly, human destructiveness lives in the dynamic struggle with creative and productive forces, the forces of love and connectedness. Who in their right minds would destroy a fellow human being in the name of love (that is, sexual abuse inside the family, the private holocaust; not to mention endemic domestic abuse), or kill a fellow world citizen in the name of democracy, or in the name of a different creed, or in the name of being the wrong gender?

If we are able to get that baseline right—that is, admit that we can be destructive, and therefore enter into an ethical understanding of ourselves—then we will have a deeper understanding of what love really means: the connection between people, the dependency on the community we live in but also on the world community, the human race, which can only survive if we show concern for each other, and for the planet we live on.

* * *

Richard Flanagan's narrow road

The Australian author Richard Flanagan's *The Narrow Road to the Deep North* (2013) is at once a historical novel and an autobiographical one.

An eventual Booker winner, it took a good twelve years to write, on account of the author trying to come to terms with the harrowing legacy of his father, who had survived a Japanese prisoner of war camp on the Thai-Burma "Death Railway" in 1942 (Raine, 2014). At a fluent narrative pace, it describes, with an economy of words and sensory vividness, the atrocities committed by the Japanese, which left thousands of prisoners humiliated, robbed of their humanity and dignity; but for many it ended in being beaten and starved to death. More died on the insane railway project than at Hiroshima, not to speak of survivors who, later on, back in Australia, mysteriously died in car crashes, by suicide, or of serious illnesses—victims of post-traumatic stress disorder, trying to recover from severe traumatisation.

In the face of such atrocities the author remains at a level of detachment that reminds us of Primo Levi's ability not to pass vindictive judgement on his Nazi tormentors in the concentration camp, remaining committed to providing an impassionate account of what happened, being a chronicler rather than a judge. Flanagan's narrator also manages to get into the mind of the Japanese guards, such as Lizard, a notoriously brutal officer, who is always on the lookout for necks suitable for decapitation by the force of his sword. And yet, we learn, he is also capable of enjoying poetry, which leaves the reader with the author's notion that it is the brutal system the Japanese perpetrators found themselves in that is evil, not the individual.

Flanagan's choice of title relates to Japanese poetry. "The Narrow Road to the Deep North" is the title of a collection of travel haiku by the poet and Buddhist monk Matsuo Basho (1644–1694). Whereas Basho takes us into the varied landscape of Japan and into his own interior (Basho, 1966), Flanagan's narrator takes his characters into the path of death or, in the protagonist's case, survival and its dire consequences for later life. Flanagan's capital as a writer is his own life. But here, as it touches upon his father's severe traumatisation and the thinness of his survival, it has become, so he says, a "strange stone within me which grew bigger, choking me" (Buruma, 2014). The conundrum of his father's survival, and what he has passed on to his own son, became a heavy load that had to be unburdened by way of writing. But it was not easy; it not only took twelve years to complete but cost Flanagan a great deal, as he was terrified of writing it. Significantly, the day he completed the book his father died. And later on, three weeks after he had learned that he had won the Booker, his mother died.

The process of writing had become a mysterious cycle of publication, recognition, and death. In the aftermath of having written *The Narrow Road* Flanagan felt depleted, or, in his own words, "diminished by the sum of his stories" (BBC1, 2015). Again, this is a reminder of Primo Levi's work of historical journalism and reportage, of having become the chronicler of human evil and depravity in *If This is a Man* (1959). Happy to have found, in his surviving years, a medium by which he could bear witness to human destructiveness, Levi never was quite able to rise above bouts of malignant depression, finally, in later life, giving in to his wish to die rather than live (Thomson, 2002). Flanagan, of course, survived, but at great cost, leaving behind a remarkable document of yet another chapter of human aggression, not to mention a monument to his father's history.

The search for love

"Everything that I know ... I know only because I love"

—Leo Tolstoy, *War and Peace*

Love is the most essential human experience. To be is to love. Love is what makes us human. The ability to love makes us immortal. It is the very stuff we leave behind in the minds of other people when we're gone. Love is what makes connections between people but also, within the individual, between the conscious mind and the psyche, that is the individual's relationship with her internal life: her unconscious, her dream life, her fantasy life, her life of imagination, and her soul life. And then there is the devastation of love. Love is stirring. Love hurts. To love, and be loved, means that all that which is you might come out of hiding, reaching in to challenging and traumatic life experiences that have previously taken the course of amnesia and repression. Both the beauty and the devastation of love make us more whole, more rounded, people.

Love shows that we are social animals. We are driven towards making connections with others. It was psychoanalyst Ronald Fairbairn, living in splendid isolation in Scotland, who placed the love-seeking intention of human beings (which unfortunately he called "object-seeking") in a more central position in psychoanalytic theory (1944). It had taken the profession dealing with the reparation of love relations fifty years to arrive at such a common sense notion. It did not help that Freud, the biologist of the mind, had developed a narrow view of love as being solely in the service of the sexual instinct and the gratification of sexual tension. Some people might reach enlightenment through the tantric practice of erotic and sexual union but it is not everybody's cup of tea. Sexual desire and passion are only a vehicle to the opening of the heart. Love, in essence, is the path of the embodiment of the soul and spiritual practice. If you give yourself deeply to another person you will be changed forever.

Love is a primary human drive. In its most elevated form the experience of love is not solely focused on physical gratification, nor, on the emotional level, on the self and a few select people around us, but is directed towards humankind, to include all people, a notion that psychoanalyst Erich Fromm, also a Marxist and a political activist, made available to a wide readership (some thirty million) in the late fifties (1957). His shrewdest notion is that love is not a given, something that just is, part of our basic equipment as human beings; it is an art form, and therefore requires hard work, effort, and knowledge. In his view, the way we can learn about an art form is to first understand its theory, then embark on its practice, followed by ultimate dedication and commitment: "there must be nothing else in the world more important than the art" (ibid., p. 4). Love in that sense becomes a primary aesthetic project, a piece of art that requires labour, attention, and preoccupation.

* * *

Fromm's notion that love is an art form can also be applied to our relationship with dreaming. Dreams are an art form. They are autobiographical fictions. That they write themselves in nocturnal instalments should not be a cheap way out of the responsibility the dreamer has for the well-being of dream life. Dreams are part of us, they visit us every night, whether we want them or not. They are as much part of our instinctual lives as breathing, eating, and sleeping are. But they amount to more than that. They are the guardians of our emotional lives, and from there they move us on to the psychic ladder of self-development, to autonomous thinking, the search for beauty, the "will to power", and to spiritual development.

If we just let dreams be, let them get on with their nightly duties of restoring physical and emotional health, we do not utilise them for the purpose of living a life of urgency, potency, and creativity. Dreams require a dreamer, as much as a lover requires another person. And a dreamer requires her dream life. As she starts to take care of her soul life, she is prepared to look after her dreams, rather than simply forgetting them, or rubbishing them for being a nuisance. And in exchange for her gifts of attention and appreciation, even in the face of nightmares, dream life will become more generous and outspoken, not unlike a companion, a good friend, intent on carrying on the perpetual conversations of friendship, holding the dreamer, supporting her, illuminating her path to self-discovery.

If we are willing to take care of our dreams, which are our most precious possessions, then dreams will not dry up. The drought of dreams might easily lead to their disappearance, a sense of deadness, and, if we are prone to giving in to hatefulness, ultimately to the corruption of the dream function. If we do not exercise our bodily selves we might become obese, immobile, and depressed; if we do not stick to a healthy diet we might kill ourselves slowly with fast food; so why should we not exercise the dream function? The dream function, that is, dream thinking, is the engine of our psychic lives. You have to take your vintage car out for a ride, otherwise it will get rusty.

However, to start taking your dreams seriously is not all there is. There is more at stake. It is a matter of choice, of living productively or living destructively. It is a matter of life and death. If we remain unconscious dreamers the dream function still serves the restoration of the body, recharging the batteries; it still deals with the rough edges of emotional conflict, keeping us away from the edge of insanity. So far, so good. The dreamer does not have to do anything to reap the rewards of dreaming. But that is on a primitive level of emotional functioning. If we want more from life, if we are prepared to face up to its challenges, we have to embark on a deeper union with our dream lives. It is no less than having to love them, to embrace them as the most precious thing that has been given to us by human evolution, if not by the universal design of creation.

* * *

Case study: Alicia

> "Love is not love
> Which alters when it alteration finds."

—Shakespeare, *Sonnet* 116

Alicia had one of her epic dreams. She and the other group patients were lying on beds or couches in a hall, generously spaced out. Her analyst tests the patients by pressing with his hands all over their bodies, which worries Alicia as she has got a shard of glass sticking in her skin that might bleed on impact. A seven-foot-tall woman enters the hall wearing stunning head gear, like the plumage of a bird with huge, colourful feathers. Her face painted, she looks like an exotic bird. The tall woman plays musical instruments, one of which is an accordion on stilts, and the analyst joins in playing music that sounds both scary and thrilling.

A large crowd of people comes into the hall to form a procession that is led outside by the tall woman, into a countryside of rolling hills. From a ridge they are able to see a beautiful valley. In the foreground stands a May tree in full blossom, the landscape behind a lush green, heaven-like, paradisiacal. "Behold! The world of the analyst!" the tall woman exclaims with extended arms. The procession weaves its way back into the hall. The analyst stands on a low stage beckoning Beverley, Alicia's daughter, over to him. Alicia is not so sure, feeling worried, saying to her, "Take care", which turns into "It'll be alright", followed by "It'll be good".

* * *

What else is analytic work other than the pursuit of truthfulness? First the lies, then a gradual realisation that one has built a whole life around assumptions that are not true. When talking about lies here, I am not suggesting that patients are liars as such, I am simply stating the fact that it is part of the human condition that we easily give in to assumptions, myths, and storylines about family history that do not hold up to the scrutiny of analysis nor to the suffering of the heart.

Alicia had, of course, throughout her life rationally understood what both her parents had inflicted on her, but it took her the best part of four years in group analysis to realise the emotional impact of her recollections. So her intellect was telling the truth whilst silencing the centre of her being, which is her heart and soul.

> Truth is the nourishment of the mind, and lies its poison. (Bion, 1962a)

Her psyche, in order to organise chaos, fragmentation, and high vulnerability, had built a Berlin Wall around the most cherished part of herself. She had learned early in life to soldier on, to give short shrift to emotional need, and develop a "will to power" that kept her going despite the nightmares. Not infrequently in the group, when others wished to get anywhere near her vulnerability, she issued public warnings of the menacing kind without words.

Do not cross the line. Do not jump the wall. I will remain untouched.

During the first interview, before joining the group, Alicia was taken aback, if not dismissive, when I said that her suffering showed, that it was visible to the person prepared to see it. One of the definitions of neurosis is "not to see the obvious". And how obvious her vulnerability had become. Her preference, though, was to maintain an air of cool detachment, control, and of being untouchable. And yet her life's fictions spoke for themselves. It took her the best part of three sessions before I was able to get a word in, such was the urgency in the delivery of her life story. There was also a feverish urgency to join the group. It was as if I had to hold the reins of a thoroughbred horse, gone wild by sensing an incoming storm, hell-bent on galloping back to the safety of the stables, whilst I tried to calm her down.

During the period of preparing Alicia for the group she had two dreams. Dreams at the outset of analysis are initiation dreams, they show what might be coming, what the actual work might look like. In that sense, initiation dreams are prophetic, but, almost mockingly, leave both patient and analyst in the dark. At this stage a dream cannot be fully understood, as it will take the course of the analysis to unravel its full meaning. In the first dream she is with her daughter on a beach by the sea. She realises a tsunami is coming, a huge, terrifying wave moving in rapidly from the horizon. They clamber up the cliff face to the top, narrowly escaping the gigantic wave. Looking down they realise that many people have drowned. In the second dream Alicia is asked to gas a number of people. She administers yellow poison gas willingly and with joy.

Later on in the group when, story by story, she led us into the shocking details of her early life, the group was affected but *she* was not, as if the stories she told were not hers. They were stories without an author but in desperate search of one. Again, her mind, barricaded off from emotional torment, gave away the gift of emotional connection and put it inside other people to experience, and possibly to safeguard. Such a mechanism—employed by the psyche so that it remains in a state of dissociation and assumed safety, and yet is strangely bemused by what the recipient is showing, as it appears so familiar—is known as "projective identification": getting rid of the bad stuff so that the rational mind stays in control, if not flourishes in triumph. Alicia seemed to be impersonating someone sitting in a cinema—which, as an ardent cineaste, she loved—watching other people break down under the weight of her own, disowned, suffering. If you don't own your own emotions, the emotions come to you, they look at you from the other side of the room, as if something foreign desperately wants to find its rightful home.

She had been abandoned by her mother aged two-and-a-half; her sister Fay was only six months old. Her mother had left the family for another man, if not for her fiercely held self-possession. Both parents being indifferent to the children's needs, the siblings were shipped off to their grandparents for a number of years. Aged five, Alicia was asked, by a person who mediated between the warring parents, with whom she wanted to stay from then on. "With your father? With your mother?"—a double-bind question she could not answer. The only thing she knew was that she wished to stay with her grandparents. And what she didn't know was that her grandmother wanted her to stay.

The sisters were taken in by their father when Alicia was five, by now having started a new family with two more children. Living in a large, middle-class house, Alicia and her sister were subjected to extreme forms of physical and emotional cruelty by their father and stepmother. Once, she was beaten up so badly by her father that she fainted, fearing for her life. Closely resembling her mother in appearance did not help; it infuriated him, and was at the top of the list of things that could arouse his volcanic hatefulness, which could erupt, over banalities, at any moment.

The sisters were forced to grow up in a parallel universe; prevented from joining the others at meal times, they had to eat separately, living on cheap food. Kept hungry, they were also hungry for love. Frequently Alicia and Fay were punished over nothing and locked for hours in a dark cupboard underneath the stairs, fed on bread and water. They had no access to the family's sitting room, which meant that they spent most of the time in their unheated bedroom during the cold season. In winter they were told to go outside, into the garden or the streets, so the sisters roamed the neighbourhood, hungry, cold, beaten by despair, as if orphaned.

If This is a Man, Primo Levi's book on surviving Auschwitz, springs to mind, in which he sharply interrogates humanity's recent moral history. It refers to the moral degradation of sadistic camp guards but also of inmates who, after prolonged exposure to cruelty and starvation, collapse into hatred and self-hatred in the place once held by human dignity. And now, last words, last words of victims being led to the gas chambers should be mentioned: *Ich bin doch ein Mensch!* meaning "I am a human being, am I not?"

Once, when the other members of the family went away, leaving the sisters behind, Alicia put a sign up in a window that was overlooked by the neighbours. *Help us!* Alicia and Fay waited, never to be rescued. There was no rescue. Alicia might have been waiting all her life in futile expectation, except for the redeeming factors of prayer, the words of Shakespeare, the exuberance of sport, and making things alongside her grandmother, who loved knitting, knitting together her grandchild's fragmented mind.

Chronos is the deity of time. Throughout her analysis Alicia struggled to be on time. Typically she would be ten minutes late, which did not go down too well with other group patients, nor with her analyst. It took her years to get anywhere near the epicentre of the dilemma. With the help of a dream that was both of a sexual and a violent nature, the doors of perception opened. She remembered a time when she was thirteen, fourteen, doing sports in the evening. Once, her coach gave her a lift home, and on arrival they kissed, entering the forbidden land of Eros. Her father had waited up for her. She was ten minutes late. For the following two-and-a-half weeks she was locked in her bedroom, curtains drawn, being fed only on bread and water.

Hannah Arendt, a German-Jewish philosopher who wrote on the trial of Adolf Eichmann, one of the main perpetrators of the "final solution", came up with the notion of "the banality of evil" (Arendt, 2007), by which she meant that there is no limit to the depths to which any of the assumptions and world views uttered by the Nazi grandees could sink. There is no thinking, no reflection, no moral consideration, no links with other fellow human beings; just primitive assumptions held. Alicia always reflected on her father's cruelty but did not find any indication as to the reasons for his hatefulness other than the love of sadism, if not the triumph of evil over young and nascent life. There was no scope to his thinking, only banality. Another of his behaviours was sadism, in the shape of emasculation, towards his son from his second marriage. Alicia's stepbrother took his own life in his forties, which was during Alicia's analysis, an event that deeply affected her. Not only was it difficult to mourn her brother, but also she was in turmoil as to the reasons for her father's continuous demolishing of her brother. There was no answer. Only the banality of evil.

Her father's cruelty occurred with the knowledge of her mother, who had made a new life for herself with a wealthy husband and two children. When she saw her daughters once a month, their expectations ran high but she remained untouched. The icy seas of her narcissism lay in-between well-practised impersonations of motherhood and her being repulsed by the demands of the children. Alicia remembered that she had loved her mother as a child, being drawn to her beauty, but was rebuffed by her mother's hatefulness and envy: "You're no good. You were an awful child from the beginning." In her mother's disturbed view, she saw in her daughter that which she had violently evacuated from her mind and deposited in her, whereas what the young girl wanted most was to touch her mother and be touched. But her mother could not tolerate any tender bodily contact.

At a later period in her analysis Alicia realised that her mother had struggled with her from the beginning. Alicia had a dream about small creatures, worm-like, unformed, embryonic, held in a membrane, slithering about. A fat worm was greedily devouring the wriggling little worms. She was disgusted, thinking that her mother had an aversive response to her even in utero. The sentiment that the intra-uterine dream evoked in the dreamer, namely disgust, was a leading feeling in her mother, who had hated the pregnancy and the nascent life inside her. Her mother had always been disgusted by her daughter's physicality; she could not bear being touched, hugged, or anything to do with bodily touch and abandon.

This was in sharp contrast to her mother's active sex life. With men she could be sensual, seductive, erotic, with an enormous sexual appetite, turning into a devouring parody of Venus, the goddess of love and beauty. However, the intention behind her highly sexed life was to dominate men, to harvest the rich fruit of sexual seduction and power, in order to import wealth and status. Young Alicia, as an onlooker, was not able to comprehend that she could not be on the receiving end of her mother's sensuality.

Feeling rejected, Alicia developed another set of "lies", which were biased theories about herself, such as being unlovable, and that there was something fundamentally flawed about her. Children tend to carry everything, to take full responsibility for bad things happening. To perceive mother as utterly mad, disturbed, and hateful would be too catastrophic a view to hold, so all of the parental failure is taken inside and used against the self, as a theory of fake security and an argument for reliable self-hatred.

Frequently, in the analysis, Alicia would ponder her failure as a child.

Was I too bright? Was I too wild? Was I too testing?

At that time she had had a number of tiger dreams. A tiger approaches the door to her bedroom. She is afraid, cowering. The tiger breaks down the door, comes up to her, and, surprisingly, lies down with her, intent on snuggling up. She ends up lying in the crescent of his soft and warm belly, being held by his big front paws, and, as he purrs, his claws show. She is terrified. *Was I too tigerish as a child?* Always seeing the basic fault-line in herself. The tiger who insisted on coming to her, making contact, turned out to be a symbol of her own power. In the past she had not identified with the power of her rational mind, her fierce intellect, but now something inside her had shifted away from the denial of her emotional self to a gradual acceptance of the need to trust her emotions rather than be afraid of them. She also came to understand that the tiger inside was a formidable weapon against her mother who, in adult life, made theatrical overtures to her of eternal motherly love but always ended up dismantling her with hateful comments. The more Alicia opened up her heart the more she realised that she had to stay away from her mother. The tiger kept the boundary well. Not only that. There were other dreams with powerful animals, such as sharks, that helped her to establish a demarcation line between her and her mother, so that she was able to come to terms with her own "sharkish" nature. More of that later.

* * *

"To thine own self be true"

—Shakespeare, *Hamlet*

Alicia had an early infatuation with Shakespeare. In the face of adversity and severe traumatisation, healing forces tend to arise, if the individual is prepared to apprehend an opening. The child, forever bound to the idea of guilt and shame, taking all the blame for the bad, paradoxically, also conjures up a world of fantasy, a redemptive world that forms a counterpoint to the experience of nameless dread. A primary redemptive feature in Alicia's early life was her belief in God. She prayed and found solace. During prayer, as her mind found the quiet waters of contemplation, God's voice took one detail of her nascent mind and made of it a foundation stone for her later life. She had always had a sense that there was something wrong with her narcissistic mother and her sadistic father, making an island of truth out of the ruins of a childhood of terror and quiet desperation. As it was, she remained a speaker of truth right through to adulthood.

This was her *intuitive* apprehension of truth. She stumbled across a more developed concept of truth whilst finding redemption through the written word. In a library, at the age of nine or ten, she found red leather-bound books of Shakespeare. *The Merchant of Venice* (1623) was her entry-point into the works of the great bard; the character of Shylock, the loan shark, who is after a pound of flesh from his debtor, became a first attempt at conceptualising her father. During lunchtimes she recruited some of her friends to play, in secret, in a world that pulled her in but which she did not fully understand. Props for the play, such as tights and a wooden sword, were hidden in a locker.

From then on she was eating up Shakespeare's words like a starving caterpillar, and as the words formed a substance inside she turned into a butterfly, always on the search for a better word. This apprehended her internal reality but did not, as yet, yield the power of comprehension nor consciousness. In Hamlet she found words that in her early life were signs but they could not be understood. She was now pairing her unconscious wishes with a spoken word that sprang from the poetry of reflection. "To thine own self be true." And things started to make sense. The entry of Shakespeare's words into Alicia's early life opened her heart and allowed the future to come in. And with it the possibility of comprehension and redemption.

* * *

At times life's downers are the prelude to real change, towards an upward movement on the heavenly ladder of self-improvement. Alicia had been dismissed at work for allegedly breaking the rules. She worked in a prison, being in charge of the inmates' education department. Shocked and devastated by the allegations, which were, in fact, fabricated, she went through a breakdown, spending seemingly endless time at home in bed, unable to function, unable to think, unable to look after herself properly, except for attending the group where she cried inconsolably, allowing herself to be untogether, wide open, and raw. Unwillingly, she had entered the *Via Crucis*, the "path of the cross", and suffering. Without it no redemption, no healing can occur.

> Things fall apart; the centre cannot hold. (Yeats, 1992, p. 235)

Her breakdown turned out to be the single most important turning point in her analysis. Whereas she had always dissociated from the traumatisations of her early life, she was now overwhelmed by fear and despair. In the group she asked for reassurance but was not given easy closure. Descending into one's own private holocaust, and the feeling of connection with it, does not offer a safe return ticket nor an immediate solution. She feared to go mad, but where she really went to were historical places in her early life that now made the demand to open up to what had happened, to find retrospective concern for what she had gone through; in short, she witnessed the return of the universe of the little girl, who had been discarded, overlooked, not listened to, made to disappear into concealment and quiet desperation. First, by her own parents, and later on, by herself, as she had not been ready to experience the feeling impact of her mother's mind, had tried to wipe her out, along with her father's cruelty.

Within a few days, her façade of togetherness, sublime intellect, and her air of untouchability had evaporated. And in this interim phase of nothingness she was unsure if she wanted to be in this place of not knowing herself any longer. She had put all of her trust in the group but struggled to see if she would ever reach the other shore.

> I am nothing
> I shall never be nothing
> I can't want to be nothing
> Apart from this, I have in me all the dreams in the world.
>   (Pessoa, 2006)

And "all the dreams in the world" came out of hiding. In her case the dreams were nightmares. As she re-entered her history in reverse, moving from the present day to things of the past, her dream world made stopovers at crucial times on the timeline.

Back now to the initial dream of her analysis. Together with her daughter she had survived a tsunami. A prophetic dream. As we know, in her early life she had survived the tsunami of unbearable emotion. Not only that. Later on in life, not once, but twice, she had survived certain death. During the latter stages of pregnancy she was so ill with cancer that it was suggested she terminate in order to survive. But she hung in there, and both she and the baby survived. And if that was not enough, some twenty years later, she and her daughter survived a near-fatal car crash.

She survived the violence of her childhood, she survived cancer, and a road accident, but as a consequence she did not trust the deep waters of her own emotional world, cutting off from it. What was required was not to run away from the swell of emotion any longer but to give in to it, to surrender, to immerse herself in the base element of water.

And so it happened. In the course of analysis she became less afraid of the terror, humiliation, and degradation suffered as a child. The solution is always inherent in the problem. Instead of standing up to frightening waves of emotion she thought about swimming the seas or surfing the waves.

Another dream with the element of water in it saw her wading through low water on the beach, then immersing herself in a large rock pool with clear and beautiful water. She had a sense of her mother being around. The tsunami had turned into shallow water. Now she was able to cry, to shed tears. At the time, on the way up to the consulting room, she went past a delivery of boxes of tissues. Piles of them. She said, jokingly, "Now I can cry. There are so many tears kept inside in need of shedding."

* * *

Dreams walk easily on the timeline of personal history, making connections between the past, present, and future, a phenomenon typical of dreams that is called multi-temporality. In other words, we are of all ages. At all times we inhabit a world, and not only in dreams, that is about the continuity of being in time. In order to live contentedly in the present we have to call upon the whole curvature of time, to link up the beginning with the end. Past, present, and future always are a continuum, which also means that there is no single dream. All dreams are connected, from intra-uterine dreams to the dreams of the baby to the dreams of the toddler to the dreams of the teenager to the dreams of the adult and the dreams preparing the dreamer for death. All dreams are "omnibus" dreams that constitute the unseen but solid ground we walk on throughout life.

We are beings of history, shaped by history, and dreams, more than anything else, are the arbiters of historical consciousness. By way of dissociation we become deprived of history, erasing what has been and also what could have been, and what might be in the future, leading to a thinness of being in the present. History, consciousness, and identity are intertwined in a nocturnal *convivium* of dreams. There is no better entry point to the experience of multi-temporality, and therefore the reclaiming of one's identity, than a temporary breakdown, a regression into the unconscious seas of our being. That is the Neptunian side of dreaming that issues states of undifferentiatedness, unknowing, and uncertainty, in short, the infinity and unboundedness of dream cosmology. Alicia, who had so far survived severe traumatisation by living in a world of rational one-pointedness, now allowed herself, reluctantly and with trepidation, first to paddle, and then to dive into the strong currents of the continuity of time, in which nothing remains untouched nor unseen.

Alicia's immersion in the deep waters of her emotional self, historically kept at bay by dissociation, made her realise one simple thing. That it was okay just to be. To be with herself in a different way, to experience the quietude of Alicia-ness. Instead of brushing off the feeling memory of past trauma she now landed firmly in the present with a wide open heart. States of being are more difficult to attain than states of doing, as they originate in the early mother-infant relationship that allows the child to play in the presence of an unintrusive mother, to use a Winnicottian idea. The pertinent states of fear that she was now experiencing made plain to her what, historically, had got in the way of the lightness of being that should have been the child's prerogative. She had been afraid of her own mother, not to mention her father: a tsunami of fear. And now she learned how to be with unbearable feelings and to build a container for them.

Another reward for her suffering was the opening up of her world of dreams. One of her dreams had written another fiction: "Now I can die"—a paradox, if you think that she had just started to be more fully alive and in the present. The phrase referred to a traumatic time in her life, almost thirty years ago, that was mentioned, fleetingly, earlier in the text. She had been pregnant, and during the middle stages of the pregnancy she was diagnosed with cancer. Being faced with the dilemma of having an abortion that would save her life or risk dying, she decided to go for a full term, which meant that she could easily have died from complications and put her foetus at risk. She went against the opinion of her consultant, and found herself a private consultant, who assisted her in her desire. Not only did she survive the pregnancy, giving birth to her daughter, but she also survived the cancer. Her "will to power" proved so strong that she had been prepared to give her own life for the nascent life inside, in sharp contrast to her mother's agenda of disgust and hateful feelings towards her when she was inside her mother's womb.

Why the dream's puzzling fiction—"Now I can die!"? Both mother and baby surviving was a godsend but also led, from then on, to a psychic conundrum: they developed a deep and loving relationship but on some level it became too intense, too dependent, too enmeshed. Alicia realised she had to sever the ties, let her daughter go, so that she, in turn, could be freer and more independent. Now that she walked on the shaky but rewarding *Via Dolorosa*, the path of suffering, Alicia had found a home in herself, and she had found another strong companion, namely her dream life. The mysterious "Now I can die!" she learned to understand as a way of letting go without falling into the abyss of fear and nameless dread.

From psychoanalyst Winnicott we know that if the infant goes through the unobstructed cycles of anxiety and recovery from it, she will eventually learn that anxiety can be transformed into something resembling peace of mind. What it requires is a good-enough mother who is capable of dreaming in the infant's distressed presence, wide open to her needs but not shaken by them. She understands that such states of mind are nothing more than tempests: however strong, they blow over. They belong to the chaotic weather systems of emotion. The infant now attains a fluid sense of self that surfs the waves of emotional upheaval, or in Winnicott's words, it is a "self that can afford to die" (1956a, p. 304).

This had a double meaning for Alicia, as she found in herself the healthy cycles of anxiety and the recovery from it, but also now emotionally connected with the historical anguish of having sailed so close to the edge of life when she and her daughter survived; when death and birth had become one and the same thing, welded into a singularity, and now had to be separated, allowing her to sense retrospective sadness, terror, and the beauty of the nascent life that had sprung from it.

Paradoxically, she also had to recover from her own "will to power": when she stood up to a berating consultant, she was almost shocked by her own resolve, asking herself, "Who is doing this? Am I doing this?" in disbelief over her own strength in the face of adversity. Also, she bravely looked death in the eye, prepared to give her own life for the life of her daughter. Only now did the magnitude of her resolve sink in. Yeats wrote on this same theme of a person's elevation at times of great upheaval. In his poem on the Irish Easter Rising in 1916, the refrain "A terrible beauty is born" (1916) encapsulates the lives of ordinary people who, in the face of great political change and danger, stood up against the repression of the British and thus made history. Sixteen of them were executed, and became symbols of Irish history and imagination, laying the foundations for an independent state.

Now being more in possession of her dream life she made sense of the initial dream with the tall woman's dream fiction: "Behold! The world of the analyst!" The woman was a priestess, a dream priestess who had initiated her into the world of the analyst, which is the dream world. The priestess wore headgear that made her look like a bird. Birds, in the canon of ancient dream consciousness, stand for the apparition of the soul and the soul's journey, during sleep, out of the bodily self. During the time of her soul returning in her dream life she consulted a shamanic healer who performed rituals, leading to the retrieval of her soul. In ancient disease theory it was thought that the soul leaves the bodily self in the face of severe traumatisation. And healing means soul retrieval, the return of the soul into the bodily self (Ellenberger, 1970).

"The world of the analyst" is, she came to understand, the world of dreams and, by means of connecting with it, she stepped right into its inherent process of dream thinking that helped her to make sense of her emotional insertion in this world. She also reflected on music being made in the dream. Music, again in ancient dream cosmology, represents the presence and movement of the soul. Alicia linked it with another Shakespearean fiction: Music is the food of love.

This made her think of one of the redeeming factors of her mother. From her she had learned about the appreciation of beauty, and about the aesthetics of food. He mother could produce delicious food but was also an outstanding baker. For as long as she could remember, Alicia had always had a sweet tooth; for her, eating cakes or sweets meant a treat, a delight of sorts. But what she was really after was to fill the emptiness inside in place of motherly love.

In the last part of the Behold! dream Alicia negotiates her daughter moving away from her over to me. The analyst has beckoned her. Alicia is not so sure, feeling worried, saying to her daughter, "Take care", which turns into "It'll be alright", followed by "It'll be good". The fictions of dreams maps out the dreamer's evolving relationship with her analyst: from being worried—and who would blame her, given her cruel father—to a sense of rightness, and, eventually, hope. Would she be able to trust her analyst sufficiently to entrust the little girl to the analytic endeavour? This depends so much on the analyst's capacity for loving kindness, on the ability to stand the heat of hatefulness, not to retaliate in return, to tolerate uncertainty, and on the scope of his understanding of the human condition.

If the Behold! dream is lined up next to one of her initiation dreams into analysis then we arrive at a different picture. In the second initiation dream she is asked to gas people, which she willingly and triumphantly does. Subsequently she is appalled by her own dream, reluctant to claim ownership, which goes hand in hand with the late arrival in her analysis of the notion that she herself could be destructive, hateful, and violent. She is, after all, the daughter of a hateful mother, and of a sadistic father, having taken in their poisonous stuff in the place of love. Dreams, for ever contrary and humorous, sowed in her mind the seed that I could be destructive, after all. Her land of glory, the assumed land of the analyst, dreamland, as it were, could be poisoned by the gravitational force towards German history under the Nazis, who were capable of gassing their own kind, Germans who happened to be Jewish. So in her dream world there was the possibility of me turning out to be like her father. The dream expert gassing the dreamer in his charge.

Her dream about the shark also came out of the storage room of the vast universal library of dreams. In fact, following her time working in prison, she realised that she had become part of a brutal regime that was making some of her staff redundant. She used the chopping quality of the shark, making short shrift of other peoples' livelihoods. After her breakdown, when she made a deeper relationship with matters of the heart, she woke up to the sobering realisation about her own propensity for destructiveness.

* * *

What is the origin of art? Where does creativity spring from? The making of art springs from dreams and dream-related states. Dreams are makers. They take the raw material of emotional chaos, an overload of sensory impressions, and thoughts in search of an author, and make from it images, symbols, metaphors, and fictions. This can be said about the origin of anything productive and creative: painting, music, poetry, prose writing, scientific innovation, architecture, the discovery of new theorems, etc., can be traced back to dream states. So, it seems that, in order to get the creative process going, it is just a matter of employing and harnessing one's own dream world.

However, if one's creative propensity has gone underground and become dormant in the face of severe traumatisation, as was the case with Alicia, then it might require an external stimulus for it to be reawakened. Hers was a horrific awakening. Some twelve years earlier she and her daughter had been involved in a fatal car accident that left both of them traumatised. It took her a good two years to recover, not surprisingly, as the trauma at the time brought back memories of historical cumulative trauma. Dreams, at the best of times, are succinct reminders of our mortality. Alicia was overwhelmed at the time with dreams about death and dying and attendant questions such as "Is this what it's like to die?", "If I were to go now, is this my life?", "If this is it, is that all there is?"

If you sit long enough with eschatological questions that are existential questions, "last" questions, as it were, reaching into the inevitability of mortality, then, paradoxically, questions of aliveness, being in life, living life to the full, come to the fore. Alicia experienced a kind of awakening, an opening of her senses to the beauty of the world. She was compelled to do art work. And her art was specific, unique. It was all about the written word, and the display of the word, using Shakespeare and her own words and phrases that sprang from dreams. As a child she had liked being taken to museums by her mother, who let her roam freely, taking in the atmosphere of natural history and art. She took a liking to display cabinets that had glass fronts and solid wooden frames, showing a vast array of insects, butterflies being her favourites.

In her new-found art she displayed, in entomology cabinets, words that had historically saved her from the agony of early life. In one of the installations, which reaches across an entire wall, she wrote in bold letters *You Are The One*. Layer after layer of laser-cut, precise writing alternates with flowing handwriting that is copied from her private diary entries. The background to the display of words is mirrored, so that if you look at the work you start to see yourself. "You Are the One" turns out not to be the other but the self. A reflection of the self, parts of which cannot be made out, is lying in the shadow, in concealment, if not dissociation. Alicia connected this piece of art with a poem by Derek Walcott, "Love after love", in which true love is described as the love for the self, taken back from projections on to other people. There is no profound love of the other without finding a love connection with oneself. Walcott describes the alienation from the self and the gradual rediscovery and celebration of one's own uniqueness. "You will love again the stranger who was your self" (Walcott, 2014, p. 227).

As a child Alicia had displayed in the window of her father's house a sign with *Help!* written on it, a sign that had never been received, never attracted an audience. But now, instead of pleading for help, she had found a most precious thing, namely Alicia-ness. Friendship with the self. Hannah Arendt talks about an essential step taken into one's own humanity, if you start to make friends with all of that which is you. And that includes the human fault-lines, failures, and shortcomings. But by the end of the day, you start to like, if not love, all of that which is you.

Another piece of her evolving art was connected with the same idea, namely love. Taken from Shakespeare's sonnets, she displayed in large letters, in the same style as before, the phrase

> Love is not love
> Which alters when it alteration finds.

At the time in her forties she was keen to find what love was. She had found motherly love but equal and mature love with a man still eluded her, despite having been in long-term relationships. By rediscovering the written words of Shakespeare and the sudden eruption of art into her life, she had found ways of conceptualising something she had never experienced as a child.

However severe the traumatisation at the hands of both her mother and her father, the actual human catastrophe in her early life was the absence of love. To have been repeatedly abused was bad enough but the emptiness in the place of love turned out to be more hard-hitting and formative. Walcot's poetry offered her reflections on self-love, and the attempt to befriend that part of herself that she had dissociated from, namely the feeling memory of parental hatefulness and cruelty.

Earlier on I mentioned Hannah Arendt, whose concept of friendship entails the idea of redemption if we manage to make friends with precisely those parts of the psyche we are not very fond of, such as: being hateful toward beloved ones; dissolving in fear in the face of adversity; not being grown up when called upon to do something responsible; being dismissive of others; not tolerating uncertainty; being grumpy, and altogether unbearable. It was such a friendship with her other half, the dark side, that Alicia was after. After the breakup of her more recent relationship, which had stirred up her daemons of contempt and hatred, she decided to stay single for as long as she could, in order to find solace in herself, self-love, and something resembling solidity and continuity. Had Shakespeare not said, "Love is not love/Which alters when it alteration finds"? A love "That looks at tempests and is never shaken".

The search for knowledge

Wishing to make sense of the world is part of the human condition. The search for knowledge is a primary motivational force. Knowledge, in this context, should not be mistaken for book knowledge, academic pursuit, or the vast amount of information now available on the internet. The latter is more like undigested clutter resembling the inside of a fragmented mind. By contrast, knowledge is defined as the search for oneself, personal truth, and universal truths. In this way it stands in the tradition of Humanism and the history of learning. Its movement is towards emotional understanding and emotional intelligence. It occurs at the interface between thinking and emotion. Its entry point is the understanding of our primary emotional drives, which are fear, love, and aggression, before it moves to higher levels of human knowledge, namely the development of the ethical sense, searches for family history, cultural identity, and into the far reaches of abstract thinking, such as being able to conceptualise complex scientific problems, if your talents happen to take you there.

Whether we like it or not, the most advanced forms of thinking in the service of problem-solving have their origin in the murky waters of the bodily self and primitive emotions. Similarly, in the face of adversity and emotional impasse, we always have a longing to return to mother, if not to the womb. Freud at the very height of his powers still visited his mother every Sunday afternoon for Viennese *Kaffee und Kuchen*, paying homage to a Jewish mother who had favoured him as a child, believed in his extraordinary talents, but, most importantly had given birth to him. She was the physical and emotional origin of his life, forever to be the object of reverence and devotion.

Just giving in to emotional states does not lead anywhere if we do not know where our states of misery come from and what we can do about it. The expulsion of reason leaves us emotionally immature and empty. We do not want to turn into emotional drama queens, always deeply hurt by the minutest of rebuffals, or give in to tantrums more appropriate for a toddler; by contrast, the expulsion of emotion, with its consequence of only thinking rationally about ourselves and the state the world is in, is not very useful either. It easily leads to dissociation and detachment, and, in its extreme form, to the celebration of glacial states of mind and the triumph of cynical self-removal from the human condition. The driving force behind our emotional and cognitive maturation, that is, our world of dreams, is after a holy marriage between the two faculties of human experience: reason and emotion looking out at the world sitting alongside each other, rather than opposite each other, tearing into each other's flesh.

* * *

Epistemophilia is the love for knowledge (Hinshelwood, 1989). In the development of the canon of psychoanalytic theory reflection on the development of thinking, understanding, and the search for knowledge was a rather late addition, prime place having been taken by theories about the infant's bodily and emotional development, giving credence to the psyche-soma entity, rather than to thinking.

However, Freud set an early tone, at the beginning of the twentieth century, in saying that understanding is key to psychoanalytic therapy, by which he meant that the conscious awareness of the chaotic unconscious is paramount in the therapeutic endeavour, or, in his words, "Where id is, there ego shall be", which amounts to the rule of consciousness over the instincts, mind over body. He also saw sexual curiosity in children, their sexual searches, as the first rudimentary form of self-knowledge (1905d). Melanie Klein, in the 1920s and 1930s, picked up on this theme of infantile sexuality as the foundation stone of the desire to know. Such instinctual searches for knowledge, aimed at the bodily self and infantile sexual tensions, are inevitably frustrating, as emotional maturation is not quite up to the task.

It is a theory that makes sense if you imagine a person searching for his identity but not finding it, as was the case with Matt, who never knew his father, wanted to know about his paternal identity, but hit a stone wall of silence from his mother who had held the information (Chapter Two). Matt became increasingly cynical about the notion of paternal lineage, rubbishing it at every opportunity, but felt relieved when his stepfather stepped in to disclose family secrets.

In the late fifties and early sixties Bion was the first to develop a comprehensive theory of thinking (1962a). He elevated the epistemophilic instinct, the desire for knowledge, to the status of connections of love and hate between the individual and her internal life, and other people. The wish to know, the longing for love, and the conundrum of hate are all emotional links between the psyche and the external world. Bion thought that a psychoanalyst's ability to understand the patient might be more important than his capacity to love and hate. To know about oneself and the world presupposes to be known by another.

Thinking, in Bion's terms, is to make sense of our confusing and chaotic emotional world. Thinking is the confluence of cognitive function with emotional subtlety, and its inception and growth reaches right back to the early mother–baby relationship.

Let us imagine that the baby is rattled by a nightmare, screams, not for the first time that night, and wakes up her parents. The husband turns round, shrugs it off, embarks on another bout of snoring. By contrast the mother has been hit right in the pit of her stomach, as if someone has ripped her heart open and left a swarm of butterflies in the middle of her body. She dashes to the cot and picks up her most precious possession, which torments and delights her in equal measure. The baby has no intention to stop screaming; it is as if all the babies in the world have joined its chorus of despair. The mother feels scared but knows that there is no reason to feel scared. It is just a routine scenario: the baby screams, the mother offers peace of mind. Now the staggering thing that is happening is that the baby communicates without words, or writing, or conceptualisation. It cannot say,

Mum, just had a nightmare. A crocodile was about to have me for supper as I went for a swim in the murky waters of the Australian outback.

Initially, the mother knows nothing about what happens inside her charge's nascent mind, but she perceives, in a somewhat crazy state of mind, something resembling dreaming, in images that are succinct and sharp and closely observe the baby's dream fiction. And, as mentioned before, in the pit of her stomach lies proof, a somatic implant, as it were, of the dilemma, the actual dream thought in the costume of a physical sensation—

Get me out of here!! Or I will be eaten by a croc!!

—that made the baby cry in the first instance. It is sheer, unadulterated fear, so much of it that it could easily have derailed the young mum. But the mum has developed an extra sense during pregnancy, before giving birth, and after, something resembling a kangaroo's pouch, as if being pregnant with emotions that are not hers but are very familiar. She is, in fact, on the receiving end of the baby's unbearable emotions, which have squatted inside her without asking. It is, of course, the baby's prerogative to be carried by everyone, as if employing a small army of helpers, not unlike donkeys that are able to carry the sorrows of the world without collapse or complaint.

Whilst mother and baby are engaged in some primeval form of communication, characterised by heavy density and heightened sensitivity, close to an unconscious infection, the husband carries on snoozing in the marital bedroom, having snug dreams—of *Schadenfreude* and thinly disguised revenge on his wife for not having slept with him for weeks, and on his baby for disturbing his sleep and emotional equilibrium, having driven him mad for all to see. And, if that were not enough, his manhood has been inexplicably stricken by bouts of impotence, despite feeling aroused at all hours of the day. All in all, this is the illness of early fatherhood.

Whilst husband has taken refuge from emotional intensity, the two others involved in the nightly family drama carry on regardless, enclosed in a time zone that drags on endlessly. The young mother is processing emotionally what has been put inside her by the baby, realising that a fear of falling apart is not the end of the world but the beginning of a cycle that is the overcoming of fear. The more the mother metabolises her own fear, and the inserted fear in her pouch, the more the baby will be able to survive its own primitive emotions. The best the mother can do is to dream in the baby's distressed presence; her reverie is the holding and containing agent of her baby's repeated cycles of anxiety and the recovery from it, so that eventually the baby develops a "self that can afford to die", to use Winnicott's words. The baby is now able to relax into an existential sense of ontogenetic security.

Such unconscious exchanges are known as projective identification. The idea is that something unbearable, when expelled, can be transformed, in the recipient, into something more bearable, and then be taken back by the projecting baby so as to lead to peace of mind (Ogden, 1979). This very same process is occurring during dream states, when unbearable emotions are being contained and worked through. The truth is that the mother's willingness to hold inside her the baby's catastrophic emotions and make them more bearable has its origin in her ability to dream, which is, of course, something we all possess. By way of dreaming we are all part of this creative process of transformation. But this is not all there is to say, because the actual redemptive feature of dream thinking lies in the repeated cycles of recovery: recovery from fear, from the rebuffal of love, from the onslaught of hatred. If our primitive emotions can be survived, if converted into something productive, then we reach into a sense of existential security, into quiescent states of mind, into states of being, living lucidly in the present, not unlike living in a lucid dream that has become reality.

However, if the dream function has been corrupted by the preponderance of hateful feelings, cycles of recovery turn into cycles of destruction, whereby feelings, good and bad, are being evacuated from the mind, leaving the dreamer feeling empty, hopeless, and fragmented and leading to firmly held theories that the stuff of loving another can destroy the other. That fear is paramount, the only substance there is, and it is as if one has entered a pact with Mephistopheles, going on the rampage with missiles of hatefulness. During such mad states of mind it is felt that the cycles of destruction cannot be exited, that there is no return ticket to sanity, to a sense of relief, nor to the belief of redemption.

Dreaming is both a state of being and a state of doing: being, in so far as it is the recipient and repository of somatic and emotional experience; doing, in so far as it is processing a large amount of information in the brain, and in its physical and emotional residues. The active part of dreaming, also reflected in high cortical arousal during REM states, is called dream thinking.

To summarise: Bion said that the search for knowledge and thinking, to whatever level of sophistication we take it, always originates from our primitive sensory and emotional insertion in this world. By way of dreaming, that is, in a creative and transformative state of mind, we arrive at an emotional understanding that is the platform for further development, such as the ethical sense, symbolic thinking, the use of metaphor, abstract thought, and thinking fit for scientific enquiry. Without dreaming at the outset of emotional development we would not climb up the heavenly ladder of sophisticated thought processes.

* * *

When I was engaged in a community project, funded by the then health authority, which entitled patients in primary care to free access to group analysis, I was surprised by the results of the research undertaken in tandem with the treatment. The GP surgeries involved fed back that the group patients showed a significant reduction in the use of medication and in the frequency of consulting medical staff during and after group treatment. In questionnaires collected a year after completion of a two-year period in group analysis the participants gave frank replies: such as "I'm not necessarily feeling better but now I'm able to think about why I feel miserable in the first place. Which at times does away with the bad feelings"; or, "I'm still depressed. The Black Dog still sitting next to me. But now I take the dog out for a walk"; or "I never could stand sitting still. Now I quietly talk to myself and try to find what's inside. Instead of running away."

So the ability to think about one's emotional predicament does help alleviate some of the suffering. If anything at all, it offers a different perspective, a meta-perspective, which is an emotion-free zone fit for observing and monitoring the part of the self that so easily gets out of hand. The last questionnaire statement referred to reaching into states of being, to being with oneself, doing one's researches into one's physical and emotional states. If we sit with it long enough there might spring from it understanding, or in Bion's words a "selected fact", a thought that makes sense of it all; like a mother remembering the anniversary of her baby's death some twenty years earlier, an event that will always be inscribed on her canvas of loss, and a realisation that will give her permission to go easy on herself, and to take a break from the demands of a busy life, if only temporarily, in order to commemorate the short life of a human being that she had grown inside her body and mind.

* * *

So far I have explored the search for knowledge (K) in the service of ordinary emotional development. However, from Bion, who worked with very disturbed patients, we know that the mind can attack itself, fall apart, and create a fantasy world that is full of bizarre events and characters. Its currency is not love or peace of mind but emotional torment, hatefulness, the expectancy to be persecuted, and the fear of annihilation. Nothing makes sense. The psychotic mind, instead of being able to process difficult emotions, is engaged in the project of evacuating fragmented emotional matter. It truly is a project of self-ruination and the hateful dissembly of the lives of beloved ones. We are now in the territory of "–K", a term coined by Bion.

The reader, who is by now sitting back comfortably, taking in information about the broken mind, snugly thinking *Madness hasn't got anything to do with me*, will be reminded, by another of Bion's notions, that we are all capable of going mad. In fact, the deepest stratum of our unconscious, so he said, is psychotic. I can assure you we are not talking about full-blown mental illness; it is more the recognition that there are pockets of our being that can be quite mad. For instance, instead of practising loving kindness, we find ourselves giving in to hateful thoughts about other people and the world.

The most popular way of expressing hateful thoughts is through the detour of personal knowledge. If we know another person well then we have enough ammunition to use it against them. Take the other's vulnerability, a favourite entry point of demolishing the other with just a few comments, such as

You have to pull your socks up. You've been mourning that child for long enough. You have to get on with life.

All in the name of well-intended advice from the amateur psychologist. Who was the patient's husband, to not welcome the fact that his wife, Lucy, had started the process of mourning, belated though it was, some twenty years after the event, but in the knowledge that by engaging in healthy mourning she would be able to shift her depression over the loss? And let the baby's soul go, and find liberation.

Another way of stabbing another in thought is to play judge on a person's calamity and thoroughly enjoy it, a pastime the Germans so emphatically call *Schadenfreude*. For instance, George lives in a small house in Oxford, a long way from the splendour of the colleges. He is married, and the father of four small kids. The car plant he has worked in for decades is closing down for economic reasons, wrecking the livelihoods of hundreds of families. His neighbour, leaning over the fence and on a fat pension as a civil servant, having worked under-ground all his life at the Bodleian as a librarian, imparts his wisdom:

> Don't worry, George. You'll find work again. Saw an ad, they're looking for car park attendants at Tesco's. Fabulous choices nowadays. The economy still running smoothly.

George feels stabbed, but puts on a good impression of a smile, which inside curls into a grimace, wishing to punch his neighbour who, he recognises with quiet disdain, continues living in the tunnel of his own small mind but enjoys playing the judge.

Another example of the banality of hateful thought: a professor of literature who doubles as an external reader for an eminent publishing house is asked to pass judgement on a debut novel. Struck by its fresh-ness, innovation, and style, if not the richness of characters, which finds mention in the report in a single barren line, the professor cannot help but nudge the fledgling writer on with some well-meaning comments. Such as:

> There is promise in the debut writer's prose style but it is marred by a plot too complex for the liking of the modern reader who prefers a lightness of touch. The story starts strongly but it peters out after one third. Towards the end the question needs to be asked if the novice writer really has got the writerly talent and promise exhibited in the first few pages which will carry through the whole length of a novel. Maybe he is better suited for the shorter prose form, the novella.

Unbeknown to the novice writer, the external reader's objectivity has been brought to an abrupt halt by a bout of envy vis-à-vis obvious tal-ent, and the nagging memory of his own failure as a novel writer, never having got past the novella stage, forever bound, as he is, to teaching literature rather than writing.

This consortium of hateful thoughts, driven by cynicism, envy, and the sheer joy at having a go at somebody else, is called epistemic vio-lence. You kill by poisonous thought. You dismember by cutting com-ments. Best of all, you hide it in metaphor.

> The downward spiral of poverty you're trapped in leaves you no option but to take on any job.

So continues George's neighbour, if only in thought.

The examples given above are taken from ordinary daily life, which is a matter of concern. Plainly put, violence of thought is not owned by the mad person's mind alone, it is part of all of us. The ubiquity of violent thinking springs from a widespread reluctance to utilise our dreams. As we know, at the root of dreaming lies the process of dream thinking, which is an active process of converting difficult emotions into something more contained and productive. By not engaging with our dreams in waking life we throw away the opportunity to work on overcoming the tyranny of our shameful emotions, such as fear gone out of control, the rebuffal of love, and the reign of hatefulness. As I mentioned earlier, we are sitting on a goldmine and we refuse to mine it, that is, our dream life, which is so generous and productive. But it needs to stay in a mutual relationship with the dreamer, and the dreamer need to be willing to remember dreams, to live by her dreams in waking life, to make dreams the primary source of self-improvement.

Case study: Maria

Maria, a patient of mine, pondered, towards the end of her analysis, how she would sever the ties from the group, which made her sad and thoughtful. Having been in a twice-weekly group for almost seven years, she had made good progress, mainly coming to terms with the violent deaths of two of her brothers, and her ambivalent relationship with her father, who could be loving, humorous, and generous but then suddenly turn violent, creating a menacing and unpredictable atmosphere in the house, and openly taking his fits of rage out on his five sons. What brought his violence into sharp relief was his caring and bohemian side. He would go out to a bookshop and come home with a large box of books that were devoured by the kids. He would break out into infectious laughter and sing Irish songs, setting the tone for shared times of happiness. But always this fire was smouldering.

> Always this energy smolders inside
> when it remains unlit
> the body fills with dense smoke. (Whyte, 1989)

Maria, being the youngest of eight, was not in the direct line of fire but was obviously traumatised, which had taken her a long time to realise.

Typical for sufferers from severe traumatisation, the abuser remains protected by outlandish theories that do not make sense. For instance, Maria had fantasies about her father in which she deified him: he was god-like, if not the son of God, handsome, charismatic, inhabiting the upper regions of human existence, not far from Dante's *paradiso*.

By contrast, toward the end of her analysis, she had converted paradise into purgatory, thinking at times of her father as the mass murderer Fred West, and her parental couple being not unlike the Wests, Fred and Rosemary. The pendulum had swung the other way. One act of internal labour remained, which was to make her deified father and the maligned father land on the ground of reality, making him a real person. His personification went hand in hand with her analyst showing signs of human vulnerability in the face of hateful and abusive treatment by another patient, which Maria picked up on, as the fine needle of a seismograph would.

She had a dream in which a man throws a puppy high up in the air. It crashes on to the tarmac, dying. Another puppy he throws up in the air lands heavily but survives, limping off. Maria wondered what part of her had died off in the presence of her father's violence, relating it to her mastery of being cut-off from other people, and her capacity to have very hateful thoughts, about her own achievements as an academic, and ones of love in close proximity. A memory came up from the depths of her dream. When she was eight years old the children had taken in a stray kitten, which they kept in the garden shed. As soon as her father, who did not like the idea of pets, got wind of it, the kitten disappeared. Everyone in the family knew he must have killed it. But no one dared to say.

She thought the dog that escaped was her getting away from the threat of violence in her family but also, unintentionally, from a working class milieu, this being a mixed bag of proud identity and reminder of intense emotional drama. At the time she had brought in a photograph that showed her in her early twenties, vacant looking, spindly thin. Another patient thought she looked disembodied, *As if your soul has left*. She looked shell-shocked, the trauma of her early life still imprinted.

Engaged with leaving the group, Maria wondered what she had achieved in her analysis. *I feel loved by the group*, she said. To be loved is much more difficult than to love, as it goes right back to the primary relationship with mother, which might, on the one hand, turn out to be a nightmare if mother is unable to engage with the baby, or, on the other, be something resembling ordinary beauty, the good-enough love relation with mother. In Maria's case she was not sure how much her mother had connected with her. It had taken her seven years in individual analysis to establish a not so hateful relationship both with her internal mother and with her real mother. Maria surely was loved in a robust kind of way but the verdict remained open, given that her mother by then, having given birth to her eighth baby, had been running on low batteries of motherhood. In any case, the entire family had welcomed the baby, choosing her name in a shared ritual, no doubt fussing over the new arrival, passing her on from one adoring person to another, before the next episode of violence erupted.

The entry to analysis and the final furlong are significant events. The entry point is like embarking on a marriage with one's internal life, with the purpose of healing, or at least finding some redeeming features in one's attitude towards the suffering in one's life history. In general terms, if we engage with a new project that is meaningful it will bring up dreams that go right back to the beginning of life, to the moment of birth, and to the foundation myth, the actual emotional context of the baby's conception in the parents' minds, which will provide us either with an internal backbone, or with a sense of being ill-equipped for the task ahead. It could turn out to be the dawn of renewal or the dawn of oblivion.

Equally dreams at the caesura of new life will bring to the fore a theme that will accompany the new project; nothing less than the title of the opus to come. The work that will be undertaken is given a name. And in the naming of it, not unlike an act of baptism, it will lose some of the anxiety that surrounds it, and will enter the world of consciousness.

And in the end, when the work is done—which, paradoxically, it never is, as it stretches over a lifetime of self-improvement—it generates dreams about separation and loss, and calls into life an acute phase of mourning, if not the urgent need to come to terms with mortality. Mourning is about the realisation of an absence, and an absence is always a fertile catalyst for thinking.

Bion (1962b) said that a human being's first thought is the "non-breast", which means the baby starts thinking in the absence of the desired object of gratification. Absences as stimulants for thought accompany us throughout our lives. It is as if we drink the strong coffee of an absence, which makes us aware of the lost person, event, or thing's inherent qualities.

Here the thing is, of course, the relational matrix of the group: thinking; laughter; fighting; lucid dreaming; emotional drama; periods of hatefulness and the recovery from them; times of insight, duly forgotten the next session; daftness, playfulness with ideas; humour in the face of adversity; sadness and melancholy moods; embarrassment; the fictions of dreams, some epic, some short fictions; the declaration of love eternal; crazy states of mind, all mixed in with moments of great beauty during which it seemed so possible to be a human being in full flow, simultaneously fabulous and ordinary. Another of my patients, on her last session in the group, summed it up with the words,

> Now I relinquish with regret something so beautiful, so extraordinary, and yet so simple: to be a human being in the presence of others.

In Maria's case, she had a dream at the outset of therapy that was about her eldest brother, Luke, who was a violent man, being part of gangland life, racist, and emotionally unapproachable. He held the firearms of a gang, and, by accident, killed himself whilst handling a gun that had been used in an armed robbery. In the dream she was close to him, even intimate, in sexual embrace. She woke up from it in horror, knowing that she always kept a distance from him, and hated him for being so violent. Over time, from the brotherly dream, image after image peeled off, revealing the likeness of her father and his violence. She thought that his violence and alcoholism had indirectly destroyed the lives of her five brothers. The second-born, a drug dealer, died of a heroin overdose; the third died of the consequences of severe alcoholism; the fourth, again to do with alcoholism, suffered a stroke and became severely disabled; the fifth again succumbed to alcoholism, ending up unemployed, in his sixties still living with his very old mother.

Maria's group initiation dream had set the tone for the work that lay ahead of her, namely to confront the traumatic nature of her family's violence but also her own relationship with destructive impulses and hatefulness, which tended to raise their head at moments of achievements in her work as an academic. She was not able to enjoy the good but was intent on tearing it up in attacks of self envy. A few furlongs into the therapy she had a dream in which Freud showed up telling her

> You have to confront it! The violence and your mortality!

And confront it she did.

At the time when she was preparing to leave the group she had another dream, in which she had an intimate and loving relationship with her second oldest brother, Rob, touching him tenderly on the shoulder. There were sexual undertones but sex was not consummated. Their relationship remained a secret in the family but everybody had a hunch about it. In one dream-frame Maria and Rob were flying to an island in the Hebrides; it was a bumpy flight. Maria was overcome with feelings of love, sadness, and a sense of certainty. Of what, she did not know.

In real life her brother, who had died only two months after the death of his elder brother, Luke, had a gentle nature and Maria and he were able to have a supportive sibling relationship. As a child Rob loved flying, and his passion led him to hanging around pilots who took him up into the sky.

Dream images of birds, birds flying, people flying, and flying planes are usually connected with the movement of the soul. The ancient dreamers assumed that the soul, during sleep and dreaming, is escaping its bodily restraints and wandering into unbounded space up in the skies, touching base with its divine origin. Now Maria, becoming aware of the full extent to which the violence of her family of origin had impacted on her, thought that from an early age her soul had left her bodily self, as could be seen in the photograph that showed her in her early twenties. A soul had been retrieved in the crucible of the group, so that it could return into her bodily self and open her heart. The bumpy flight in the dream would indicate the rough re-entry of the soul into her physical being, which brought back memories of its departure such a long time ago, and its traumatising circumstances. The return of the good always has in its wake the return of the bad.

If you compare Maria's initiation dream with her ending dream it is striking that, initially, she was attracted to forming a relationship with somebody destructive, resembling her father's hatefulness and her identification with her own hateful feelings. The dream with Rob the pilot revealed that, having worked hard at overcoming her own destructive feelings, she was open to the prospect of profound love, to love and be loved in the face of beauty. Beauty is destructiveness overcome.

> Art, if only by implication, bears witness to the world of depression
> or chaos overcome. It would otherwise possess no perennial attrac-
> tion. Calm beauty is nothing without the collapse from which it
> arose: or, rather, it is mere prettiness. (Stokes, 1978)

Maria also had, over the total arch of her analysis, dream after dream in
which she had sexual relations with me, her analyst, which she found
difficult to tell the group about, given that a group always reflects
the internal *and* an audience, not unlike going public with something
deeply embarrassing and shaming. Her sexual omnibus dreams, however, were exactly the entry point she needed in overcoming the broken
heart her father had inflicted on her. She realised that her father loved
her but also that he had become too close to her with his sexual desire.
As a young child she would be allowed into the bedroom, snuggling
up with him when he returned from the night shift for a sleep. In the
grey zone of human relations he had a passionate connection with his
daughter, not acting on it but being caught in something forbidden and
troublesome. It led to his abrupt turning away from her as she entered
early puberty; unable to tolerate his daughter's sexual development
and nascent sexual power, he had recoiled from her.

Maria, who had a tendency to somatise emotional conflict, developed a heart condition that kept her off work for five months. Usually
an ardent runner and known for going for lengthy hikes in the mountains, she was hardly able to get out of bed, take the dog for a walk,
or do household chores, being out of breath, developing scary palpitations, and chest pain. It was an altogether scary situation to be in but
equally perplexing, as the heart specialists were unable to find physical
evidence of her striking symptoms, making her feel like a fraud.

In the group she realised that something had to give. Her body had
created compelling somatic fiction for all but herself to see. She had
been blinded to the fact that she did not follow her heart in what she was
doing. Running around in the long corridors of academia had become
a burden. She had invested too much of her underlying problem of
dissociating from violence and trauma into academia. There was the
lure of rational thought, "were it not that she had bad dreams", to use
Shakespeare's phrase. Academia was a way out, but not the solution.

Hers was the search for knowledge. She loved research into sibling
relations, she loved teaching psychoanalytic theory. Nothing wrong
with that. But Maria felt suffocated by the bureaucracy of university

life, in hot pursuit of funding targets, and blind academic targets such as having to produce a flood of papers every year, losing out on quality and beauty of thought. It is impossible to think when the whip of furious pace is out, unless you are a sprinter. A layer beneath professional life she realised her way of being in everyday life: being emotionally disconnected; doing an impersonation of warmth and connection, but directed by an icy queen; giving in to the triumph of emotional dissociation, even in relation to her husband with whom she had a loving relationship. And just underneath the layer of ice, she found her troubled relationship with her father. Historically, she had to remove herself from a volcanic family constellation, especially her father's threats of violence, and his highly sexed being.

Her physical breakdown, her scary heart condition, had in its wake an emotional breakdown. The body is usually the last domain of sanity and emotional equilibrium. The bodily refuge gone, Maria descended into the frightening waters of her unconscious life as never before, becoming wide open, highly sensitive, and fragile. She now had entered the *Via Crucis,* the path of the cross, if not the *Via Dolorosa,* the path of suffering. Her old defences did not hold. Her strong identification with her searching mind broken, she had become a citizen of "gaga land".

There is nothing wrong with the search for knowledge as such, but, in extremis, it can lead to such a degree of dissociation from one's emotional world that one departs from human connection and belongingness. Not only that. A good intellect with ferocious appetites can easily lead into epistemic violence, meaning that one can easily wipe out another person by hateful and vicious thinking. There is nothing easier; the triumph of a glorious mind. Having climbed the heights of grandiosity, the descent into humanity, connectedness, and belongingness is rather scary.

Her descent into the openness of her broken heart allowed Maria for the first time to actually feel the traumatisation from which she had suffered in her early life. It is a sign of maturation as a human being to develop a "friendship" with one's own being, to borrow an idea from philosopher Hannah Arendt.

Reflecting on the substance of her work undertaken in the group, which was in the presence of other people, she said,

I will miss the thinking together, making sense of things.

And went on to say,

I'm dreaming my life. I'm in life and dreaming. Dreaming is reality.

What she was referring to was, by no means, what we call dreamy states of mind, when we are deranged, sitting in an uncertainty cloud of unknowing, or daydreaming as children, cats, and dogs do so well. There is nothing wrong with unbounded mental states, if not altered states of consciousness. There is always a right time to take a break from the demands of everyday life, to give in to the need for nonsense (Winnicott, 1971), meaning to make no sense of things.

But Maria was referring to something entirely different, which was lucid dreaming, not only being aware of dreaming whilst dreaming proper in the night but dreaming lucidly in the day, making your nocturnal dreams become reality in waking hours. The gift of the dream might be to dream of dogs. She repeatedly dreamt of dogs. In real life a dog lover, her soul being touched by four-legged canine loyalty and adoring eyes, she used the dream symbol of the dog to carry a diversity of meaning, such as dogs being cruelly treated, or dogs turning into a lover (one a German shepherd), or dogs acting like a nightclub bouncer. All in the name of self-understanding.

One aspect of dreams is their language. Dreams play with symbol and metaphor, and it is up to the dreamer to receive the word behind the dream. The group joined in the fun of free association and played with the word "dog". As it turned out, Maria was described as "dogged", not allowing anybody else's opinion to cross hers, holding on to the bone that is her view of the world. Doggedly she had taken the fight to her analyst, who had dared to utter an opinion of his own. Doggedly she had gone into battle with her husband who returned the favour with

Do you want to be happy or right?

Being ruthlessly honest, especially with herself, she described herself as being *dog*matic. In the world of academia she doggedly hung on to her own ideas and her beliefs of what academia is. Of course, being able to hold on to your own opinions is a godsend, but it also a curse, especially if it serves the purpose of defending against emotional content. This came to the surface when she described her father as *A dog of a man*.

His emotional legacy was that he was a man of high sexual tension and coiled up aggression that could erupt at any moment.

Not only should we receive the gift of the dream but we also have to put into practice the actual process of dreaming and make it available in everyday life. We have to remind ourselves that we spring from dream life. Foetuses spend considerable time dreaming. Babies dream themselves into existence. So do we in adult life. This cycle of creating dream fictions and, from it, the fictions of fulfilling waking life, only ends when we engage in the dream fictions of death and dying, which, of course, does not just belong to the final furlong of life. The question, *Why do we dream?* might be answered by *Because we try to come to terms with mortality*, which is a life-long task that helps us to better engage with life and living, the cause of great fear, possibly greater than the fear of death.

The bread-and-butter task of dreaming is the processing of sensory impressions, raw emotions, and scattered thoughts in search of an author in such a way that we are free enough to have a meaningful life. The psychosomatics of dreaming done, we are heading for the higher echelons of lucid dreaming and dream thinking, which we might be able to transfer to the lucidity of waking life. And from the stuff of dreams, that is, symbols, metaphors, and fictions, we make a life around it: becoming the authors of our feelings, thoughts, and actions; being fully in the present; seeing the beauty of the world; and having a sense of belonging to other people and the environment we live in, which is the foundation stone of soul life. We do this so that we do not have to sell our souls to the deities of vulgar and empty temptation, such as giving in to monetary greed, to blind consumerism, and living under the illusion that individual greatness rules over the social and cultural environment that has made us in the first place.

Maria had, with the help of the group, reached into searching for mature love, which entailed the impossibility of love in the face of hatred, but she had also become a conscious dreamer in everyday life, making dreams work for her, which is tantamount to making sense of the world she lives in. She had finally understood *the* dream; the nature of dreams. The sense of certainty in the dream about Rob the pilot, in which love and sadness figured, was about the certainty of love. Once she had moved beyond the emotional dissociation from the family trauma she was open to receive the gift of love. Apart from the approach of death, there is nothing more certain than love. Had Freud not said to her in a dream, "You have to confront it! The violence, and mortality!"?

The substance of the group, as it turns out, lies in the land of the invisible, not visible to external view or scrutiny but only experienced by the individuals who have taken part in the adventure. The poet Rainer Maria Rilke talked of artists as being

> the bees of the invisible. We madly gather the honey of the visible
> to store it in the great golden hive of the invisible. (Rilke, 1947)

There are, of course, yardsticks for the success or failure of the analytic endeavour. On the side of achievement there is the ability to be more able to relate, to curtail one's hatred toward self and others, to do the chores of everyday life gladly, not to take one's own bad moods out on vulnerable people, to be able to forgive one's destructive inclinations, offering friendship, not condemnation, and to engage with a task in life that is productive and serves other people—Sartre's "fundamental human project". Not to forget finding replacement strategies for the triumph of hatefulness and violence that is loving kindness. The list is long, and takes a lifetime to achieve.

Last thoughts. The "bees of the invisible" in the group are also engaged in something entirely different that goes beyond the hard graft of self-improvement on the emotional level. It reaches into the spiritual, into aesthetic experience, and the life of the soul. As we enter what Einstein called "we-consciousness" (see Chapter Three) we realise how pathetically small a view is governed by the demands of the ego and of narcissistic self-enclosure. It is only in the experience of "infinite connectivity" with humankind, and universal love, that we gain full freedom from the tyranny of tormenting emotion.

The search for beauty

So far we have seen that dreams help us to come to terms with our primitive emotions, such as aggression and fear, and elevate them to a higher level of mental functioning, if we are willing to put the work in. One could say that dreams are born out of fear: the fear of mortality, the fear of insanity, and the fear of separateness. We dream ourselves into life as it were, into mental health, and into the domain of relatedness, in order to set counterpoints to existential forms of fear.

The fear of mortality, once worked upon, still remains a lifelong companion but it will change our outlook on how to live a more fulfilling life. The fear of insanity, once recognised in its ubiquity, will make us see with the sharp eye of Bion that, deep down, we all are capable of falling apart, giving in to disintegration and undifferentiatedness, and from the chaos of the mind we might land again on the solid ground of reality. The realisation of our existential separateness, without a sense of the possibility of its redemption through the union with another, is terrifying. Thus, on the way to becoming a more rounded human being we have to face up to the demands of mature love, which, in part, alleviates our fear of separateness but piles on us another dilemma: once engaged in a meaningful and equal relationship, we experience the devastation of love; we will be changed forever, which goes against the grain of habit, as it is part of the human condition that we do not want change. Having negotiated the perilous currents of relatedness we might become open to the beauty of the world.

We cannot live without beauty, which is a bizarre statement because beauty does not feed us nor does it offer a flesh and blood relationship, nor does it figure in bank accounts of material affluence. It belongs to the world of the invisible. As do thoughts, ideas, images, symbols, metaphors, and dreams, for that matter. Beauty feeds the soul. Enzo Ferrari said that "before I became Ferrari I've dreamt of being Ferrari". So from the world of the invisible he became the maker of beauty and reality. Primo Levi, Italian writer and holocaust survivor, thought it was arbitrary that he had survived the concentration camp, but he remembered that during periods of great humiliation and the fear of dying he had fantasies about what might lie ahead if he were to survive. He never believed he would make it, but something like a dream had taken hold of his mind: the desire to become a writer, and, by writing, being able to tell the world about the atrocities in the camp; a dream that, unbelievably, became reality. However, he never really recovered from the dehumanisation he and others were subjected to, suffering from debilitating spells of depression, and in old age he took his own life in an act of defiance against the sinister forces that had already destroyed part of his humanity. As it was, for a few decades after the war he had lived his dream, a beauty he had created in the midst of utter destruction (Thomson, 2002).

* * *

Let us make the distinction between internal and external beauty. The distinction does not hold up to close scrutiny but is useful for our enquiry for the time being. What we can say for certain is that the experience of external beauty is as important as the apprehension of internal beauty.

We love the beauty of nature: stunning vistas from alpine mountain tops; the calming and redemptive proximity of the sea; the rugged mountain areas of Crete blessed by pines, meandering kri-kri goats, and olive trees with fossilised trunks; the sacred red rocks of Ayres Rock, called Uluru by the Aborigines, in the Australian outback; the views from an aircraft high above the clouds; the starry heavens at night-time that make us think of other galaxies and the infinity of space. The list is long.

* * *

My habit of making lists of things is similar to one of Umberto Eco's favourite occupations. He is an Italian semiotician, philosopher, and mediavalist. In *The Infinity of Lists* (2009), he talks about the dizzying sense that open lists engender in us because of their sense of infinity. The idea of catalogues has been around since the beginning of human culture. "A culture prefers enclosed, stable forms when it is sure of its own identity, whereas when faced with a jumbled accumulation of ill-defined phenomena, it starts making lists," Eco says, which means that we make lists in an attempt to create a semblance of order in a chaotic and complicated world. Eco distinguishes between the poetics of "everything included" and the poetics of the "et cetera". Even a shopping list, at first sight finite, might in its intention be the poetics of the ordinary "et cetera", depending on the level of starvation. Famously closed lists are in the *Iliad* where Homer lists, ship by ship, an armada about to go into battle. James Joyce in the penultimate chapter of *Ulysses* draws up a list of things contained in the drawer of Leopold Bloom's kitchen.

One such "et cetera" catalogue that makes one's head spin are dreams. There is no such thing as a single dream. Every dream is connected with a previous one which is connected to a previous one. In short, from the present to the past, to early family history, to intra-uterine life, to the family history of previous generations, to the precipitate of cultural identity and history, and right back to the history of humankind. *Voilà.* Yet another list. Not to forget the futures expressed in dreams, the life that lies ahead, what the ancient dreamers called prophetic dreams.

And, if we look bravely ahead, even past our own death, we will be the stuff of dreams in the minds of people, still alive, and touched upon by us during our shared lifetime.

So the catalogue of the dreams of a lifetime, accumulated over some 50,000 hours of dreaming, is never a closed list. To use the Italian title of Eco's book, *La Vertigine della Lista,* the catalogues of dreams truly are vertiginous. In the knowledge of the interconnectivity of dreams, if we try to understand one single dream, draw it out of the murky waters of unknowing, we will be able to understand all of our dreams, and therefore our psychic, social, and historical insertion in this world. One dream saved from oblivion means that we have saved the whole humanity of dreams.

* * *

Returning from the detour to make sense of lists, we are still pondering aspects of external beauty. We have talked about nature's beauty. Dreams draw up internal landscapes of staggering beauty, mixed in with locations of haunting ugliness, modelled on the natural world in which we live. The inner landscapes of dreams reveal the spatiality of the psyche: we either live in open spaces when we are in touch with love and beauty, or we head straight for an enclosed space, a claustrum, if in the grasp of depression, recovering from traumatisation, or giving in to epistemic violence.

We are also drawn to the beauty of animals. Our aesthetic experience of them is always connected with their ability to unashamedly be themselves, without judgement, always close to something that tends to elude us, namely being fully immersed in the ontology of the present, that is, being rather than doing, a state from which we emerge at the caesura of birth. So we end up going through life climbing the steep hillsides of the illusion that doing things, soldiering on, always paying tribute to the minor deity of activity, is the panacea for life's demands. In its extreme form, we end up in the cul-de-sac of thoughtless careerism and greedy materialism, making money for money's sake, in tandem with amnesia about the fact that we might be driven to high performance by an underlying trauma, an impoverishment of sorts, or an affliction of the soul.

Dreams, being the arbiters of truthfulness, come upon us with images of animals. First, to remind us of an imbalanced life, so we might rein in activity for activity's sake, and also give in to states of contemplation, seeking peace and quiet. The answer lies in finding the right balance between being and doing. Animal dreams seem to precisely point out this dilemma. There is an economy to being: you hunt when hungry, then you rest. Also, the beauty of animals lies in their instinctual nature, so we are reminded of our own origin in the caves of prehistory. And animal dreams show us another aspect of beauty, which is power (see Chapter Four).

The principal exponents of external beauty are the fine arts: music, dance, poetry, prose, painting, sculpture, and architecture. In the contemplation and experience of the fine arts we are never far away from its source, its origins in terms of its underlying ideas and its process of realisation. In the chapter on the fictions of dreams (Chapter Two) I made the point that the creative processes behind writing are dream states, as can be seen in Kafka's fictions. It is my view that everything we see manifested in the visible world of the fine arts has its origins in the world of the invisible, which is the dream world. Dreams are inspirational and at the root of the creative process, be it the realisation of a piece of art or scientific discovery.

* * *

We are now talking about internal experiences of that which is beautiful. Nelson Mandela referred in his inauguration speech to what internal beauty is, borrowing a quote from Marianne Williamson's *A Return to Love*:

> Our deepest fear is not that we are inadequate. Our deepest fear is that we are powerful beyond measure. It is our light, not our darkness, that most frightens us. We ask ourselves, who am I to be brilliant, gorgeous, talented, fabulous? Actually, who are you not to be? You are a child of God. Your playing small doesn't serve the world. There is nothing enlightening about shrinking so that other people won't feel insecure around you. We are all meant to shine, as children do. We are born to manifest the glory of God that is within us. It's not just in some of us; it's in everyone. And as we let own light shine, we unconsciously give other people permission to do the same. As we're liberated from our own fear, our presence automatically liberates others. (Williamson, 1992, p. 90)

In the chapter on hate (Chapter Four) I made the point that there is one fundamental flaw in the human condition, which is the paradox that we tend to recoil from good experiences, as if we cannot tolerate something good and beautiful, as if we don't deserve it. Worse still, under the rule of envy, we tend to attack the good and beautiful. We are capable of tearing to pieces the prospect of love, achievements in professional life, peace of mind, a stunning birthday cake, or a present given from the heart. In the main, if we give in to envy we attack the beautiful. The attributes of internal beauty are truthfulness, consciousness, and meaning.

* * *

Rilke and Lou Andreas Salomé

> For beauty is nothing but the beginning of Terror we're still just able to bear and why we admire it so is because it serenely disdains to destroy us. (Rilke, 1957, p. 629)

Why should beauty be unbearable? For Rilke this was the case. Aged twenty-one he was in love with Lou Andreas Salomé, fifteen years his senior, a Russian noble woman of German descent, a psychoanalyst and known writer, living in Berlin, and, to make matters worse for young Rilke, she was a very attractive woman. She entertained friendships with some of the most distinguished thinkers at the time, among them Nietzsche and Freud. Nietzsche, desperately in love with her, suffered a breakdown after she refused his intrusive and inflated attentions, and two rebuffed marriage proposals. His family duly responded by blaming her for the philosopher's descent into insanity. After he had overcome his chagrin Nietzsche wrote one of his masterpieces, *Thus Spoke Zarathustra* (1883), inspired by the loss of his muse (Hollingdale, 1969, p. 20).

Having established herself as a writer, on hearing about the new craze in Vienna—that is, psychoanalysis—Salomé decided simply to show up on Freud's doorstep in the Berggasse. *Me voilà*. She was taken into the family, and joined the famous men-only seminar group on a Wednesday night. The men were duly impressed by the sharpness of her mind, if not by the Freudian undercurrents of desire she engendered. She qualified as an analyst in the shortest time possible, between

1912 and 1913, following combative debates with the men, and lengthy walks with Freud, not to mention indulging in *Kaffee mit Schlagobers und Sacher Torte* provided by Martha, Freud's wife, as they discussed patient work and theories. Nowadays it would take a trainee a good decade to qualify as a psychoanalyst, not to mention the question of professional boundaries; Freud cut short her training and elevated her to a well-deserved status amongst equals, quickly recognising her talent for understanding the human condition. She had become the first woman psychoanalyst in history.

Lou Andreas Salomé was married to a professor of linguistics, though the marriage remained unconsummated. She openly had affairs with a number of eminent men, such as Rilke. She was not very flattering about his early poetic work, which spurned him on to take his art to a higher level. On her instigation he also changed his first name from René to Rainer, which she thought sounded more masculine, forceful, and Germanic. They undertook two extensive excursions to Russia, one with her husband in tow. When, after some three years, she ended the relationship with Rilke, saying that "the passion was over", he used the loss of his great love to good effect, taking his art to the high altitude of poetic facility. His muse, now in absentia, inspired him to his first great masterpiece, the *Duino Elegies*, followed by another masterpiece, *Sonnets to Orpheus*. Rilke and Andreas Salomé remained friends up until the end of his life, when he was only fifty-two (Leppmann, 1984, pp. 57–91).

Maybe unsurprisingly for a man in his early twenties, Rilke was in awe of this beautiful, confident, and rebellious woman who broke a range of taboos for a woman of her time, setting the tone for women to emerge from the enclosure of male repression.

Let us go back to the beginning of this section, when we questioned why beauty should be so unbearable. Why bring up the Rilke–Andreas Salomé story? As a woman, she had it all: she was strikingly beautiful, in control of her romantic life, and she had found, first one fundamental project in life, her writing, and then another, psychoanalysis. She was unafraid in the pursuit of her destiny. She did not play small. But also, in her relationships, she remained committed to the people she cared for. She remained Rilke's confidante, friend, and muse throughout his life, even after he married the sculptor Clara Westhoff. Her marriage with Friedrich Carl Andreas continued for over forty-three years. As it was, they became very close towards the end of his life, a fact Freud, in one of his numerous letters to his outpost in Berlin, was very pleased about. Her life-long connection with Freud endangered her life when the Gestapo started to hassle her over her practicing the "Jewish science", confiscating her library just a few days before she died in 1937. As we know, those who destroy books go on to destroy people.

Young Rilke found Andreas Salomé's beauty as a woman almost unbearable. "For beauty is nothing but the beginning of terror we're still just able to bear", as he says. Beauty is not unlike love in its devastating impact on the psyche. No doubt Andreas Salomé was also physically attracted to this troubled and handsome young man. If we move from the physical to the interior, in terms of beauty, Rilke was stunned by her human qualities. She lived her dream, and she engaged in lucid dreaming in everything that she did. She engaged in the art of living by consistently challenging herself and others, along the lines of beauty, whose attributes are truthfulness, consciousness, and meaning. Without her aesthetic impact on his life Rilke would have stayed a minor poet, surely forgotten by now.

The "will to power"

The "will to power" is a concept that Nietzsche elevated to being the main driving force in humans. In his view, the "will to power", *der Wille zur Macht*, has to do with achievement, ambition, and the striving to attain the highest possible position in life. His concept is closely linked with sublimation and what he called "self-overcoming", which is the conscious chanelling of a raw force of nature, *Kraft*, for creative purposes. Nietzsche first coined the phrase "*Wille zur Macht*" in *Thus Spoke Zarathustra* (Nietzsche, 1883, p. 138).

The borrowed term "will to power" has at once philosophical, psychological, and psychosocial implications. At a base level it is about the intentional, willful engagement with the human project of self-improvement, giving one's life a purposeful shape, such as the overcoming of adversity and physical disability, not giving in to setbacks, rising again from the unmade bed of depressive bouts; seeing financial bankruptcy as a starting point for renewal; and seeing loss as an ultimate gain, in short using the "will to power" as a resource for the overcoming of impasse, and the demands life makes on us, without going under.

But the engagement with the "will to power" also extends into the much wider conception of the social world we live in. We cannot touch upon happiness and contentment in life without giving it all to a "fundamental human project", in Sartre's sense. To be immersed in a fundamental human endeavour is to move in the stream of social life, a purposeful movement, beyond individual identity, with its intention of making a contribution to the lives of other people.

Typical dream narratives linked with the theme of power are sexual dreams, dreams about wounded masculinity or wounded femininity, and dreams that are about the separation from identifications of being the ill one, the self-hating individual, or the one forever bound to debilitating fear and anxiety. The theme of power emerges through images, symbols, metaphors, and fictions, making this demand on the dreamer: to wake up to the urge of living a life more in keeping with power, authority, achievement, and affluence. Not infrequently dreams associated with the search for power are populated with powerful animals but also with mythological figures such as solar and lunar deities, and representations of light and the luminous.

The emergence of power animals in dreams takes its starting point in human suffering, during times of great crisis. They form a counterpoint to suffering, offering choice, a different outlook, a different perspective. It is safe to say that along the path of suffering, the *Via Dolorosa*, healing powers might arise, the possibility of a different life. The consortium of power animals will fortify and enrich internal life, so that from a position of increased internal solidity and grounding in life futures can be built that move beyond the tyranny of unbearable emotion.

Dreams are generous, they give us the gift of a black panther hidden in the dark of night, a tiger on the prowl, a white lioness lazing by a king's throne, a shark showing its splendid teeth, a female elephant, the matriarch of her herd, a crocodile hovering just underneath the water line, eying up prey. The sheer beauty of such animals lies in their power, giving the dreamer permission to think about finding her own sense of power, getting up from the bed of depression, standing up to domestic violence, or confronting a bullying boss.

Animal dreams also figure in the mental rehearsal techniques of athletes. David Hemery, the ex-sprint hurdler who won an Olympic gold medal and held the world record, always imagined being a greyhound, an image he had taken from his dream life. Roger Bannister, the first sub-four-minute-mile runner, imagined being both a lion and a gazelle. They both need to run—the lion to catch the gazelle, the gazelle to outrun the lion. He had fortified himself for both occasions: staying in front, or, if in a calamity such as being caught by an opponent, to come from behind. Again his mental rehearsal technique originated from dream images that had become solid reality. During races he had become the lion chasing prey, or the gazelle running for dear life into the history books of athletics.

Ted Hughes' animal consorts

Literature, especially poetry, is populated with symbols and metaphors of power animals, evoking and conceptualising the "will to power" in the Nietzschean sense. Ted Hughes thought that the origins of his creative life as a poet started with a single early poem that determined what was to come, or in his words, it was "a compact index of everything to follow" (Bate, 2015, p. 93); not unlike a series of dreams that originate in a signature dream when, in a single moment, the door of perception opens and lets the future in. "The Thought-Fox", written in 1955, was Hughes' signature poem and, being a writer drawing inspiration from a vivid dream life, the symbol of the fox sprang directly from a dream. During his student years in Cambridge, as he tried to write yet another essay but, in a biting cold night, was left with an empty page, he dozed off and on waking up found himself in the company of a burnt fox, "a sudden sharp hot stink of fox", a wounded fox, the dream so vivid and visceral he looked for blood marks on the empty page (Hughes, 2003, p. 21). In the dream the burnt fox had said "Stop this—you are destroying us", a dream narrative that had lasting consequences (Bate, 2015, p. 76).

Following the dream, Hughes decided to abandon his studies in English literature, which paved the way for his full commitment to poetry. His primary marriage was always to the art, always to poetry. A poet was born through a power animal, though a wounded one, wounded by the rigour of academia; but the wounded fox also stood for and anticipated his own vulnerabilities as a person. He had realised that he was well able to produce impressive essays of literary criticism, always tempted to dismantle a text, mindful of his own sadistic impulses, but it meant that his creative work was stifled. His art, he realised, came from another place, not from his sharp mind but from his life-long immersion in nature, going back to his Yorkshire roots, the outdoors, fishing and hunting, and his internal companions, the world of dreams, astrological symbolism, Jungian mythology, and the magical.

In a single dream he had found his foundation myth. It is a reminder of Freud's signature dream of "Irma's injection", a programme dream that was the foundation stone for his self analysis and the discipline of psychoanalysis, setting the tone for all later developing theories (Anzieu, 1986).

However, "The Thought-Fox" did not stand on its own. Two consort poems, written during the same formative period, also lived on animal symbolism. In "The Hawk in the Rain", the title poem of his first acclaimed poetry collection published in 1957, the hawk hangs in the air, seemingly effortlessly, and with the sharp eye of the predator oversees the world beneath, as if "his wings hold all creation in a weightless quiet" (Hughes, 2003, p. 19). The hawk hovering, watching from high above, gave expression to Hughes' ability to stay coldly detached from emotionally charged and explosive images that preoccupied his poetic mind. Deep down he remained affected by his father's depressive moods stemming from war traumatisation. A self-revelatory, confessionalist poet he was not. Only in his mature work, foremost in his late farewell to Sylvia Plath in Birthday Letters in 1998, did he abandon his clinical attitude towards the personal, intimate, and autobiographical aspects of poetry. The symbol of the hawk, taken from the perspective of ancient dreamers, stands for the retrieval of the soul and the emergence of soul life. By turning away from the constraints of academia he had found his own territory, up in the skies shared with his hawk, and in mythical amplification of the hawk he found Uranus, the Greek sky god, ruler of emotional detachment, conceptualisation of reality, and higher principles that govern the world. Uranus, in the guise of the hawk, became apparent in the emotional restraint he put on himself following the suicide of Sylvia Plath and the ensuing attacks on his personal integrity. He waited for over thirty-five years, approaching his death, to give a very private poetic answer to all his critics in the public domain.

The third of Hughes' formative poems, in the eyes of his "unauthorised" biographer, Jonathan Bate, the signature poem, which was "a compact index of everything to follow" (2015, p. 94), was "The Jaguar" written in 1955. The jaguar, despite being caged, remained wild and free, no space big enough to contain the beautiful beast's unbroken will to prowl, hunt, and devour. "The world rolls under the long thrust of his heel" (Hughes, 2003, p. 19).

Hughes' cage was conventional life, the bounds of marriage, and the poetic convention he was up against as a modernist writer. The jaguar prowls in his carnal bodily self, in his dreams and vivid imagination. His is a dark and dangerous charisma, as if Eros has given him no choice but to act as his ambassador, moving from one sexual relationship to another, giving in to his vulnerability towards women. The stability of marriage was always pitted against female muse figures, the two worlds never really finding a unison of purpose, except during the period of the early Plath–Hughes relationship. The jaguar in Hughes wounded women but *he* remained wounded by his own folly of promiscuity, a sexual appetite that could never be satisfied. But it was not all about his base carnal self and his prey: vagina, sex, and gratification. He was seeking more than that. His search was also a writerly one, one of poetic inspiration, if not spiritual contemplation, and what he pursued was an *image* of woman, the deepest of which he found in the presence of Sylvia Plath, calling her the "White Muse". The jaguar had anticipated and unleashed his love for women and the transformative role they were always to play.

Plath saw him as the panther, the predator; she was his prey. The moment Ted Hughes and Sylvia Plath set eyes on each other at a party in Cambridge in 1956 both their lives were be changed forever, the animal attraction so strong that she had bitten him in loving embrace. In her poem "Pursuit" Plath gives in to youthful idealisation, describing Hughes as a panther on the prowl, stalking her, his sexual appetite so huge it ignited her own flames of passion, and yet, she says, prophetically, "One day I'll have my death of him" (Bate, 2015, p. 105). Not that he literally killed her, but her experience of him upped the stakes between the forces of life and death inside her, all wide open and raw, giving in to the devastation of love and its companion experience of being changed for good. And as she was able to endure mature love in the service of her art, she was given more to endure, and then lost the strongest anchor and artistic muse in her life, giving rise to memories of the loss of her father and her eventual collapse into the terror of her mental illness.

The internal consortium of fox, hawk, jaguar, and panther, not forgetting Plath as mentor and catalyst of his poetic craft, led Hughes into his ascendancy as a poet, finding the power that culminated in the publication of his first poetry collection in 1957, *The Hawk in the Rain*, published by Faber & Faber. Power animals in poetry and dreams initiated him into his "will to power". At the start of their relationship it was Plath who was published, an award-winning American poet. It was she who opened not only his floodgates of passion but also his belief in himself. In return, Hughes, kind and protective towards her work, paid close attention to her development as a poet initially technically accomplished but without emotional power. In his containing presence she overcame frequent writing blocks, dark moods, and psychotic emotional states, becoming by way of the *Via Dolorosa*, the path of suffering, a powerful, passionate writer, always on the verge of slipping into the abyss of her illness, the daemons of darkness, her hatefulness of life, and obsession with death and dying. Paradoxically, being so drawn to the dark, she also had a deep appreciation of beauty and a joy for life. She had carved out a life of reaching into the light of marriage, motherhood, and poetry from the forces of darkness.

Crow (1970), written following the suicides of both Sylvia Plath in 1962 and Assia Wevill in 1969, is possibly Hughes' masterpiece. He had to accept and digest, as a person but also as a poet, the human character trait that is the most difficult of all human fault-lines to declare, namely destructiveness. It is a huge blow for anybody to lose not just one but two life partners to mental illness and self obliteration. It left him bruised, despairing, and enraged but also made him think about his own tendency to destructiveness in the shape of promiscuity, giving rise to an all too familiar archetype of the "daemonic husband". In the poetry collection Crow, the protagonist, is given unbridled reign over the daemonic side of the human condition, as if evil were the reigning principle of the world. Crow outwits, dismisses, and defeats Death, Love, God, and his Creation, in a litany of destruction and a triumph of contempt. But Hughes' poetic statement about the human condition— that we are capable of anything—also had in its wake the apprehension of the overcoming of human destruction, and with it the attainment of beauty and the ethical sense.

Birthday Letters, published in 1998, only seven months before his death, bear witness to his personal and poetic recovery. It is testament to the redemptive force of mourning the loss of his most fertile muse, the "White Muse" of his early writerly life. It shows the passion, love, and creativity that marked the intense and passionate six years he and Plath spent together in an unprecedented artistic collaboration and intimate relationship. From death to death we go, rounded with a life.

* * *

Case study: Stephanie

Stephanie, one of my patients, who had lost her father aged five and grew up with a severely disturbed mother had her first great moment of self-realisation a few years into her analysis. *I love hating myself*, she announced out of the blue, as if pleased with herself. A terrible beauty was born. She had just realised that she tends to spoil her experience of good things in life.

In the privacy of my mind her moment of truth sounded more like popping a bottle of champagne. There are moments in a patient's hard work that are in need of appreciation, if not celebration. To be able to recognise that one is inflicting harm on oneself by hateful thoughts is a big step towards recovery and the development of the ethical sense. You cannot even begin to love yourself if you are deluded about the fact of self-hatred.

Stephanie's realisation of *I love hating myself* did not come out of the blue. It came from the script of a dream that fell into her willingness to learn about herself. In the dream she has the urge to go into a cathedral and there is drawn to step close to the sarcophagus of an ancient king, who might have been medieval. She touches the cold white marble, which shows signs of minute engravings, possibly done by visitors over hundreds of years. There she finds an inscription written in the very hand of the dormant king: "My child, let go of your self-loathing".

That made me think, that really made me think what I'm doing to myself,

Stephanie said. She was thinking about her mothering skills. Having recovered from an acute phase of breakdown she put everything into reconnecting with her children who were at first stroppy, but quickly forgiving, as children can be. But Stephanie never knew if she was doing the right thing, repeatedly checking in with me as if I were supernan, and heavily laying into herself for making mistakes, forgetting on the way that parenting, like analytic work, is an ongoing exercise in managing failure, if only in part. From her new perspective of hating herself she read through the pages of her book of life and saw it with different eyes.

When she first started analysis Stephanie was hardly able to get out of bed, giving in to depression, neglecting herself physically, not being able to look after her three young children, who were taken care of by her husband. When I said that she was going through a breakdown she was puzzled by what I meant but cottoned on to the idea that she was very ill. In fear of retaliation, none of her friends, nor her husband, were able to feed back to her what was obvious.

As time moved on from her rough beginnings she had a dream in which she is one of a twin. One of them is shy, withdrawn, in awe of and frightened by the other who casually rips open her chest to take her heart out and eat it. As she is lying in a pool of blood her twin sister gives her milk to drink, which she spits out, and it erupts in a fountain of milk. The white of the milk and the red blood mix, turning her white dress pink.

Stephanie quickly rushed into the territory of the dream, saying that she had always hated drinking milk, giving a plausible impression of being disgusted but not knowing from where her aversion stemmed. Then she remembered that her mother had always referred to her as a twin when she was a child, treating her only child as a confidante. *We are one, aren't we?* Stephanie thought this bizarre but not surprising. There was a pay-off in being the twin, the two of them laughing in unison at the expense of others. *Devilish laughter*, she went on to say, looking concerned. When pressed about the pink dress, she replied without hesitation

That's the dress I wore when my mother was hospitalised. I've got a photograph of it. I was two years old.

Her mother had to be hospitalised following a psychotic episode during which she tried to kill Stephanie, throwing her against a wall and kicking her whilst she was lying on the ground bleeding. Her father had intervened just in time. Only hours before the tragic event a family friend had taken a photograph of the three of them posing as a happy family in the small garden of their semi-detached house. On the insistence of her father, both mother and daughter went into a psychiatric observation unit where her mother, under close scrutiny, was taught how to relate to her daughter without inflicting harm on her.

The treatment programme turned out to be successful, on the level of curtailing actual physical harm, but did not protect young Stephanie from her mother's hateful thinking, lingering threats, and outbursts of rage.

Back now to the organising ideas of Stephanie's dream life. The fictions of her dreams were written by the search for beauty, with its attributes of truthfulness, consciousness, and meaning. In the course of her treatment she worked herself out of the abyss of her mother's severe mental illness towards finding her own beauty in life, her own human idiom. To be living with and growing up alongside a disturbed mother quite literally means for the child to be living in her mother's mind, which is like a claustrum, a confined space without an exit route. It is a hateful and frightening place and also means that what remains of the child's own personality is intruded upon, violated, and taken possession of by her mother's invasive mind, which, instead of relating, offloads her own sinister and unwanted stuff into her child's nascent psyche.

Her dreams relentlessly reminded Stephanie of the truths she had shied away from all her life, but she remained depressed and paralysed, unable to engage with life. The first realisation was that her mother was the mad one, not herself. Her mother had *made* her mad, a notion that was brandished by her mother, especially during Stephanie's teens when she started to stand up for herself and get into rows with her mother. It came as a relief to change her perspective on herself. *I've been suffering but I'm not mad.*

Bion said that truth is the nourishment of the mind and lies its poison. Stephanie had the habit, from the outset of treatment, of saying *I like that!* whenever I was making any comment about what was going on, simple remarks, commonplace statements, never reaching the glorious heights of interpretation: as if thanking me, as if bowing her head in prayer. *I like that.* When she reflected on what she was doing she said, *I like your small morsels of truth,* which was tantamount to saying that she had been starved of any positive reflection.

The actual human catastrophe is what happens to love. Her mother, the twin, ripping her heart out and eating it had been a recurring theme in Stephanie's dreams since her teenage years. But it had never been open to understanding. She had to work through layer upon layer of ordinary human development. With her father dying when she was five and her mother sunk in a narcissistic personality disorder she had

no chance of ordinary maturation. Stephanie had to shed the legacy of
her mother hatefully attacking her beauty, her capacity to love, and her
aliveness as a child. The daemon of her mother's envy had to be kept
at bay.

This mockery of what were her best assets had led to Stephanie hating herself from early on, without her being aware of it. The first champagne moment of her therapy occurred exactly in that territory of her
mind—*I love hating myself!*—when truthfulness had become her internal consort, setting the tone for other realisations, for instance, that she
could be very hateful to other people. And that included her children.
Beauty is destructiveness overcome.

After giving due understanding to her own hatefulness she became
more open to matters of the heart, such as sensing for the first time that
her husband loved her. He stuck by her during her breakdown and her
subsequent, limp attempt to find a solution to her internal conflict by
going off with another man.

Stephanie always referred to me, her analyst, as a loving father, needing to idealise me. By doing so she made her father spring to life in the
consulting room. She now understood the marble king of the dream to
be her father, risen from the dead and become a flesh-and-blood being.
Instead of glorifying him, she now had a real person sitting alongside
her in the consulting room and with relish she began to take in the good
stuff of fatherly compassion, famously complimenting my morsels of
truth with *I like that*, but still making demands on a father she could not
have. In the process of making her father a person, rather than hanging
on to fantasy, she had another champagne moment, this time of pure
beauty. *I really think my father loved me!* The realisation that a significant
other loves us is possibly the most difficult form of love to be attained,
more difficult than loving an other, or the love of self, or universal love.
Raymond Carver put it succinctly in "Late Fragment" when contemplating what might be the most important experience in one's lifetime:
"To feel myself beloved on this earth" (Carver, 2009).

Not only that. She had a number of dreams in which her father, in
real life a womanising entrepreneur, picks her up in his open-top sports
car and takes her to the seaside, where they swim together and sit on
the beach nattering. He is keen to get to know her husband and her
children, he confesses. In the face of depression she had not been able
to mourn the death of her father. Depression is an antidote to healthy
mourning. And mourning is the slow process of defrosting glacial

states of mind. Forever clinging on to the idea of the dead father, she had forgotten how alive and loving he had been. Her hatefulness had not helped. You cannot mourn properly if in your mind you have killed off the loved one.

Her mother, not surprisingly, also did her best to wipe out her late husband and, therefore, rubbish the profound, if periodic, connection between father and daughter, not facilitating Stephanie's grieving process at the time. Now the multi-temporal nature of dreams that walk easily on the timeline of past, present, and future brought her one dream after another in which her father talked to her, urging her to get up from the sick bed, to enjoy motherhood, and find herself a job. In one of the dreams he is holding her lower back with his right hand. In fact, she had developed chronic back problems from her teens, which now seemed to relent.

As her internal life grew to incorporate a connection with her father, she was more able to endure the notion that her mother did not love her. That her mother had hated her, that she had tried to kill her as an infant, was difficult enough. But that her mother was unable to love her was the actual human catastrophe. The dream in which her mother had ripped out her heart and eaten it now made more sense.

Stephanie had a heart devoured, a heart taken from her, an absent heart, a part of her that she frequently described as her coldness, her cruel and triumphant emotional dissociation. In a dream at the time she sees a small bird of beautiful plumage—it might be a goldfinch—flying towards her as she is standing by the marble sarcophagus of the old king. Unlike in previous dreams the king turns into an ordinary man on his deathbed, breathing the bad breath of dying. The bird perched at the headboard of the bed chirps away and then flies straight into her body in the area if the solar plexus, making her glow and feel warm inside.

There are ancient shamanic traditions that understand the onset of mental affliction as an expulsion of the soul from its bodily host (Ellenberger, 1970). In this ancient disease theory the healing up of the afflicted person lies in soul retrieval, meaning the shaman performs rituals that will help the soul return back into the body. There are modern forms of treatment for severe traumatisation, such as energy psychology (Mollon, 2008), that work on the energetic level of the body, with the intention of releasing the traumatic imprint from the body's subtle system, so that the soul of the person might return to its primary home, the bodily self.

Ancient dreamers thought that during dreaming the soul goes on a journey away from the body, not being comfortable, at the best of times, being tied to a body, and returns when daylight strikes. Birds, in ancient cosmology, were seen as the symbol of the soul, able to fly from the world of the body to the dream body, and explore the nightly freedom of soul life, bringing back from its journey divine messages, if not prophecies.

Stephanie had a sense of being more whole. Her soul had returned home. She is now "having a father"—*habemus papam*—albeit dead but not gone, an internal father who helps her out with finding self-love and repairing her broken heart. The more confident she grew the more she was able to sort things out with her internalised father, taking him to court over his human fault-lines; such as getting angry with him for letting down her mother, going off with other women, not protecting her enough from the madness of her mother, and only spending time with her as a child when his amorous timetable would allow.

I guess now he is having it off with angels. The bastard!

But always we return to mother. The final furlong belongs to the maternal. Always the need to link the beginning with the end. Freud, who had the good fortune of a feisty mother who firmly believed in him and his talents, always returned to her right into his late adult years. Freud was born with a caul, which, in the Jewish tradition, imbues the new arrival with magical properties, as if to say, "Your son is born for great things to come". This was a notion his mother fully believed in. Even when *der Herr Professor* had established himself and his brain-child, psychoanalysis, as an influential cultural force in the 1920s and 1930s, was comfortably set up in private practice in Vienna's bourgeois Berggasse, and had a family life with wife Martha, her sister, and five kids, he visited his mother every Sunday afternoon for *Kaffee und Kuchen*, to pay homage to his roots and solid anchor in life (Clark, 1982).

So why do we return to mother? The search for mother is a return to our first dwelling. It is where we come from. We spring from mother's body and mind. Not only that. The biology of foetal development gives us the staggering detail that, in the formation of the genders, we all start out in a female shape. Ancient mythology starts off with matriarchal goddesses before any of the patriarchal gods are anywhere to be seen. The French painter, Gustave Courbet, in 1866, painted a woman lying naked on her back displaying her vagina, calling it "the origin of the world", *l'origine du monde.*

Not surprisingly, towards the end of any long-term analysis the patient returns to the primary relationship. To the beginning of life. More so, the return is an attempt to link the beginning with the end, to intervene in the script of life that is determined by a birth, a life dreamt into existence, and mortality; to be able to write a lifetime's fiction that makes sense, which has meaning alongside the facts of suffering. By stating one's maternal foundation myth, the patient appreciates her identity as being linked to the generations beforehand. A woman, in that sense, never is a singleton; she is an integral part of the female line of her ancestors.

In Stephanie's case that was not an easy way to think. She could not, with an open heart, nor with any conviction or pride, say *Look, that's where I'm coming from.* Once, when she allowed herself to think that she came out of her mother's body, she vomited violently, as if ridding herself of such a thought. She came from a broken mind, a mother who issued hateful thoughts in the place of love. But Stephanie had taken in the substance of analytic work over a decade. The small morsels of truth had eventually formed the substance of her psyche. She had restored her internal mother from the ruins of murderous thoughts, in the main through dreams that fortified her in the struggle to survive her mother.

In one dream her mother had come to visit her, no longer the menacing, mad surgeon of previous dreams who, with great pleasure, had dissected bodies with a scalpel. In the dream Stephanie notices that her mother has shrunk. She is fragile, looking old, her life force spent. Proportion in dreams is significant. Developmental dreams typically seem to depict the dreamer as small, hinting at the historical nature of the dream material. From the perspective of a toddler, the world looks huge, but such a view becomes more accentuated in the face of traumatisation. When the self shrinks, the heart recoils, and the infant's thoughts have lost ownership and meaning. In the dream, the reverse movement had occurred; Stephanie was towering over her mother, which meant that her mother was losing her considerable powers of madness.

Around the same time that Stephanie was ready to separate out from her mother's grasp, more dreams were given her to enlarge her repertoire of resolve. In one dream she is riding a black horse, a beautiful creature that is able to talk. On their rides out they natter away, enjoying each other's company, making sense of life, in short they create a new fiction in Stephanie's psyche. On horseback she felt strong, the fear of her heart being ripped out and devoured by her mother faded, and she found her power as a woman taking on a responsible job. Gone were the days when she had hardly made it out of bed. Then she had another dream about a pack of wolves in which she became the alpha female.

Fortified inside by her dream fictions about power animals Stephanie was now ready to enjoy motherhood, to be open to the love of her husband, and plot a future in which she saw herself starting up her own business. She was also keen to convert a derelict outbuilding in the garden into her own study and studio space so she could return to her long-neglected art of sketching and painting. From the ruins of her early life she had, with the help of a vivid dream life, restored a life once lost and given up on.

As a final thought let us return to the organising ideas of Stephanie's dream fictions. Her dreams were seeking beauty, and she was quickly taken on board. Internal beauty is governed by truthfulness, conscious-ness, and meaning. The untruth she had to confront was that she thought she was mad. As it turned out the author of untruth was her own mother. The opposite of the assumed theory was true, as dreams revealed that her mother had impulses to kill her, treating her with hatefulness and contempt.

Stephanie also had to come clean over her pertinent self abuse and hateful thoughts about her own achievements. Confronting the mad stuff, the propensity for destructiveness, she could walk the ground of the ethical sense, having an inclination about what was good and what was bad for her. She invited into dream contemplation a truth of stag-gering beauty: that her father was only dead but not gone, that he had remained a silent companion in her tormented life, that he had loved her all the way; a realisation that opened her heart to the experience of being loved by her husband, by her kids, and friends, if not the world, something of which she had starved herself.

The dreams of the final furlong of her analysis, of her shrunken mother, the black horse, and the pack of wolves, had brought into her conscious mind different ways of thinking about herself. Through the emergence of power animals she reached into the Nietzschean "will to power". She not only had the tools for fending off her mother but she had found a horse with which to ride into a future of her own making, accompanied by a howling pack of wolves, eager to join the hunt for knowledge, beauty, and the spiritual.

During times of greatest despair, Stephanie was frequented by epiphany dreams. In one of them she goes up into the sky, propelled by a rocket, and lands in an altogether paradisiacal place, a cottage in the midst of a beautiful garden full of blossoming flowers, chirping birds, water flowing from a well. A figure shrouded in light moves towards her. It is God himself, dressed in a loin cloth, accompanied by his wife— who looks like a farmer's wife, rotund, red cheeked, an image of rude health—and a lustrous band of angels who play the harp and heavenly trumpets. The party approaches her, God is talking to her, offering kind words and solace.

I'm on the mend, I'm on the bloody mend!,

Stephanie said, as she recounted the dream of the apparition.

* * *

The case study demonstrates that power animals have a tendency to show up in the final furlong of a patient's analysis, which is tantamount to saying that the psyche on the way to recovery needs to be strong enough to entertain the idea of the dreamer coming into her own power. When dream images of power animals come into consciousness and make demands on the dreamer, something needs to be in place first: the prerequisite to inviting power into one's life is a solid emotional foundation made up of self love, kindness, compassion, and generosity, not to mention the establishment of the ethical sense and spiritual inclinations. Without this, power rests on shaky foundations and will become a destructive force as it directs fear, hunger, greed, and hatred outwards.

The spiritual searches

From Biblical Nebuchadnezzar's use of dream revelations and dream exegesis we can learn about the spiritual source of dreaming that is still relevant nowadays. The king's learning curve had to do with the realisation about where real power lies. Does it lie in the material world, in the showing of military might, in the deification of golden statues? Or does it lie in leading a spiritual life, appreciating the power of God? Whenever I mention, during long-term analytic work, the fundamental human desire and longing for spiritual development, I am met with raised eyebrows, thinly disguised ridicule, and consternation, if not irritation. *No thanks, religion is not for me!* Or, *Oh God! God is not for me!* Our spiritual longing, in its final analysis, has little to do with being part of an established church or religion. What matters is that in the privacy of the mind we are drawn to something that is bigger than ourselves. The search for the spiritual is a fundamental human drive and therefore should be included in the practice of counselling, psychotherapy, psychoanalysis, and group analysis, that is, in whatever form of treatment.

An elucidating fact about patients who have suffered from severe traumatisation is the simultaneous regression to the actual origin of the trauma (which might mean to the experience of dissociation, numbness, and a barrenness of affect) and an emergence of spiritual experiences; following acts of brutalisation, the patient may find solace in prayer. One person reported the apparition of an angel, telling her that she would survive the darkness. Another patient described how, having fallen into an abyss of despair, she had a sense of illumination, a warm glow of light seeming to flow through her whole body, upwards inside the spinal column, exiting at the crown chakra. At moments of greatest despair healing forces might arise.

In the analytic setting we are, in the main, dealing with emotional restoration, when the patient catches up with historic fault-lines of formative childhood events. But emotional life is not all there is. The patient needs to develop strategic thinking; this is important, in order to counter the strong currents of an established illness, or the tyranny of the child, forever screaming. The patient needs to actively engage with what it means to relate to other people. She also needs to learn to endure the beauty of the world. But, most importantly, the patient needs to move beyond understanding the world from a purely emotional perspective. The spiritual opens up vistas that are much bigger than healing our self-indulgent affected egos. We need to develop a moral sense, that is, in the main, to truthfully confront our tendency towards destructiveness. We need to learn about the sacrifices of compassion, loving kindness, and social responsibility. And what about happiness?

The Dalai Lama, in *The Art of Happiness* (1998), said that "the very purpose of life is to seek happiness", which, of course, differs from hedonism and instant gratification of needs and requires mental and ethical discipline in the overcoming of complex negative and harmful mental states. The search for happiness leads to experiences of beauty, to peace of mind, in the knowledge that destructiveness can be overcome, and converted into something productive. It is like looking up from the small world of one's ego and discovering the suffering in the world, and thus entering we-consciousness; noticing the kinship with other people, and realising that, fundamentally, we are all interconnected through the large pool of our immortal souls.

The American philosopher and fiction writer David Foster Wallace insisted that we are driven to worship (1997). We do not have a choice in the matter. The only choice is *what* we worship, be it the lure of sex, the triumph of war, the attraction of monetary wealth, or, in a more spiritual manner, to believe in the redemptive power of love, the view that we all belong to the same human race, that nothing happens in isolation, that the suffering in the world is our own suffering, that the starvation in the world is the starvation made by us.

Mordecai Himmelfarb's apostasy

One of Patrick White's favourite characters in *Riders in the Chariot* (1961), Mordecai Himmelfarb, a Jewish holocaust survivor and ardent intellectual, arrives in Australia only to be humiliated, yet again, this time by his fellow workers. In a scene that shows the cruelty of Australians against foreigners (and White himself was not exempt from being treated like an outcast), Himmelfarb is subjected to a mock crucifixion at the factory, which leaves him devastated and without the prospect of recovery. There was an outcry in Australia against such a savage depiction of the country's own shortcomings. White himself, at the time, was acutely aware of his own indifference as to the fate of the Jews when he had spent time in Germany in the 1930s, oblivious to what was going on. His writing showed moral and historical consciousness in the tradition of the great Russian writers.

With his character Himmelfarb, White shares the experience of faith, the renunciation of it, and finally the rediscovery of God. Himmelfarb's apostasy lay in the discovery that his vast intellect did not help him to get out of the human conundrum of the concentration camp. He witnessed himself and fellow human beings rapidly descend into the base self of shattered humanity with hatred, fear, and humiliation a constant companion. As it was he found his "chariot", not in the wisdom of books, but in the revelation of man's bestiality in war. As bombs were falling, dropped by RAF planes, he found inside "an ecstasy so cool and green his own desert would drink", as the narrator describes.

Patrick White, in his book's underlying exploration of faith, carries on the reflection:

> "What I want to emphasize through my ... 'Riders' ... is that all faiths, whether religious, humanistic, instinctive, or the creative artist's act of praise, are in fact one." (Marr, 1992, p. 360)

CHAPTER FIVE

The father of modern dream analysis

The foundation myth

A foundation myth is about the universal search within all of us for the very origins of our existence. It is the search for our identity. Where do we come from? The ethnic and cultural origin of the generations before us are significant markers of identity. Most pertinent, though, is the question of one's family history where generation after generation of ancestors have converged into the parental couple.

We spring from the minds of our parents. How did we come into being? By two people appreciating each other, being passionately in love; or were we a mistake, a late arrival in the family; or were we made out of a reparative idea, the relationship needing to be rescued by yet another child; or were we conceived in a haze of drunkenness or at the godlike heights of coke addiction? Both our human fault-lines and the beauty of our being can be traced back to the very beginning, when we only existed as an idea in our parental minds.

Death, loss, and mourning lie at the root of the psychoanalytic profession. It belongs to its foundation myth. If Freud had not lost his father towards the end of the nineteenth century he might not have had such revealing dreams about him, nor his realisation of dreams being the *via*

181

regia (the royal road) to the understanding of internal life, nor would he have composed his major work, *Die Traumdeutung* (*The Interpretation of Dreams*). His father's was a timely and far-reaching death. Mourning usually brings about a flurry of dreams about the nature and significance of the person lost, but it also brings to the fore the shaping forces of the culture in which the deceased has lived.

Mozart, who composed his masterpiece, the *Requiem*, after the death of his father utilised dream states for his compositions. Thus Mozart and Freud had in common that each produced, from dreams and dream-like states of mind, a masterpiece as an edifice to the loss of his father. Mozart's *Requiem* and Freud's *Interpretation of Dreams* are nothing but dreams gone solid.

Didier Anzieu, in his study of *Freud's Self-Analysis*, gives an account of the turning point in Freud's inner life, when, after the funeral of his father Jacob in October 1896, he had a dream that made him embark on a self-analysis and write a book on dreams (1986, p. 169). Here, for the first time, he found a dream of a personal nature: he was in a train station where he saw a printed notice saying "You are requested to close the eyes", or "You are requested to close the eye". In a letter to his friend Fliess, Freud recognised his guilt feelings toward his father, which eventually took him to an awareness of patricidal feelings. In the same letter he professed to a good relationship with his indulgent father:

> "I valued him highly, understood him very well, and with his mixture of deep wisdom and fantastic light-heartedness he had a significant effect on my life." (Ibid.)

What Freud omitted here was his critical, if not condemnatory, view of his father as a Jew who had not stood up for himself when frequently humiliated by anti-Semites during the arduous assimilation of the Jews in the Austro-Hungarian Empire. Freud, being Freud, found his new insight into patricidal fantasies liberating, and he also understood a previous dream better, the dream of "Irma's injection" (24 July 1895), which turned out to be a programme dream about his future theoretical and professional development. What he had not understood at the time was his level of guilt. Now he was able to link it with his infantile guilt feelings over his murderous fantasies toward his father.

The "Close the eyes" dream was a steep learning curve for Freud. We can learn from his inaugural dream experiences. That he linked two dreams, some one-and-a-half years apart, shows that there is no such thing as a single dream. They are all interconnected, providing the substratum for the continuity of life when we exist from moment to moment, from day to day, from year to year, rounded by a death. In the history of modern dream analysis this was the entry point to the understanding of omnibus dreams, dreams as interrelateded clusters, not unlike galaxies of the mind.

Mozart was able to string together notes "who liked each other" in order to compose entire symphonies; so the link between the first note and the last one in his oeuvre is the presence of love, liking being a subdivision of love. In the symphonies of dream life there is a thread connecting dreams we have had in intra-uterine life with the dreams we have had in childhood and teenage years, dreams we are having in midlife, and dreams we are going to have in the final furlong of life, before death calls. Dreams are signposts for the permanence of life, when we are able to connect the beginning with the end.

Freud's awareness of the connection between dreams, and his being able to see a previous dream in a different light, also demonstrates that the interpretation of a dream can never be fully exhausted. I believe in the first "fix" of understanding, the second "fix" of comprehension, and so on, to use the jargon of the builder who, hopefully, starts on the foundations of a house and works up to greater heights, without the walls collapsing.

* * *

On a level beyond the emotional, dreams encapsulate not only hidden meaning but also the mysteries of life. Or is there *a* mystery of life? *Who would have expected that?*, a patient said in awe of her own dream when, during a prolonged bout of depressive despair, a dream of beauty emerged: she is riding on horseback on a sandy beach that stretches out in front of her for miles, and alongside her trots a young lioness, her soft fur brushing against the rider's leg. The lioness is a companion, talking away to her, in a voice familiar to the dreamer, who understands that she is engaged with mourning the mother she lost when she was only four years old. She realises that the dead are only dead, they are not gone.

> The dead are invisible, they are not absent. (St. Augustine, in (Hollingworth, 2013))

The lioness, serving dream memory, dug out memories of a childhood lost but also of the years she had had with her mother before cancer cut short her life. Naturally, a life event such as the early loss of mother is traumatic, so the dreamer, in order to survive, has dissociated from the unbearable loss.

However, such a protective mechanism has also done away with the memory of good experiences, which are now coming back. The life of her mother, and the four years shared, were no longer a mystery. Mourning, a creative state of mind, gives the gift of memory, not only of painful life events but also events of deep connection, moments of beauty. In her mind the patient is now fortified by having a lioness companion alongside her, the sound of her mother's voice, and the memory of a gaze between the two of them, just before she died. A gaze held in the name of love.

The patient also found that after intense months of grieving her depression had lifted to such a degree that she was able to face working again. The process of healthy mourning is *the* panacea for alleviating states of depression, even deeply engrained ones.

* * *

The emotional relief Freud experienced from accepting hostile feelings towards his father, which constituted the first glimpse of his later concept of the Oedipus complex, were considerable. "He stopped complaining of fatigue, moments of depression, or an intellectual block", in Anzieu's words, able to start on a good run of creative work for some six months (Anzieu, 1986, p. 175). In aesthetic terms, one could say that the overcoming of destructive feelings might lead to an experience of beauty. Internal beauty is the recognition and appreciation of a process in which transitions are taking place. Beauty is destructiveness overcome.

The foundation myth of psychoanalysis is closely linked with Freud's father's death, and the writing of his major work, *The Interpretation of Dreams* (1900), which he carefully product-planted at the turn of the nineteenth century, somehow apprehending its seminal influence. But his dealings with death and mourning also brought about, some seventeen years later, another major publication, in which he escaped his own metapsychological claustrum of instinct theory by thinking about "Mourning and melancholia" (1917e). There he set the tentative ground for the later development of the theory of "object relations" by talking about internalisation; this meant that the Freudian infant was no longer in the ancient cave of instinctual gratification, but destined now to emerge and experience the riches of real people, experiences that can be taken inside, into the bank of internal affluence, to widen the scope of relatedness.

If we lose somebody and mourn him we might be able to reinstate him in our internal life. To the grieving of his father Freud owes the investigations into three of the most creative states of mind: dreaming, mourning, and, possibly, humour. (He was too much of a rationalist, and a depressive, to allow into his range of investigation the productive nature of play: this was an area that Winnicott excelled at, creating a theory around it; and Einstein, who played the violin to stimulate his right-brain hemisphere, walking on the endless shores of playing with ideas) Another creative state of mind that Freud relied on was hypomanic subject immersion, giving in to his manic swings by engaging in a punishing work schedule.

Freud's dream of dreams

Freud's dream of "Irma's injection", which came to him on 24 July 1895, was the foundation dream of psychoanalysis. It was a programme dream that anticipated the core concepts of psychoanalysis, and offered an intimate view of Freud's private life and his struggle to make it in the world. Few dreams have become the subject of so much attention and analysis. Freud himself wrote twenty-four pages of free-associative comments on his master specimen.

As with all great works of art, dreams are deeply rooted in the economic, social, and psychic circumstances of the time of their creation. Didier Anzieu, in *Freud's Self-Analysis* (1986), provides us with a psycho-historical account of Freud's courageous self-analysis through the interpretation of his own dreams during the years from 1895 to 1899 leading up to the publication of *The Interpretation of Dreams* in 1900. From Freud's outpouring of dreams Anzieu deducts the anticipation of the major concepts of psychoanalysis (such as the Oedipus complex, the primal scene, castration anxiety, and the theory of the psychical apparatus). Anzieu also refers to Freud's close relationships with Breuer and Fliess (friends, co-workers and co-authors), and the grieving process over his father's death.

> The study of dreams may be considered the most trustworthy method of investigating deep mental processes. (Freud, 1920g, p. 223)

Ellenberger, in *The Discovery of the Unconscious* (1970), insisted that Freud suffered from a "creative illness" during the time period that Anzieu refers to as Freud's initial period of self-analysis, an illness of the creative kind that also befell Jung, following his breakup from Freud and his time of seclusion and feverish work on his own theories. Freud had looked upon Jung as his crown prince, the person who would be capable of spreading the psychoanalytical gospel in the world, in part because he was not a Jew. This was a shrewd judgment on Freud's part, given the endemic anti-Semitic sentiment of the 1920s and 30s. But it was not to be.

Margaret Little, one of the leading proponents of the psychoanalytic Independent Group, who was in analysis with Winnicott, also went through a form of creative illness. She suffered a breakdown that led to a surge of creative activity as an artist and analytic writer, writing with high sensitivity, capturing the early states of the infant's mind, which she called "primary undifferentiatedness".

Kay Redfield Jamison, a leading researcher into manic-depressive illness, notes, in *Touched with Fire* (1993), that a large number of artists have been affected by manic-depressive illness and related conditions. The list is long: from the poets William Blake, Samuel Taylor Coleridge, P. B. Shelley, T. S. Eliot, Charles Beaudelaire, John Keats, Sylvia Plath, Dylan Thomas, to the prose writers Charles Dickens, Graham Greene, Ernest Hemingway, Hermann Hesse, Malcolm Lowry, Leo Tolstoy, and Virginia Wolf. Poets show the highest suicide rate amongst artists.

Jamison was able to see that certain types of mental afflictions can be the very driving force of art, and in that sense are productive. And, if one is immersed in the creative process as a normal-neurotic artist, the daemons of madness also might arrive. As soon as you are engaged with a fundamental human project, there is no way out. Such a project makes ruthless demands on the artist, inducing states of disintegration and an abdication of ordinary ways of seeing reality.

Art is built on sufferance.

> "We of the craft are all crazy ... [s]ome are affected by gaiety, others by melancholy, but all are more or less touched." (Lord Byron, in Blessington, 2011)

Jamison, a professor of psychiatry and herself a life-long sufferer from manic depression, which she documents with refreshing honesty in her memoir *An Unquiet Mind* (1997), refers to the ancient belief of "fine madness", one of the oldest and most persistent cultural notions describing the possibility of a connection between the artistic genius and madness. The Greek philosophers Socrates, Plato, and Aristotle held the belief that profoundly altered states of consciousness and raw feeling states in the artist, conducive to great art, could only be obtained through some kind of "inspired madness", which required a union with the gods or the Muses. This "divine madness" would set in motion a loss of consciousness, an affliction with psychic illness or states of "possession", which would open up the artist to her creative imagination, enthusiasm, and inspiration.

Such states of "fine madness" in the working artist are not unlike what mothers experience during late pregnancy, during birth, and in the long, long weeks after giving birth. A "state of heightened sensitivity, almost an illness", in Winnicott's words, comes over young mothers, taken by surprise by experiences that are frightening and relentless (Winnicott, 1956a, p. 302). And no one seems to have prepared her for this "very special psychiatric condition", which Winnicott calls "primary maternal preoccupation". It goes on alongside other experiences: of sheer physical exhaustion, being in a constant feverish state of mind, a sense of utter isolation, and, let us not forget, the amazing moments of the baby's beauty, and her fragile and wondrous ways of entering this world. Intriguingly, Winnicott goes on to say that "it is not easily remembered by mothers once they have recovered from it", but is by fathers, who have stood quietly in the background supporting their wives gone mad.

What drives the mother to despair and delight in equal measure are the baby's demands. Emotionally speaking, the mother has to hold the baby's internal world of primitive emotions and somatic states, dominated by fear of survival, if not a threat of annihilation, even if the going is good enough. Solid mothering holds the baby's untogether self, with the prospect of recovery in mind. If the mother can give in to such states of reverie, the baby's self will develop a sense of recovery from states of fear. "The self that can afford to die", as Winnicott puts it.

My opinion is that what the ancient philosophers described as "fine madness" and what Winnicott describes as "primary maternal preoccupation" is nothing other than immersion in dreams and dream-related states of mind. The artist engages deeply with her art, which induces inspired madness; a mother engages deeply with her baby, the first human project, and goes mad over it, and on the way she learns to dream and be in the present: the dreamer engages deeply with the deity of dreams, Asclepius, and makes herself open to the madness of dreams, an altogether creative state of mind, where she is immersed in the task of uncovering more and more from within the depths of her psyche. If you allow yourself to be touched by a piece of art, by the baby's demands, and by dreams that might not at first sight make sense, then you open yourself up to being changed forever.

* * *

One of my patients, Rose, who lost her mother when she was only three years old, rediscovered her mother when she engaged with her dream life. Initially this was frightening, as one nightmare after the other lined up to rattle her old perceptions of herself as a child. She always insisted that the loss of her mother had not affected her but made her stronger, an aspect of her vocational life that could not be argued against. But it had been at the great cost of losing touch with her fragility.

She had shied away from relationships, putting everything into a successful career as an editor at a publishing house. Her dreams, acting like a can opener, left her wide open to the unbearable feelings she once had as a child and had repressed in order to survive. Her father, at the time only interested in extending his business empire on an international scale, had had her looked after by her aunt and uncle. In fact, she lost her mother, her father, who had been absent before, and her early environment, the family house in which they had lived. Her relatives were good enough people but emotionally vacant and distant, not unlike her father.

The return of the bad in adult life made her lose it at times in the work place, blowing her top, replying sharply to colleagues' concerns and worries, being grumpy and moody, her image as a balanced and reliable person disappearing quickly. However, in the analysis she made good progress, making some inroads, through the process of mourning, into building a relationship with the bereaved three-year-old girl. In her grief she had a sense of what she must have gone through as a child, and had repeated dreams in which her mother appeared. Now alongside her in her dreams, her mother held the young child in her arms, played with her, brushing her long hair, telling her bedtime stories, and watching over her during the night. This came as a huge relief to the night terrors she had had for as long as she could remember but had never made sense of.

Now that she had her mother in her dreams Rose became more engaged with me in the consulting room, allowing me in rather than rebuffing me the way her father had. Jokingly she said that now she might try out her green fingers, growing plants in her attic flat and on her roof terrace. The next task was trying out a pet, possibly a cat, and then she might be ready for her first relationship, at the age of thirty-seven. She followed more closely her mother's words, which came from the world beyond:

Let your heart be open. Let your soul be touched.

* * *

Once Freud had engaged with his fundamental human project, namely the understanding of dreams, he was driven by curiosity, the search for knowledge, and the mystery of life—nothing short of being touched with fire—like Einstein, whose thirst for knowledge was so enormous he wanted to find out about nothing less than the finer mechanisms of God's creation. Later on, when Freud was assured of his position in the world, being the regent of the psychoanalytic world he had created (excepting his vicious treatment by the Nazis in occupied Vienna), he knew that he had come across one of the fundamental human mysteries, that is, dream life. And he was willing to make its propagation his life's task, becoming a modern day servant of Asclepius and Psyche, the deities of dreams, the ancient dreaming couple.

Freud was able to convert his "creative illness" into something tangible, a contribution of some magnitude toward the thinking of the twentieth, and the twenty-first, centuries. His life at the time of the dream was fragmented, and he was desperately searching for a unifying factor, which he found in the analysis of his own dreams. The secret of dreams, and of unconscious life, was revealed to him through the dream of "Irma's injection", Freud himself claimed.

A large hall—numerous guests, whom we were receiving. Among them was Irma. I at once took her on one side, as though to answer her letter and to reproach her for not having accepted my "solution" yet. I said to her: "If you still get pains, it's really only your fault." She replied: "If you only knew what pains I've got now in my throat and abdomen—it's choking me"—I was alarmed and looked at her. She looked pale and puffy. I thought to myself that after all

I must be missing some organic trouble. I took her to the window and looked down her throat, and she showed signs of recalcitrance, like women with artificial dentures. I thought to myself that there was really no need for her to do that. —She then opened her mouth properly and on the right I found a big white patch; at another place I saw extensive whitish grey scabs upon some remarkable curly structures which were evidently modelled on the turbinal bones of the nose. —I at once called in Dr. M., and he repeated the examination and confirmed it ... Dr. M. looked quite different from usual; he was very pale, he walked with a limp and his chin was clean-shaven ... My friend Otto was now standing beside her as well, and my friend Leopold was percussing her through her bodice and saying: "She has a dull area low down on the left." He also indicated that a portion of the skin on her left shoulder was infiltrated. (I noticed this, just as he did, in spite of her dress.) ... M. said: "There is no doubt it's an infection, but no matter; dysentery will supervene and the toxin will be eliminated." ... We were directly aware, too, of the origin of the infection. Not long before, when she was feeling unwell, my friend Otto had given her an injection of a preparation of propyl, propyls ... propionic acid ... trimethylamin (and saw before me the formula for this printed in heavy type) ... Injections of that sort ought not to be made so thoughtlessly ... And probably the syringe had not been clean. (1900, p. 107)

At the time of the dream Freud was plagued by a number of issues: he felt anxious about his health, job, and family life; he suffered from a number of psychosomatic complaints such as heart trouble and dysentery; working as a neurologist in private practice he struggled financially; and he was not overly enthusiastic about his wife's pregnancy with their sixth child, fearing that Martha would have another thrombosis, as in previous pregnancies.

The expected baby turned out to be Anna, one of his most ardent followers in later life. Freud named her after a patient and family friend. Intriguingly, he had reserved the name Wilhelm for her before her birth, expecting yet another son. In his own written associations with the dream he admitted harbouring the desire for miscarriage: "the toxin will be eliminated." The psychoanalytic community should be pleased that his infanticidal wishes did not materialise, and that the toxin turned to remedy. Also, if we apply the concept of the foundation myth, I wonder what Anna Freud would have made of her origins in her father's mind. She must have figured that out in her own analysis, dreaming inexplicably about somebody called Wilhelm, her psychic twin, and of being gotten rid of, the latter, of course, joining up with historical consciousness concerning the fate of the Jews.

The day before the dream, Freud had met the son of a patient to whom he had given an injection and who subsequently became seriously ill, most likely because of a dirty syringe, as is expressed in the last phrase of the account of the dream. Embarrassment and guilt was compounded by the fact that Freud, himself experimenting with cocaine, had at the time recommended to his friend Fleischl the medicinal use of cocaine, which ended tragically with Fleischl taking a fatal overdose.

The very night before the dream Freud wrote a letter to Breuer (Dr. M. in the dream), his mentor, in order to defend his analytic treatment of Irma. Breuer was the co-author of Freud's first impressive work, *Studies on Hysteria* (1895d), and a close witness of Freud's diagnostic and treatment errors. To Freud's additional consternation, Breuer did not show any inclination to accept his psychosexual aetiology of hysteria. Another dream figure, piling up the pressure of professional accusation, is Otto. In real life, Dr. Oscar Rie, a family friend and paediatrician, had pointed out to Freud that he thought that his treatment of Irma, who suffered from hysteria, was not going anywhere, which no doubt irritated Freud.

In those early days of psychoanalysis boundaries were kept very loosely indeed: the Irma of the dream was in reality Anna Hammerschlag-Lichtheim, a favourite patient of Freud's, a widow and family friend, invited to Martha's thirty-first birthday two days following the dream. This aspect of the dream reveals that Freud had a response to Irma's desire (in her phantasy life) to have a child by him, her own father-analyst. He must have harboured erotic phantasies about his "available" patient, her being a widow, in conjunction with the possible deadly outcome of Martha's pregnancy.

Such hidden phantasies must have initially unsettled him, and yet stirred his thinking about the Oedipus complex, moving from the smallness and singularity of the consulting room to the development of generalised theory. The sexual undertone of the dream also brought to the fore the later developing centrality of working with the transference (i.e., experiences from the past that are "carried over" to the present). And the allusion to pregnancy in the dream might have carried his unconscious wish to "conceive" lots of children, patients, ideas, even a new science—a metaphorical expression of his productivity to come.

Anzieu pointed out that the dream appears to be like a court hearing. In the dream Freud stands accused by a burden of evidence of previous and current professional malpractice. The dream becomes a defence speech in which the key question of the human tragedy is: Who bears the responsibility? Freud summons up witnesses to demonstrate his innocence. At the root of Irma's continuing illness is her rebuffal of his solution. Poignantly she does not accept his interpretations, suggesting her lack of sexual satisfaction.

In his summary speech he advocates the concept of the sexual origin of neurosis, an idea he elevated to the very formula of life (trimethylamin). There is a hint of Freudian grandiosity and a sense of destiny in his manner of describing the chemical structure of $N(CH_3)_3$. "And I saw before me the formula for this printed in heavy type" is reminescent of Kekulé von Stradonitz's famous inspirational dream in 1890 in which the molecular structure of benzine, a closed carbon ring, appeared to him, a fact well known to Freud.

> "Again the atoms were juggling before my eyes … my mind's eye, sharpened by repeated sights of a similar kind, could now distinguish larger structures of different forms and in long chains, many of them close together; everything was moving in a snake-like and twisting manner. Suddenly, what was this? One of the snakes got hold of its own tail and the whole structure was mockingly twisting in front of my eyes. As if struck by lightning, I awoke. Let us learn to dream, gentlemen, and then we may perhaps find the truth."
> (Quoted in Freud, 1900, p. 138)

Despite being plagued by grave self-doubt and an expectation of a hostile response to his new ideas, Freud maintained a deep sense of destiny and a craving for a great discovery that would bring him fame. Such a sense of grandeur and destiny had been instilled in him in his infancy by his beautiful, authoritarian, and abrasive mother, Amalia, who showed a boundless admiration for her first-born son Shlomo Sigismund (Clark, 1980). The mystique around his birth was compounded by the fact that he had been born with a caul, an amniotic membrane, traditionally a sign of good fortune, and supposed to preserve against drowning.

Usually dreams tend to be dominated by visual and auditory sensations. Not so Freud's dream, which is richly populated with sensory impressions, governed by the body sense or the sensation function, not unlike the guiding perception of horse riders excelling in dressage. Earlier in the text I pointed out Asclepius' rulership of dreams and his association with the body of the dream, the dream soma. The image of the body takes centre stage in the theatre of Freud's dream. In the Freudian paradigm of the mind, the body is the home and origin of psychic life. Being a paradoxical thinker, he meant this both in a literal and metaphorical sense.

In *The Ego and the Id*, Freud said that "the ego is first and foremost a bodily ego" (1923b, p. 451). It is the seat of "reason and common sense" and tries to regulate instinctual impulses from an archaic and murky unconscious where "the passions" lie, the passions of sexuality and anger springing from the somatic id. He goes on to say that "a person's own body, and above all its surface, is a place from which both external and internal perceptions may spring" (ibid., p. 450). Consciousness for Freud is born out of the body and dependent on an ego that is acutely monitoring somatic-emotional impulses from deep inside and from external perception.

That Freud, in his biological model of the mind, should have given so much attention to sensory perception as the origin of human consciousness and knowledge, makes him intrinsically part of the tradition of philosophical aesthetics.

Aesthetics and the body

Terry Eagleton, referring back to the originator of aesthetics, Alexander Baumgarten, says that "aesthetics is born as a discourse of the body" (1990, p. 13). Aesthetics at that time had no intention to elaborate on art; it was mainly concerned with the domain of human perception and sensation, as the Greek *aisthesis* would suggest.

> That territory is nothing less than the whole of our sensate life together—the business of affections and aversions, of how the world strikes the body on its sensory surfaces, of that which takes root in the gaze and the guts and all that arises from our most banal, biological insertion into the world. (Eagleton, ibid., p. 13)

Our "biological insertion into the world" was contemptuously overlooked by classical philosophy, which wanted to see the human idiom under the absolute rule of reason and conceptional thought. This oversight was partially corrected by Baumgarten's aesthetic theory, which placed the aesthetic right in-between the universal laws of reason and the subjectivity of the senses (1750). Or, in Eagleton's words, Baumgarten's contribution was an appreciation of

> the body's long inarticulate rebellion against the tyranny of the theoretical. (Eagleton, 1990, ibid.)

Aesthetics was no longer just a prosthesis to reason; it became a discipline in its own right. Freud's biologism of the mind went one step further. His human aesthetic intrinsically demystifies the entire classical aesthetic heritage of the "rich, potent, serenely balanced subject" by saying that "our drives are in contradiction with one another, our faculties in a state of permanent warfare, our fulfilments fleeting and tainted" (ibid., p. 263). At the very root of human existence he placed an instinctual murkiness, where sexual desire and the death instinct are embraced in a dynamic tête-à-tête of considerable volatility—a vast underground region of the mind Charles Levin used to call "a kind of primitive substance of social process".

Back to Freud's dream. Back to the body of the dream. In his intrepid pursuit of comprehending the origin of hysteria he was the first person in modern psychology to ask questions about how neurotic illness in adult life might be connected with actual sexual abuse in childhood. His "seduction theory", which he later revised to include seduction fantasy, was a landmark in the acknowledgment of early traumatisation and its somatic imprint. The origin of the word hysteria is in the Latin and the Greek words for womb. Thus the most productive female organ is seen not only as the giver of life but also the carrier of traumatic memory.

CHAPTER SIX

Sleep research

The guardians of sleep

One of Freud's assumptions on dreaming, that "dreams are the guardians of sleep", was proven wrong by sleep researchers. Freud's notion
was that one of the functions of dreaming is to preserve sleep. The
researchers found the reverse to be true, namely that "sleep is the
guardian of dreams" (Jouvet, 1999, p. 52).

On the level of ontogenetic security, the dream state is a potentially
perilous situation for the dreamer, given the increased threshold for
arousal (the dreamer is less able to sense his environment) and muscle
paralysis (the dreamer cannot take flight). There is a significant cor-
relation between the amount of dreaming and factors of instinctual
security. We cannot fall into dream states during deep sleep without a
complicated biological preparation.

One could almost see the ontologically fragile and mentally highly
productive dream state as requiring a certain amount of biological "parenting" by deep sleep. Dream consciousness uses more energy than
waking consciousness; it uses so much energy that its reserves need to
be refilled during deep sleep. Energetically speaking, deep sleep is the
provider and caretaker of dream sleep.

The redeeming explanation for Freud's lapse is that, in his time, little was known about the physiology of dreaming, and, as an ardent biologist of the mind, he was prone to emphasise the somatic aspects of the dream state, preferring to see the dream state as dominant over deep sleep. He may have had a valid point. In my view, dream activity, which in the main is a highly developed mental function, might also have a quietening effect on deep sleep. A quiet mind leads to a relaxed body; a relaxed body leads to a quiet mind. The two states of mind, the psyche and the soma entity, are, in reality, interdependent.

REM states

Physiologically, there are three states of brain activity or states of consciousness: waking life, deep sleep, and dreaming. The dream state was discovered as an autonomous state of mind only in 1958 by Michel Jouvet, following nearly a century of neurobiological research, which, unsurprisingly, happened in a rather insular and disjointed manner.

In 1880 Jean Baptiste Gelineau described narcolepsy, that is, the almost total absence of muscular tone, without realising that he had landed on one of the four physiological signifiers of the dream state. It was Freud himself, in 1895 who, without resorting to physiological evidence, first suggested in his *Project for a Scientific Psychology* (1950/1895) that the dream state might be accompanied by atonia or motor paralysis. In 1937 Klaue discovered that cats, in defined periods of deep sleep, showed rapid electrical activity in the cortex that differed significantly from the usual slow cortical activity of deep sleep—it was, however, not related, at the time, to dreaming.

In 1944 Ohlmeyer discovered a periodic cycle of penile erections in males during sleep, again without relating it to dream states. Dream research at the time failed to draw the right conclusions because it worked on a biased paradigm that was unable to afford dreaming an autonomous status. Dreaming was seen as a state of half-waking and half-sleeping. When in 1953 the Chicago school of Nathaniel Kleitman, Eugene Aserinsky, and William Dement discovered that during sleep there were periods of rapid eye movement (REM), accompanied by dreaming, they were still unable to give dream activity its rightful status as an autonomous state of mind. Jouvet calls the dream state "paradoxical sleep" because of the simultaneous occurrence of intense cerebral activity and muscle atonia (Jouvet, 1999).

Sleep deprivation

The very rare disease of the brain, fatal familial insomnia (FFI), involves progressively worsening insomnia. The sufferers are unable to go beyond light sleep stage one and never enter light sleep stage two, nor deep sleep stages three and four, nor REM states. Their brains do not get the rest they need to revive, as most reviving and repairing processes of the body are believed to happen during these sleep and dream stages. The enforced absence of dreaming leads to emotional disintegration, states of fear, an upsurge of hateful and paranoid feelings, experiences of depersonalisation, and dissociation from reality, in short, to insanity. And prolonged sleep deprivation leads to the deterioration of the body and utter exhaustion. This total collapse of the psyche-soma entity finally leads to death, which usually occurs between six to thirty-six months after the onset of the illness.

From Bion we know that one of the great instigators of thinking is an absence. If we know how we deteriorate physically and emotionally during severe sleep and dream deprivation we will have some idea of the function of dreams. The presence of dreams might do the opposite to sleep deprivation: it leads to a sense of somatic and ontogenetic security, and it transforms unbearable emotions into something that feels manageable and contained. Dreaming seems to be a *psychic* process that converts looming insanity into mental health and serves the restoration of the body. Dreams are both the doctors of the soul and doctors of the body.

Sexual states of mind

I wish now to talk about sexual states of mind and dreaming. As I mentioned earlier, erections in males and clitoral engorgement in females are typical indicators of REM activity. The famous morning erection in male adults might have little to do with actual sexual arousal or wet dreams—they are simply physiological landmarks, signifying dream activity. When I made this point during a dreams seminar, a female student seemed to experience some relief at the thought that the male residents of her home for people with learning difficulties who showed the early morning "coathanger" phenomenon (her words), were possibly engaged in something more meaningful than just sexual protuberance and intrusiveness.

198 THE FICTIONS OF DREAMS

That sexual arousal should occur during dreaming provides evidence for the potency and generativity of the dream function.

Dreaming is a sexual state of mind

Robert Caper, in his paper on "Play, experimentation and creativity" (1996), makes a link between sexual states of mind and creativity. He formulates that a playful and creative relationship with reality requires the acceptance and reverence of one's "internal sexual parents", an idea that was first proposed by Klein in 1939, called the "combined parental object". The internal sexual mother stands for the capacity for receptive observation; the internal sexual father represents the capacity for active enquiry and experimentation.

> The precise state of one's internal parents, i.e., the degree to which one has been able to accept an internal parental couple whose sexuality is pleasurable, creative and non-destructive, plays an important role in one's ability to establish the kind of playful, experimental relationship to reality … (Ibid., p. 864)

The dream mind sets the scene for the dreamer getting in contact again with his internal parents. Dreams might become an audit of the nature and past experience of one's actual parents and ways in which they were internalised, in order to provide a solid foundation for one's emotional life.

Grotstein, in his essay *Who Is the Dreamer Who Dreams the Dream and Who Is the Dreamer Who Understands It?* (1981), made us think about the dream source but equally of the dream *audience*. In his view, the dreamer who dreams the dream is the infant in search of a receiving mother capable of reverie (emotional receptiveness) and containment of the dreamer's nightmares and unbearable emotions. This ménage à deux he calls the "dreaming couple". A dream never stands alone. It firmly requests an audience, a relational and social context. A dream moves from monologue to dialogue to discourse, not unlike the lines of communication in a developing group culture (Schlapobersky, 1994).

CHAPTER SEVEN

A brief history of dream consciousness

The prehistoric dreamer

Cave paintings

One of the oldest depictions of a dream state is a mural in the complex of caves at Lascaux in southwest France, painted some 18,000 years ago by our European early modern human ancestors (Aubarbier & Binet, 1997).

There we can see depicted a man asleep on the ground, body and arms outstretched, surrounded by a bird perched on a stick, and a mortally wounded bison, a beautiful and powerful creature, with its entrails hanging out, and a spear, broken in two, seeming to connect the hunter and the hunted. On closer inspection we notice the hunter's penile erection directed toward the dying bison, in touching distance of its furry neck. The man and bird, unlike the beast, are drawn in a childlike style, with thin strokes, not dissimilar to Winnicottian squiggles.

From sleep research we know that, apart from rapid eye movement, fast cortical activity, and the absence of muscular tone, penile erections in males and clitoral engorgement in females are prime biological signifiers of the state of dreaming. And birds, in prehistoric cosmology, represent the immaterial nature of the soul. So it seems that the hunter's soul has left his body to roam freely through time and space, driven by his desire to kill this formidable beast. The scene set on the wall is a dream, not an actual depiction of hunting. It describes the hunter's wish to make a kill in his next hunt. His dream thinking is concerned with a successful hunt, and a union with the hunted, showing a reverential attitude towards the beast that is sustaining life.

That the cave artists should be familiar with a delicate physiological detail about dreaming, the dreamer's erection, only proven, in laboratory conditions, in 1944 by Ohlmeyer, is a remarkable feat. It demonstrates that human knowledge and wisdom existed long before the scientific paradigm. The depiction of dreams is one of the oldest aesthetic projects of humankind. Dreams have always been our companions.

* * *

The prehistoric cave paintings of the Perigord area of France, going back to 30,000 BC, are considered the cradle of art in human history but are also a celebration of the state of dreaming. Art and dreams are companions of longstanding. While the above-mentioned ithyphallic imagery represents dream states, a much wider array of murals hints at rudimentary forms of unconscious life.

There are friezes that describe scenes of the natural habitat of the hunters and gatherers: bulls (aurochs), cows, deer, horses, bears, lions, and mammoths, shown in the splendour of their movement and vitality but also in their savage nature. Dreams not only describe internal states of mind but also represent the social world in which we live. They also produce histories, as we can see in seemingly primitive cultures that based their entire social life around the sharing and interpreting of dreams.

In modern dream interpretation we take it that animal images in dreams represent our instinctual nature, cave man and cave woman never being that far beneath the surface of refined emotional display. An image of a ranting and raving child is imposed on a palaeolithic image of serenely powerful creatures. These are images that have been on the dreaming mind of people for thousands of years. In fact, they have become as much a part of our genetic material of memory as they have a part of our psychic lineage. Over time they have become archetypes, that is, structuring symbols of internal and external reality.

A phrase such as *He's a dog of a man*, which might appear in a dream, is not only a weary, if not adoring, description of a highly sexual man, it also links up with the whole history of mankind, hyaenas, wolves, coyotes, hounds, all joining in the hunt. One animal image extends from the personal into a collective memory of ancient times. One image walks freely on the timeline of dreams. And in that sense an image is of all ages. In the same way, as human beings, we are of all ages, an idea that Einstein promoted when giving credence to the little boy within him, lurking just beneath the veneer of the impression of adulthood, the little boy who used to play freely with ideas, with the possibility of other worlds.

Apart from depictions of their material surroundings, the prehistorics also employed female sexual symbols, mainly the vulva, phallic symbolism, and the symbol of a unicorn in a panther's skin, a deer's tail, a bison's hump, with human legs and two elongated horns.

We know from much later legends that the only way of catching the fierce unicorn was through a virgin, in whose presence the hunter lost his mind and lay down in her lap, thus becoming a symbol of sublimated sexual potency. The prehistoric artists painted a world beyond the material, a world governed by the worship of nature's deities, a spiritual quest that dealt with the essentials of living, namely birth, procreation, and death.

* * *

The Sistine Chapel of prehistory

My suggestion that a large number of these murials might depict dream states is based on what one experiences on entering the caves. The prehistoric artists had at their disposal only primitive artistic means. They used manganese dioxide for the black, and iron oxides for the yellow and red ochres, and yet the outcome was staggering. Abbé Breuil, an archeologist involved in the Lascaux project, described one of the ceilings with its "bouquets" of red cows as the "Sistine Chapel of prehistory". The caves were not discovered until 1940.

One is so drawn in by the power of the paintings and the inviting underground atmosphere of their environment, that one is reminded of Bion's concept of "reverie", suggesting that the intrepid analyst should dream her own dream in the presence of the dreaming patient. It is an imperative intended to call for and enter into a mental state of healthy emptiness, calm receptiveness, and heightened sensitivity—an altered state of consciousness, not unlike that which is required from a good enough mother, if not father, meeting the baby's needs.

These prehistoric wall paintings are not only the witnesses of the origin of the visual arts but also of the appreciation and worship of dreams, and with it the idea of a maker. As John Berryman asked in his *Dream Songs*, a collection of poetry: "Does the validity of the dream-life suppose a Maker?" (Berryman, 1964, p. 339).

Aristotle and "the dawn of the science of dreams"

The historian William V. Harris, in *Dreams and Experience in Classical Antiquity* (2009), provides us with a scholarly discussion of the development of thought about dreams from the prehistoric oneiromancers to the philosophers of classical antiquity, putting into perspective the view that Freud was the father of modern dream analysis. As it turns out, Aristotle, by digesting and developing dream theories by Democritus, Empedocles, Hippocrates, and Plato, the initiators of the naturalistic approach to dream theory in the fifth and sixth centuries BC, has to be seen as the originator of the science of dreams. Aristotle's schema of dream theory is surprisingly modern and well ahead of its time, taking issue with the prehistoric notions of the divine origin of dreaming and its main task of prophecy.

What Aristotle inherited from his predecessors were a number of notions: (i) Democritus' god-excluding approach; (ii) Empedocles' theory that "dreams arise from one's activities by day" (which resembles Freud's notion of the "day residues"); (iii) the assertion that dreams take place entirely inside the individual; (iv) that dreams are closely connected with the dreamer's physical state; (v) Plato's idea of dreams as being linked with the personality of the dreamer; and (vi) Democritus' thoughts about how specific images tend to emerge in the dreamer's consciousness (ibid., p. 253). This was a move away from seeing the world of dreams in god-made, mythical terms, the dreamer being directed from outside forces, to a humanising of dreams: that is, the individual dreamer, his bodily self, and his interiority are now at the epicentre of dream life. From the gods up above to the human being down below, walking the ground of ordinariness.

Aristotle contributed three dream books to the canon of the oldest preserved texts on dreams, *De Divinatione per Somnum*, *De Somniis*, and *On Sleep and Waking*, which stand alongside Hippocrates' *On Regimen*,

Lucretius' *On the Nature of Things*, Cicero's *On Divination*, Artemidorus' *Oneirocritica* (ibid., p. 230), and the dream anthologies in the Bible, going back some 2,500 years. The pre-Aristotelians, Democritus, Empedocles, Hippocrates, and Plato, wrote about dreams, but only in a peripheral way.

Aristotle's achievement was that he took dream theory away from religious speculation and made a science out of it by way of empirical observation and investigation. In Harris' words, "in so far as scholars have evaluated ancient writing on the subject of dreams, they seem to have given the palm of honour to Aristotle ('the dawn of the science of dreams')" (ibid., p. 233). In his dream enquiry Aristotle asks pertinent questions but does not consider the function of dreams nor their purpose. But he goes beyond the mere description of dream content and arrives at a phenomenological view.

On a mundane level he formulates that dreaming springs from the bodily self and that from bodily perception images arise. He sees the heart as being at the centre of sensory perception and as the fountain of imagination. His psychobiological approach is not that far from Freud's, who put emphasis on the psychosomatic function of dreams, in its most rudimentary form, before they can be utilised for thinking and understanding, saying that "dreams are the guardians of sleep".

On another level of the somatic underpinning of dreams Aristotle makes the point that dreams incorporate the immediate sensory impact of one's surroundings on dream activity. He also observed that some animals are able to dream.

Despite being adamently against prehistoric notions of dreams as solely prophetic, Aristotle concedes that some dreams foretell the future, singling out ordinary people, rather than wise ones, and some people suffering from insanity who have the gift of prophecy.

As for dream recall, he believes that some dreamers remember dreams whilst others seem to struggle, one reason being excessive eating. In his physical theory of dreaming he seems to think that an invisible but material movement passes between things in the external world and the interiority of the dreamer's mind. As is the case in the lack of dream recall, this movement between outside and inside is obstructed by overeating. The idea of food intake acting as an obstacle to dream recall is an ancient forerunner of the modern idea of dream repressors, such as fatty foods, psychotropic drugs, and excessive alcohol.

Aristotle suggests that young children do not dream, a notion that he retracts in other parts of his writing. It is most likely that in his time children were not regarded as separate human beings nor as having minds of their own. Nowadays we know from sleep research that foetuses and babies spend considerable time dreaming whilst asleep. They dream themselves into existence.

On a more sophisticated level of dreaming Aristotle asserts that from dream images thoughts might arise. That is, of course, not mature thinking in the strict Bionian sense, which is about emotional understanding, but it might be linked with what Bion calls "beta elements", which are the basic stuff the mind is made of, such as primitive emotion, sensory impressions, and "thoughts without a thinker" (1962a).

As to the issue of lucid dreaming, which nowadays is praised as one of the high altitude achievements of dream consciousness (Green & McCreery, 1994), we need to give credit to the old masters of the past. During the time of the pre-Aristotelians, in the sixth century BC, it was the ancient Buddhists who first developed the art of using states of lucid dreaming for the expansion of the mind in deep meditation, as can be seen in *Sleeping, Dreaming, and Dying*, where the Dalai Lama explores the highest states of consciousness as linked to the moment of conception, the moment of birth, the process of conscious dying, and dream states (Varela, 1997).

Aristotle, two centuries later, points to one of the most mature forms of dreaming, which is lucid dreaming, that is, the awareness that one is dreaming whilst dreaming. Lucid dreaming in the modern canon of dream theory is linked with high levels of consciousness, self awareness, and dream thinking.

Aristotle pioneered some astounding notions to do with dream life. He talks about the multi-temporality of dreams where future, present, and past events appear in dreams (Harris, 2009, p. 259). He also refers to states of "reverie", so revered by Bion, which are dream-like states in waking life. Then he goes out on a limb by stating that "manic people ('melancholic' to be more precise), and drunks, and those suffering from fever have disturbed and monstrous and incoherent dreams" (ibid., p. 258). Again he comes up with a psychobiological theory of dream life, and lays the ground for our modern conceptions of psychotic states of mind that might underlie disturbing dreams. And, in a final act of setting the tone for all dream interpreters to come, he asserts that some interpreters are more skilled than others, using the Greek term *technikos*, which is also a word for art. Dream analysis is an art form, no less.

In summary, Aristotle's twenty or so dream notions, and the ideas of the pre-Aristotelians, make up the earliest canon of modern dream science from some 2,500 years ago. Aristotle sits on the ancient throne of modern dream theory, residing as its grandfather spirit, as it were. Freud still occupies the role of the father of modern dream science, as he brought depth psychology and the dreamer's ownership of the dream to the art of dream interpretation, closely followed by Jung, who initiated, through analytical psychology, another strand of dream analysis that might be more closely related to the ancient dreamers, as it utilises mythological and symbolic explorations of the theme of dreaming.

Artemidorus' Oneirocritica

Freud, in the introduction to *The Interpretation of Dreams*, gave credit to the masters before him (1900). He singles out the ancient dream interpreter and chronicler of dreams Artemidorus of Daldis who, at the height of Graeco-Roman culture in North Africa, collected a vast number of his contemporaries' dreams in the *Oneirocritica* (c. 150–200 CE). *Oneiros* is Greek for dream and *critica* for interpretation; its linguistic connotations might have been an inspiration for Freud's choice of book title. Artemidorus collected dreams from all walks of life, undertaking extensive travelling across the Mediterranean, mainly to Greece and Italy, for the cause of dream-interpretation and divination (Harris-McCoy, 2012, p. 31). Rather than relying on highbrow academic texts and debate with his colleagues, his preferred source of observation and research were the "diviners of the marketplace". However, one classical historian, William Harris, has gone as far to suggest that Artemidorus' dreams were all made up (2009). Even if this were true, if Artemidorus had used his fictional imagination to create fictions of dreams, he was still bearing witness to the psychosocial circumstances of his time. Any fictions of dreams spring from the dreamer's historical, cultural, and ethnic identity, to sum up the psychosocial factors of dreaming, but they also originate in the dreamer's internal life that gives rise to his autobiographical fictions. Most likely, Artemidorus, in order to arrive at an encyclopaedia of Graeco-Roman dream life, relied on a number of sources, and these included his own fantasy life. For instance, he addresses part of the book to his own son and encourages him to have a go himself at dream interpretation.

Whatever the source, Artemidorus' dream fictions are an astonishing historical document of the most private sphere and, at the same time, the public domain of ancient dreamers. The type of dreams listed read not unlike a contemporary anthology of dreams. At first sight it appears that not much of dream life seems to have changed over 1,800 years. There are dreams about sex in such an uninhibited way they could be from Freud's canon of thought; then there are dreams about flying, skinned children, physical prowess, infertility, impotency, court cases, family disputes, and the gallery of gods of classical antiquity, all coexisting in an internal world that Artemidorus describes but does not psychologise. Unlike Aristotle (384–322 BC) who proposed a psychobiological theory of dreams some five hundred years earlier, Artemidorus is not prone to developing a psychological theory of dreaming. His domain is the narration of dreams, he is a storyteller, a true mouthpiece for the dream's unbounded and, it seems, timeless fictions. Being an educated wealthy man and widely travelled, he takes possession of the dreams' meanings by interpreting them in a formulaic manner, playing with words, as if himself becoming a minor deity of dreams, as if taking a seat next to the consortium of Asclepius, Apollo, and Neptune, the Graeco-Roman triumvirate of dream gods. He enthroned himself as the maker of meaning, as it were.

That is were Freud comes in, using Artemidorus as a counterfactual to his developing science of dreams. Instead of dream knowledge resting solely in the hands of a learned dream interpreter, Freud hands the ownership of the dream, and the searches for the hidden meaning, back to the dreamer himself. There is no comprehension of dreams without the dreamer. Having said that, it is highly implausible to think that Freud took a backseat in the exploration of dreams, given his medical background, his social status, and his self-assurance about the very purpose and mission of psychoanalysis.

One compelling notion of Artemidorus' oeuvre is his statement that he will *not* begin from the gods. By doing so he puts the individial dreamer firmly in the centre of dream exploration (Harris-McCoy, 2012, p. 63, p. 435), and moves away from the prehistoric idea of dreams as divine revelations. At the same time he hangs on to the other prevalent prehistoric idea of the prophetic nature of dreams, which places him in opposition to the actual founder of modern psychobiological dream theory, Aristotle, who thought that dreams originate in the physical self and rudimentary forms of internal life (Harris, 2009, pp. 252–261).

Artemidorus' organisation of dreams centres around human development from birth to death, and in-between is about growing up, the body, body parts, "the teaching of all kinds of arts and labours and pursuits, then about youth, about exercises, about contests, about the bath and every type of bathing, about every food", etc., (ibid., p. 10). It is no less than an encyclopaedia of everyday life. Becoming at once a *vox populi*, the voice of the mundane and ordinary, and a dream expert, he exults in dream exegesis not unlike the dream priests of old residing in dream temples. His capital as a writer is the close observation of the everyday dreamer, and from it he makes theories about the meaning of the dream with its main purpose of divination, the foretelling of the future. In Harris-McCoy's words: Artemidorus' *Oneirocritica* is "an encyclopaedic treatment of the subject of oneiromancy or prophecy through dream-interpretation" (ibid., p. 1).

Most intriguing is his discourse on intercourse (ibid., pp. 137–151). Being intent on classifying and ordering the chaos that is dream life, he reports sexual dreams that are according to the law, contrary to law, and contrary to nature. As he frankly reports on the psychosocial sex life of his contemporaries he moves from sex with one's wife, to sex with female courtesans, brotherly anal penetration, sex with slaves, adultery, hand jobs for the master, and masturbation, in one clean sweep of lust, passion, Eros, and untamed carnality. His interpretations are centred around three concepts: foretelling the future, people as possessions, and social status. For instance, having sex with one's own wife in dream life is good, as long as she is willing and submissive. As the woman is seen as the property of the man, it is an indication of the good fortune of his own business to come.

"And to have sex with one's slave, female or male, is good." Artemidorus goes on: "For slaves are the property of the observer. They therefore signify that the observer delights in his property, which will fittingly increase in quantity and become more valuable" (ibid., p. 139). "And for a man to be penetrated by a wealthier man and older man is good. For it is customary to receive things of this sort. And to be penetrated by a man who is younger and poor is grievous. For it is customary to give to men of this sort. And it signifies the same thing, too, if the perpetrator is older and a beggar" (ibid.).

CHAPTER EIGHT

The ancient deities of dreams

"The dream is personal myth, and myth is the dream of a culture"

—Freud

Dreaming feeds the individual's internal life and her conscious awareness of it with unique stories collected over a whole life span, compressed through symbolisation into personal myth; equally dreaming feeds the social unconscious in a symbolic bowel movement of burning social issues. Mythification of psychological and social issues takes place in the world of dreams; it is a process of digestion and transformation of emotional experience.

The major mythological deities of dreams in Graeco-Roman times were Asclepius, Apollo, Neptune, and Zeus; the minor ones were Hypnos and Morpheus. The oldest dream deities were possibly An-Za-Oar in Assyrian, Babylonian and Sumerian mythology, and the Egyptian Imhotep.

Asclepius

"The mind tries to be its own doctor"

—Admetos in *Alcestis* by Euripides, in a version by Ted Hughes, 1999, p. 67

Asclepius is the main deity of dreams. There are two different myths surrounding the son of Apollo and Coronis. Coronis betrayed Apollo and was condemned to burn at the pyre. Baby Asclepius was rescued by his father and taken to Mount Pelion where he was put into the care of Chiron, the centaur and divine mentor, who taught him to hunt and instructed him in the science of medicine.

Asclepius, carried away by his medical quest, not only tried to cure people but brought the dead back to life. He breached the taboo of death that was, of course, Hades' domain, who brought the matter to Zeus' attention. Zeus, the god of gods, struck Asclepius off the medical register, by striking him with a thunderbolt. In turn, Apollo took revenge for his son on the Cyclopes who had forged the thunderbolt. Subsequently Apollo was banned from Olympus by Zeus (Larousse, 1959, p. 163).

At the dream temple of Epidaurus another version of Asclepius' birth was known that, again, was not very flattering to Coronis; after giving birth to her son, she took him to Mount Titthion and abandoned him. A goat that took pity on him fed him, and a dog guarded him. A shepherd named Aresthanas discovered the new-born child and was amazed by the supernatural light that surrounded Asclepius (ibid.).

The deity of dreams and health was widely regarded as the off-spring of light or fire. The Asclepian regalia was the serpent that is still the symbol of medicine today. As we heard earlier in Freud's account of the ancient method of dream incubation, a number of rites were observed at the *Asclepeia* or dream sanctuary that served to cure physical illness.

A number of aspects of these myths are relevant for Asclepius' rulership of dreams.

The dream body and the body of the dream

Asclepius is associated with medicine and therefore with the healing of the body. The relation of dreams with the body belongs to the foundation matrix of our psyche. During REM activity we regress deeply into our physical selves; we give in to what poets call "the mother of the night", the fantasy of the moon cradling and watching over the dreamer.

Ted Hughes, in his translation of Euripides' *Alcestis*, gives Admetos a voice, saying "The nerves of the married man ... are woven into the body of his wife" and to the somatic self of his offspring (Hughes, 1999). There is a physical connection between close family members and previous generations. Our psychic histories as human beings are both emotional and physical, and memory, a central feature of dream life, takes its essential and relevatory clues from body memory.

Joyce McDougall called this physical regression and its resultant illusion of fusion with the maternal object a "one-body" phantasy. In *Theatres of the Body* (1989), she describes the baby as emerging from the "body–mind matrix" of the "mother universe" to move on to the "breast universe", and, eventually, to the "symbolic universe", which is characterised by verbalisation of somatic and emotional states. This "desomatisation" of the psyche is always accompanied by the reverse psychic quest, that is, to be completely submerged in the phantasy of primary fusion with the maternal object (pp. 32–49).

This leaning into the body of the dream implies internal restoration on the physical plane first, before we restore psychic balance or mental health. Freud, through his dictum "dreams are the guardians of sleep", made us aware of the physiological function of dreaming. We dream in order not to wake up from sleeping, or in other words, dreams restore the psyche by restoring the body. In the Freudian schema, that meant the ego's labour of binding and digesting sensory impressions and instinctual impulses, such as erotic or aggressive feelings. And the Freudian ego is foremost a bodily ego.

This idea of fending off and shepherding intrusive dream thoughts, or whatever murkiness that comes from the place below, looks simplistic at first sight but it will come as a great relief to the dreamer who might be stretched to think that every single dream is meaningful. Dreams, at times, simply serve a somatic function. This is a controversial concept that allows for the somatic self doing its own healing without being interfered with by the conscious mind.

The Kleinian dream expert Grotstein suggests two theories of creativity in dreams: one is the idea that dreams are "autochthonous", that is, they create something out of themselves; the other is based on the genital intercourse of the parental couple, and the resultant Oedipus complex (1981, p. 380). At its most unintegrated, autochthonous dream activity remains on the level of omnipotent self-creativity; in its more integrated form it contributes to the mastery of psychic chaos. Bion woke us up to the fact that dreaming never ceases. Its autochthonous function is a necessary background activity during waking hours that "entertains" and puts to sleep a multitude of thoughts, emotions, and sense impressions so that we can focus on one single task and experience the ordinariness of living. It also erects sensible membranes around such avalanches of phantasies, giving the ego a skin and a shape. The psychotic psyche operates without such membranes, its dream autochthony, or autopoiesis, generates a mass of fragmented thoughts spilling into the conscious mind and overflooding it.

My suggestion is that the autochthonous activity of the normal neurotic dreamer binds difficult emotional experience not only on the level of emotion and thought but also on a somatic level. Through dream activity emotions are given their somatic home, which gives them more substance and weight. Dream states are deeply embedded in the somatic. If McDougall talks of the necessity for the "desomatisa- tion" of the psyche in the course of normal development, we know of the nocturnal movement in the opposite direction: dreams "somatise" emotional experience in a healthy way. They give embodiment to thought and affect. Nocturnal dream activity means the psyche's immersion in and inhabiting of the body.

Freud, the biologist of the mind, had a curious relationship with the body–mind continuum. In his model, emotions were secondary to instinctual experience, and not important in themselves.

> With the advent of the drive/structure model, affect was relegated to a theoretically secondary position. (Greenberg & Mitchell, 1983, p. 64)

> With the establishment of the primacy of drive, the specific quali- ties of affects were disregarded, except as they reflect the nature of the repressed instinctual impulses. (Ibid., p. 65)

This peripheral role of emotions meant that they were not consid- ered to carry meaning, and thus the Freudian theory of dreams could not conceive of dreams being generative. Freud, locking himself up in an epistemological impasse because he wanted to sound scien- tifically convincing, broke the developmental flow from instinctual body matters to a psyche that has at its centre one's feeling nature. By contrast, Bion's dream model, where the creativity of the mind lies in the generation of meaning through the digestion of sensory experi- ence and primitive emotions, is a truly aesthetic understanding of dreams.

Nocturnal detraumatisation

Dreams also build bridges to the past through their access to body or cell memory. In my work with sexually abused patients and second-generation holocaust survivors, I have come to the conclusion that dreams enable the release of lost memory.

Dreaming is traumatisation in reverse; it is the servant of detraumatisation. During severe traumatisation unbearable states of mind can be evaded by emotional dissociation and the transportation of nameless dread into the soma, where it may remain for a whole lifetime, lying in wait like a monstrous beast that might violently project the traumatic experience into the insides of loved ones.

Dissociation and alienation from the self eventually lead to the somatisation of the traumatic imprint. This traumatic introject, or "alien object" (Rheinschmiedt, 1998), leads a life of its own, out of reach of memory, thinking, and emotional linking. The traumatic introjects, once they have taken refuge in the body, can only be processed and brought to the surface from great depths through the occurrence of dream material that might trigger in the patient severe physical regression without initial knowledge of the trauma.

The taboo of death

The second aspect of the mythical Asclepius relevant to our discussion is his urge to meddle with the taboo of death that led to his downfall. He is not afraid to face the dying and the dead and tries to bring them back to life.

Dreams bring back to life the dead. This can be seen during periods of healthy mourning or in the termination phase of psychotherapy when death dreams are high on the agenda. From Donald Winnicott (1954) and Jonathan Pedder (1982) we know that the antidote to depressive states is healthy mourning.

> If in an individual the depressive position has been achieved and fully established, then the reaction to loss is *grief*, or *sadness*. Where there is some degree of failure at the depressive position the result of loss is depression. (Winnicott, 1954, p. 275, original emphasis)

The demand on the grieving person is to create a realistic relationship with the lost one, although where there has been strong ambivalence this might be not easy.

Michael Harner, in *The Way of the Shaman* (1990), describes the Native American tradition of dream appreciation where dreams are considered the mouthpiece of ancestral spirits, mainly the grandfather spirit. The spirits from the other world are regarded as guardians relevant during times of initiation and threshold experiences. For instance, youths are initiated into adulthood by being forced to survive on their own in the wilderness and having to wait for the right initiation dream to come to them. An initiation dream is meant to offer the individual a new adult name, a metaphor for his new standing and occupation in the tribe.

Apollo

"One might say of Apollo what Schopenhauer says ... of Man caught in the veil of Maya: 'Even as on an immense, raging sea, assailed by huge wave crests, a man sits in a little row boat trusting his frail craft, so, amidst the ferocious torments of this world, the individual sits tranquilly, supported by the *principium individuationis* and relying on it.' ... Apollo himself may be regarded as the marvellous divine image of principium individuationis, whose looks and gestures radiate the full delight, wisdom, and beauty of 'illusion'."

—Nietzsche, *The Birth of Tragedy*

"The origins of the cult of the Greek sun-god Apollo, in roughly 2000 BC, predates the Bronze Age. He was regarded as the representation of the sun on earth, the carrier of the sun, bearing it from east to west in his golden chariot. By the fifth century BC he was not only associated with the worship of the sun but also with diverse qualities such as the breaking of family curses, healing, prophecy, artistic inspiration, and he was the bringer of light to human beings."

—Greene & Sasportas, 1989

Consciousness

Apart from Asclepius, Apollo was looked on as the main deity representing the world of dreams. He was, essentially, the giver of inner light, as we can conclude from the inscription at the temple of Delphi that proclaimed "Know thyself". He became the foremost symbol of consciousness both in the world of religious dedication and in philosophical thinking. Pythagoras and Plato showed a leaning towards the Apollonian premise of the gathering and acquisition of consciousness as a fundamental human trait. Philosophy, in its purest and oldest form, stands for the love of wisdom. In Plato's theory, consciousness was the entry point to "eternal realities" such as truthfulness, ethical qualities in art, and "ideal beauty" as an image of divinity.

How did the mythological Apollo arrive at consciousness? He was in permanent battle with female chthonic underworld deities such as the Python and the Erinyes or "Furies", who represented instinctual impulse, fatedness, and ancestral compulsion. He became the slayer of darkness and the breaker of family curses but he also integrated these forces of darkness into the worship of the sun (Graves, 1955).

The defeated giant serpent Python, for instance, was turned into a priestess at Delphi and eventually spoke the god's oracle. The chthonic mother-deities were also revered through the establishment of the "omphalos" or naval-stone at the temple, consisting of an outer stone circle and a point in the middle of the circle, representing the centre of the earth, a sacred place where the life-sustaining sun came down to earth.

Now let us apply these mythological aspects of Apollo to our understanding of dream life. Ancient mythology and philosophy, through the idea of the omphalos, elevated dreams to the very centre of our being, making them the soul of psychic life. It assumed a core self that was not static and did not rely on one single conception, because dreams, being part of nature, are in perpetual movement and bring into the open the creative and fecund powers of nature.

Freud, in *The Interpretation of Dreams*, talked about the "naval" of the dream, "the spot where it reaches into the unknown". He meant that there is a centre of dream life and mental life that can never be fully understood, out of reach of interpretation. It is a hallmark of his respect for the unconscious that he was able to bow low to, rather than invade, the Egyptian burial chambers of psychoanalysis. This naval stands for the mystery of life that can be apprehended but never fully known.

The major attribute of this core self is consciousness, which stems from both an appreciation of the wisdom that lies inherent in our instinctual-bodily ancestry and the overcoming, or "slaying", of nature and the body. There are faint echoes of Freud's instinctual id, Melanie

Klein's internal world of fear, rage, and envy, Winnicott's hate in the countertransference, and Bion's insistence on beta elements, which are sensory impressions and archaic feelings, as the first stepping-stones out of the cave of our primitive ancestry.

The breaker of family curses

Apollo, in his role as the breaker of family curses, makes us think about the dream's position in the elucidation of trauma that originates in previous generations. We can find in dreams an inherent capacity to access memory, which, in Freudian eyes, forms a bridge to formative childhood events, cultural identity, and ancestral knowledge. Dreams have long arms, reaching into the past, and thus offer us the opportunity to get a handle on the transgenerational transmission of trauma. What the old Greeks described as family curse we can nowadays locate in, for instance, sexual abuse and the repetition of the abuse in the following generation when the abused himself becomes the abuser.

One of my patients, as a small child, had been sexually abused by her father who had himself been abused in a children's home and had a marked disinterest in, and lack of understanding of, her dreams. Initially she had no clear memory of the abuse and relied solely on her present sexual difficulties as a means to finding clues to the past. From time to time, she went into deep physical regression; she curled up in the foetal position, cradling herself with her arms, went quiet and petrified, too afraid to engage in eye contact, and she had sensations of physical intrusion and a sense of a menacing male presence. Her somatic regression tended to induce drowsiness in me and I was hardly able to stay awake. Eventually it occurred to her that her lack of contact with her dream world was linked with her fear of going to sleep. She then had dreams that became more and more explicit about the nature of the abuse. She was abused during the night. To wake up to dreams meant to be abused, the experience of dreaming and dream recall becoming welded to the trauma of abuse. She had lost contact with her dream world, a kind of alienation that also underpinned her dissociation from her body and her sexual needs.

* * *

One could also call the generational handing down of mental illness a family curse. The passing on of manic-depressive illness, especially in artistic and noble families, is well documented by Kay Redfield Jamison (1993). Being a professor of psychiatry and an adherent of a medical model of the mind, she believes that manic-depressive illness is passed on genetically. I would agree that there is undoubtedly a genetic disposition to the occurrence of madness but there is a strong psychic link between family members who fall ill. In a previous chapter on the "transmission of the survivor syndrome" (Chapter Three) I have tried to establish the psychology of the generational transmission of trauma that also entails the passing on of psychic illness.

The poet Alfred, Lord Tennyson, himself suffering from manic depression, described the frequent manifestations of mental illness and melancholy in his family, going back some five generations, as a "taint of blood", and "black blood". T. S. Eliot called him "the great master of metric as well as melancholia". The poet Lord Byron, like Tennyson embroiled in family insanity, lamented that "some curse hangs over me and mine" (Redfield Jamison, 1993).

REFERENCES

Angelou, M. (1993). *On the Pulse of Morning: The Inaugural Poem*. New York: Random House.

Anzieu, D. (1986). *Freud's Self-Analysis*. London: Hogarth.

Arendt, H. (2007). *The Jewish Writings*. New York: Schocken.

Aubarbier, J. L., & Binet, M. (1997). *The Paths of Prehistory in Perigord*. Rennes: Editions Ouest-France.

Baggott, J. (2012). *Higgs: The Invention and Discovery of the "God Particle"*. Oxford: OUP.

Banville, J. (2013). A different Kafka. *The New York Review of Books*, 24 October.

Basho, M. (1689). *The Narrow Road to the Deep North and Other Travel Sketches*. London: Penguin, 1966.

Bate, J. (2015). *Ted Hughes: The Unauthorised Life*. London: William Collins.

Baumgarten, A. G. (1750). *Aesthetica (Vol. 1)*. Charleston, SC: Nabu Press, 2012.

BBC1 (2015). *Imagine: Richard Flanagan: Life after Death*. 21 July.

Berryman, J. (1964). *The Dream Songs*. London: Faber & Faber.

Bettelheim, B. (1983). *Freud and Man's Soul*. London: Hogarth.

Bickerton, E. (2006). The road from war. *Times Literary Supplement*, 10 March.

Bion, W. R. (1962a). A theory of thinking. In: W. Bion, *Second Thoughts* (pp. 110–119). London: Heinemann, 1967. (Reprinted by Karnac, 1984.)

Bion, W. R. (1962b). *Learning From Experience*. London: Heinemann.

Blessington, M. (2011). *Conversations of Lord Byron with the Countess of Blessington*. Cambridge: CUP.

Briggs, J. (1992). *Fractals: The Patterns of Chaos: Discovering a New Aesthetic of Art, Science, and Nature*. New York: Simon & Schuster.

Buruma, I. (2014). The worst railroad job. *The New York Review of Books*, 20 November.

Calaprice, A. (Ed.) (2011). *The New Quotable Einstein*. Princeton, NJ: Princeton University Press.

Caper, R. (1996). Play, experimentation and creativity. *International Journal of Psycho-Analysis*, 77: 859–869.

Carver, R. (2009). *Collected Stories*. New York: Library of America.

Clark, R. W. (1980). *Freud: The Man and the Cause*. London: Granada.

Cox, M., & Theilgaard, A. (1987). *Mutative Metaphors in Psycho-Therapy: The Aeolian Mode*. London: Tavistock Publications.

Dalai Lama, & Cutler, H. C. (1998). *The Art of Happiness: A Handbook for Living*. London: Hodder.

Dilts, R. (1994a). *Strategies of Genius* (Vol 1). Capitola, CA: Meta Publications.

Eagleton, T. (1990). *The Ideology of the Aesthetic*. Oxford: Blackwell.

Eco, U. (2009). *The Infinity of Lists*. London: Maclehose Press.

Einstein, A. (1956). *Out of My Later Years*. New Jersey: The Citadel Press.

Ellenberger, H. (1970). *The Discovery of the Unconscious: The History and Evolution of Dynamic Psychiatry*. New York: Basic Books.

Fairbairn, W. R. D. (1944). Endopsychic structures considered in terms of object relations. In: *Psychoanalytic Studies of the Personality*. London: Routledge & Kegan Paul, 1952.

Ferrante, E. (2012). *My Brilliant Friend* (trans. A. Goldstein). New York: Europa Editions.

Ferrante, E. (2013). *The Story of a New Name* (trans. A. Goldstein). New York: Europa Editions.

Ferrante, E. (2014). *Those Who Leave and Those Who Stay* (trans. A. Goldstein). New York: Europa Editions.

Ferrante, E. (2015). *The Story of the Lost Child* (trans. A. Goldstein). New York: Europa Editions.

Ficino, M. (1489). *Liber de Vita* (trans. C. Boer, 1980, *The Book of Life*. Irving, TX: Spring Publications).

Flanagan, R. (2013). *The Narrow Road to the Deep North*. London: Chatto & Windus.

Foster Wallace, D. (1997). *A Supposedly Fun Thing I'll Never Do Again: Essays*. London: Little Brown.

Franzen, J. (2010). *Freedom*. London: Fourth Estate.

Franzen, J. (2012). *Farther Away*. London: Fourth Estate.

Freud (1895d). *Studies on Hysteria. S. E., 2*. London Hogarth.

Freud, S. (1900). *The Interpretation of Dreams. S. E., 4–5*. London: Hogarth.

Freud, S. (1905d). *Three Essays on the Theory of Sexuality. S. E., 7*. London: Hogarth.

Freud, S. (1908). Creative writers and day-dreaming. *S. E., 9*: 141–153. London: Hogarth.

Freud, S. (1917e). Mourning and melancholia. *S. E. 14*: 237–243. London: Hogarth.

Freud, S. (1920g). *Beyond the Pleasure Principle. S. E., 18*. London: Hogarth.

Freud, S. (1923b). *The Ego and the Id. S. E., 19*. London: Hogarth.

Freud, S. (1950/1895). Project for a scientific psychology. *S. E., 1*: 283–392. London: Hogarth.

Friedländer, S. (2013). *Franz Kafka: The Poet of Shame and Guilt*. New Haven, CT: Yale University Press.

Fromm, E. (1956). *The Art of Loving: An Enquiry into the Nature of Love*. New York: Harper & Brothers.

Garcia Márquez, G. (1967). *One Hundred Years of Solitude* (trans. G. Rabassa). London: Picador, 1978.

Garcia Márquez, G. (1985). *Love in the Time of Cholera* (trans. E. Grossman). London: Jonathan Cape, 1988.

Garcia Márquez, G. (1989). *The General in His Labyrinth* (trans. E. Grossman). London: Jonathan Cape, 1991.

Garfield, P. (1974). *Creative Dreaming*. New York: Ballantine.

Gawler, I. (1987). *Peace of Mind*. South Yarra, Australia: Michelle Anderson.

Graves, R. (1955). *The Greek Myths* (Vols. 1 & 2). Middlesex: Penguin.

Green, L., & McCreery, C. (1994). *Lucid Dreaming: The Paradox of Consciousness during Sleep*. London: Routledge.

Greenberg, J., & Mitchell, S. (1983). *Object Relations in Psycho-analytic Theory*. Cambridge, MA: Harvard University Press.

Greene, G. (1940). *The Power and the Glory*. London: William Heinemann.

Greene, L., & Sasportas, H. (1989). *Dimensionen des Unbewussten*. München: Hugendubel Verlag.

Grotstein, J. (1981). *Who Is the Dreamer Who Dreams the Dream and Who Is the Dreamer Who Understands it?* In: J. Grotstein, (Ed.), *Do I Dare Disturb the Universe? A Memorial to W. R. Bion* (pp. 358–416). London: Karnac, 1983.

Gunn, D. (2013). Superhuman organization: Infinite connectivity in the flawed but fascinating first novel of Patrick White. *Times Literary Supplement*, 25 January.

Harner, M. (1990). *The Way of the Shaman*. New York: Harper One.

Harris, W. V. (2009). *Dreams and Experience in Classical Antiquity*. Cambridge, MA: Harvard University Press.

Harris-McCoy, D. E. (2012). *Artemidorus' Oneirocritica: Text, Translation, &* *Commentary.* Oxford: OUP.

Hinshelwood, R. D. (1989). *A Dictionary of Kleinian Thought.* London: Free Association.

Hofmann, M. (2014). *Where Have You Been?: Selected Essays.* New York: Farrar, Straus & Giroux.

Hollingdale, R. J. (1969). Introduction. In: F. Nietzsche (1883), *Thus Spoke Zarathustra* (pp. 11–35). London: Penguin, 2003.

Hollingworth, M. (2013). *Saint Augustine of Hippo: An Intellectual Biography.* London: Bloomsbury.

Hughes, T. (1970). *Crow: From the Life and Songs of the Crow.* London: Faber & Faber.

Hughes, T. (1998). *Birthday Letters.* London: Faber & Faber.

Hughes, T. (1999a). *Euripides: Alcestis. A New Version by Ted Hughes.* London: Faber & Faber.

Hughes, T. (1999b). Poet, pike and a pitiful grouse. From a previously unpublished interview given to Thomas Pero of a US angling magazine. *The Guardian Review,* 8 January.

Hughes, T. (2003). *Collected Poems.* London: Faber & Faber.

Jouvet, M. (1999*). The Paradox of Sleep: The Story of Dreaming.* Cambridge, MA: MIT.

Kafka, F. (1925). *The Trial.* London: Penguin, 1994.

Kannemeyer, J. C. (2013). *J. M. Coetzee: A Life in Writing* (trans. M. Heyns). London: Scribe.

Kellman, S. G. (2005). *Redemption: The Life of Henry Roth.* London: W. W. Norton.

Kermode, F. (2000). *The Sense of an Ending: Studies in the Theory of Fiction.* Oxford: OUP.

Kiberd, D. (2009). *Ulysses and Us: The Art of Everyday Living.* London: Faber & Faber.

Lederman, L., with Teresi, D. (1993). *The God Particle: If the Universe is the Answer, What is the Question?.* London: Bantam Press.

Leppmann, W. (1984). *Rilke: A Life.* New York: Fromm.

Levi, P. (1959). *If This is a Man.* London: Penguin, 1969.

MacGregor, N. (2014). *Germany: Memories of a Nation.* London: Allen Lane.

Mandelbrot, B. B. (1975). *Les objects fractals: forme, hasard et dimension.* Paris Flammarion. (*The Fractal Geometry of Nature.* New York: W. H. Freeman, 1982.)

Marr, D. (1992), *Patrick White: A Life.* New York: Alfred A. Knopf.

McDougall, J. (1989). *Theatres of the Body: A Psychoanalytic Approach to Psychosomatic Illness.* London: Free Association.

Modiano, P. (2015a). *Dora Bruder*. Berkeley, CA: University of California Press.

Modiano, P. (2015b). *Suspended Sentences* (trans. M. Polizzotti). New Haven, CT: Yale University Press.

Mollon, P. (2008). *Psychoanalytic Energy Psychotherapy*. London: Karnac.

Muhlstein, A. (2014). Did Patrick Modiano deserve it? *The New York Review of Books*, 18 December.

New Larousse Encyclopaedia of Mythology (1959). London: Hamlyn.

Némirovsky, I. (2005). *L'enfant prodige*. Paris: Gallimard

Némirovsky, I. (2006). *Suite Francaise*. London: Chatto & Windus.

Nietzsche, F. (1883). *Thus Spoke Zarathustra* (translated with an introduction by R. J. Hollingdale). London: Penguin, 2003.

O'Brien, S. (2003). Essential but unlovely: Collected poems by Ted Hughes. *The Guardian Review*, 1 November.

Ogden, T. (1979). On projective identification. *International Journal of Psycho-Analysis*, *60*: 357–373.

O'Rourke, M. (2014). Lives of girls and women. *The Guardian Review*, 1 November.

Pedder, J. (1982). Failure to mourn, and melancholia. *British Journal of Psychiatry*, *141*: 329–337.

Pessoa, F. (2006). *A Little Larger Than the Entire Universe: Selected Poems*. London: Penguin.

Philipponnat, O., & Lienhardt, P. (2010). *The Life of Irene Nemirovsky, 1903–1942*. London: Chatto & Windus.

Phillips, A. (2002). *Promises, Promises: Essays on Literature and Psychoanalysis*. London: Faber, 2000.

Raine, C. (2014). He might be falling: Review of Richard Flanagan's *The Narrow Road to the Deep North* (2013). *Times Literary Supplement*, 19 August.

Raphael, F. (2010). Stench of carrion. *Times Literary Supplement*, 30 April.

Redfield Jamison, K. (1993). *Touched with Fire: Manic-Depressive Illness and the Artistic Temperament*. New York: Free Press.

Redfield Jamison, K. (1997). *An Unquiet Mind: A Memoir of Moods and Madness*. London: Karnac.

Rheinschmiedt, O. (1998). *Der Gruppenanalytiker als Fremd-objekt* (The group analyst as alien object). *Gruppenanalyse: Zeitschrift fuer gruppenanalytische Psychotherapie, Beratung und Supervision*, *8*: 2.

Rilke, R. M. (1947). Letter to Witold von Hulewicz. In: *Selected Letters of Rainer Maria Rilke 1902–1926*. London: MacMillan.

Rilke, R.M. (1957). *Die Gedichte*. Frankfurt a.M.: Insel, 1990.

Sadie, S. (2006). *Mozart: The Early Years 1756–1781*. Oxford: OUP.

Schlapobersky, J. (1994). The language of the group: Monologue, dialogue and discourse in group analysis. In: D. Brown & L. Zinkin (Eds.), *The Psyche and the Social World*. London: Routledge.

Schmidt, M. (2014). *The Novel: A Biography*. Cambridge, MA: Belknap Press.

Schoenau, W. (1968). *Sigmund Freud's Prosa*. Stuttgart: Metzlerische Verlagsbuchhandlung.

Schuetzenberger, A. A. (1998). The Ancestor Syndrome: Transgenerational Psychotherapy and the Hidden Links in the Family Tree. London: Routledge.

Slipp, S. (1990). The Children of Survivors of Nazi Concentration Camps: A Pilot Study of the Intergenerational Transmission of Psychic Trauma. London: Institute of Group Analysis Library.

Stach, R. (2013). *Kafka: The Decisive Years* (trans. S. Frisch). Princeton, NJ: Princeton University Press.

Stach, R. (2015). *Kafka: The Years of Insight* (trans. S. Frisch). Princeton, NJ: Princeton University Press.

Stewart, C. (2012). *Dreaming and Historical Consciousness in Island Greece*. Cambridge, MA: Harvard University Press.

Stokes, S. (1978). The Critical Writings of Adrian Stokes. London: Thames & Hudson.

Sutherland, J. (2011), *Lives of the Novelists: A History of Fiction in 294 Lives*. London: Profile Books.

Thirlwell, A. (2014). Suspended sentences. *The Guardian Review*, 22 November.

Thomson, I. (2002). *Primo Levi*. London: Hutchinson.

Tóibín, C. (2009). *Brooklyn*. London: Viking.

Tóibín, C. (2014). *Nora Webster*. London: Viking.

Tóibín, C., (2016). Colm Tóibín explains how he circled around Nora Webster for a decade. *The Guardian Review*, 1 January.

Trilling, L. (1950). *Freud and Literature*. In: L. Trilling, *The Liberal Imagination* (pp. 34–57). New York: New York Review Books Classics, 1978.

Varela, F. J. (1997). *Sleeping, Dreaming, and Dying: An Exploration of Consciousness with The Dalai Lama*. Boston: Wisdom Publications.

Vendler, H. (1997). *The Art of Shakespeare's Sonnets*. Cambridge, MA: Harvard University Press.

Volkan, V. (1997). *Bloodlines: From Ethnic Pride to Ethnic Terrorism*. New York: Farrar, Straus & Giroux.

Walcott, D. (2014). *The Poetry of Derek Walcott 1948–2013* (selected by Glyn Maxwell). London: Faber & Faber.

Weiss, J. (2007). *Irene Némirovsky: Her Life and Works*. Stanford, CA: Stanford University Press.

White, P. (1939). *Happy Valley*. London: Cape, 2012.

White, P. (1955). *The Tree of Man*. London: Vintage, 1994.

White, P. (1957). *Voss*. New York: Alfred A. Knopf, 2012.

White, P. (1961). *Riders in the Chariot*. London: Vintage, 1996.

White, P. (1966). *The Solid Mandala*. London: Cape, 1976.

White, P. (1973). *The Eye of the Storm*. New York: Viking.

Whyte, D. (1989). Out on the ocean. In: *Songs for Coming Home*. Langley, WA: Many Rivers Press.

Williamson, M. (1992). *A Return to Love: Reflections on the Principles of a Course in Miracles*. London: Aquarian Press.

Winnicott, D. W. (1949). Hate in the countertransference. In: D. W. Winnicott, *Through Paediatrics to Psycho-Analysis* (pp. 194–203). London: Hogarth, 1987.

Winnicott, D. W. (1954). The depressive position in normal emotional development. In: D. W. Winnicott, *Through Paediatrics to Psycho-analysis* (pp. 262–277). London: Hogarth, 1987.

Winnicott, D. W. (1956a). Primary maternal preoccupation. In: D. W. Winnicott, *Through Paediatrics to Psycho-Analysis* (pp. 300–305). London: Hogarth, 1987.

Winnicott, D. W. (1956b). Psychoanalysis and the sense of guilt. In: D. W. Winnicott, *The Maturational Processes and the Facilitating Environment* (pp. 15–28). London: Hogarth, 1965.

Winnicott, D. W. (1967). The location of cultural experience. In: *Playing and Reality*. London: Tavistock, 1971.

Winnicott, D. W. (1971). Creative activity and the search for the self. In: *Playing and Reality*. London: Tavistock.

Yeats, W. B. (1916). Easter, 1916. In: W. B. Yeats, *The Poems* (p. 228). London: Everyman, 1992.

Yeats, W. B. (1992). *The Poems* (ed. D. Albright). London: Everyman.

INDEX

227

234   INDEX